BLACK FREEDOM STRUGGLE IN URBAN APPALACHIA

BLACK FREEDOM STRUGGLE IN URBAN APPALACHIA

EDITED BY

J. Z. Bennett

Christy L. McGuire

Lori Delale-O'Connor

T. Elon Dancy II

Sabina Vaught

Copyright © 2025 by The University Press of Kentucky

Scholarly publisher for the Commonwealth, serving Bellarmine University, Berea College, Centre College of Kentucky, Eastern Kentucky University, The Filson Historical Society, Georgetown College, Kentucky Historical Society, Kentucky State University, Morehead State University, Murray State University, Northern Kentucky University, Spalding University, Transylvania University, University of Kentucky, University of Louisville, University of Pikeville, and Western Kentucky University.
All rights reserved.

Editorial and Sales Offices: The University Press of Kentucky
663 South Limestone Street, Lexington, Kentucky 40508-4008
www.kentuckypress.com

Cataloging-in-Publication data available from the Library of Congress

ISBN 978-1-9859-0187-2 (hardcover)
ISBN 978-1-9859-0188-9 (paperback)
ISBN 978-1-9859-0190-2 (pdf)
ISBN 978-1-9859-0189-6 (epub)

This book is printed on acid-free paper meeting the requirements of the American National Standard for Permanence in Paper for Printed Library Materials.

Manufactured in the United States of America.

Member of the Association
of University Presses

Contents

Preface ix
  T. Elon Dancy II

Introduction: A Poetics of Black Appalachia 1
  Sabina Vaught and T. Elon Dancy II

Part 1. "returning to sacred places" 21
  Sabina Vaught
On the Horizon 23
  Morgan Overton
Wawawpewnowat 24
  Jennifer Johnson
Grounded Justice: Unearthing the Birthright of Liberated,
Collective Black Environmental Justice Futures
in Pittsburgh and Beyond 34
  *M. Beatrice Dias, Cassie Quigley, Alyssa Lyon, Ariam Ford,
  and Ebony Lunsford-Evans*
Liberation Is Yet to Come: An Interview 47
  S. L. Akines, Win Nunley, and Robin-Renee Allbritton

Part 2. "sometimes falling rain / carries memories of betrayal" 57
  Lori Delale-O'Connor and T. Elon Dancy II
The Burgh 59
  Cue Perry
The Effects of a Black Child's Education 60
  Breanna Ewell

Emerge   63
    Morgan Overton
We're Going to Figure It Out: Reflections from
an Interview   65
    Amber Thompson, Cadence Spruill, and
    Chetachukwu U. Agwoeme
Excerpts from Slow Walking in Circles: The Struggle to
Improve African American Student Achievement in
the Pittsburgh Public Schools—A Report of the Equity
Advisory Panel (EAP), October 2020   74
    Anthony B. Mitchell, James B. Stewart, Wanda Henderson,
    and Tamanika Howze
Caste, Carcerality, and Educational Inequity: A Call to
Restore Liberating Educational Opportunities
for Black Pittsburgh   85
    Esohe Osai and Sean Means

Part 3. "renegades roam here"   97
    Lori Delale-O'Connor
The System   99
    Taj Poscé
Bridging Perspectives: Criminology, Education, and
Lived Experiences with Children from Pittsburgh
Sentenced to Death by Incarceration   101
    J. Z. Bennett and Christy L. McGuire
A Lost Soul in Someone's Body   110
    Briayelle Gaines
Black Caregivers' Educational Strategies to Avoid
and Disrupt Potential Pathways toward Criminal
(In)justice   116
    Lori Delale-O'Connor, James P. Huguley, and Ming-Te Wang
Notes from Upstream: Salmon Girl   126
    Sheila Carter-Jones
All Writing Is Political: An Interview   131
    Sheila Carter-Jones and Robin-Renee Allbritton

Resisting School Violence: Hip-Hop as Pedagogy for
Black Freedom Struggle   *142*
  Jasiri X, Christopher M. Wright, and Tiana Sharpe
In the Space That Is Not Yet: A Dialogue   *150*
  Marc Lamont Hill and T. Elon Dancy II

Part 4. "fierce grief shadows me"   *155*
  Sabina Vaught
They Always Come (A Note to My Son):
For Ahmaud Arbery and Breonna Taylor and
Those Suffering in COVID-19 and the Past, Present,
and Future   *157*
  Medina Jackson
A Requiem for Antwon Rose II: Defending the Dead in
the Afterlife of Slavery   *160*
  T. Elon Dancy II, Christopher M. Wright, and
  Chetachukwu U. Agwoeme
What They Say What They Said 2   *175*
  D. S. Kinsel
Prison Took My Daddy   *178*
  Nekiya Washington-Butler
Boy   *181*
  Sheila Carter-Jones

Part 5. "listen little sister / angels make their hope here"   *183*
  Lori Delale-O'Connor
The Flying African   *185*
  Mikael Owunna
What a Free Future Looks like to Me: A Prose Poem   *187*
  Cadence Spruill
Our People That Came before Did an Awful Lot to
Be Free: An Interview   *191*
  Tamanika Howze, Cameron Shannon, and DaVonna Shannon
Let's Go Find Out   *202*
  Win Nunley

Discipline, Punishment, and Black Childhood:
How Carceral Education Shapes Time for Black Youth   209
   Ariana Brazier
Budding Off a New Kind of Tree: An Interview   223
   Tereneh Idía, Nekiya Washington-Butler, and Chelsea Jimenez
The Journey to Freedom: A Conversation on
Freedom Struggle   231
   Sala Udin, Briayelle Gaines, and Christopher M. Wright
Happiness & Freedom   240
   Cue Perry

Acknowledgments   241
List of Contributors   245

Preface
T. Elon Dancy II

In William Turner and Edward Cabbell's watershed text, *Blacks in Appalachia*,[1] Turner argued that the presence of Black people in the Appalachian Mountains, the labor of Black people in the industrialization of the region, their needs, and the culture developed in the area were overlooked and yet to be systematically analyzed. In many ways, this book responds to Turner's clarion call to "magnify the Black Appalachian experience"[2] in order to establish Black historical presence and evaluate socioeconomic and cultural patterns. We join an ongoing dialogue about the geopolitics of racialization, sociality, and education in the region, which, before this volume, has also included Pittsburgh community scholarship.

In 1999, the Urban League of Pittsburgh published *The State of Black Youth in Pittsburgh: Perspectives on Young African Americans in the City of Pittsburgh and Allegheny County* to "tell the truth about our children's quality of life and the society in which they live."[3] The volume brought together various community contributors—professional educators, civil rights organization directors, young people, artists, and other community residents—who developed a guidebook to map tactics for eliminating barriers to youth self-determination and learning. The volume included the first Black person and woman deputy superintendent of Pittsburgh Public Schools, Helen S. Faison, whose chapter advocated for multiple community-based interventions in response to the life and educational outcomes of Black youth in Pittsburgh.[4] We situate this book within a genealogy of Black Pittsburgh and Black Appalachian struggles for education represented in that volume.

Founded just three years after the publishing of *The State of Black Youth in Pittsburgh* is the University of Pittsburgh School of Education's

Center for Urban Education (CUE). CUE's written mission responds to *The State of Black Youth*'s clarion call to transform educational opportunities and experiences through freedom and justice praxes. The Center's Summer Educator Forum (CUESEF), sponsored by the Heinz Endowments, initially inspired this book project. CUESEF is a local education conference widely attended by educators and community organizers to study the schooling experiences of the structurally vulnerable toward a vision of self-determination, collectivism, and freedom. The 2019 annual gathering, which was organized around the complex interplay of schools and prisons, catalyzed this book.

Several communities call our attention to schooling as a carceral project or having carceral elements. A more specific academic literature interrogates not just how schools' physical structures resemble prisons but also how policies, practices, and knowledges support, naturalize, and extend relationships between incarceration and schools.[5] These dynamic relations were the focus of the three-day conference on the University of Pittsburgh campus, during which more than five hundred participants from around the world explored the features of school-prison relations and discussed practices of resistance, justice, and freedom. Participants included educators and activists in the broadest sense—professional teachers, community residents, college faculty, community members, students, poets, painters, and formerly incarcerated people. The conference featured over fifty presentations including leading thinkers around carcerality, anticarcerality, and educational settings.

At least three interrelated questions were taken up and deepened in the forum: How, and in what ways, do schools use the logics of prisons, and how might these reflect larger structural designs? What is the relationship of antiblackness to the state? What are sites of intervention in Pittsburgh and the broader Appalachian region? The book is inspired by many of the forum's thinkers, some of whom appear in its pages. As we circled back to that 1999 Urban League of Pittsburgh publication, we recognized the lineage and tradition of inquiry locally and the urgency to continue struggles for freedom and map the new coalitions, ideas, and contributions that are pushing it forward.

Notes

1. William H. Turner, "Between Berea (1904) and Birmingham (1908): The Rock and Hard Place for Blacks in Appalachia," in *Blacks in Appalachia*, ed. William H. Turner and Edward J. Cabbell (Lexington: University Press of Kentucky, 2014), 11–22.
2. Ibid., 18.
3. Urban League of Pittsburgh, Inc., *The State of Black Youth in Pittsburgh: Perspectives on Young African Americans in the City of Pittsburgh and Allegheny County* (Pittsburgh: Urban League of Pittsburgh, 1999), xiii.
4. Ibid.
5. T. Elon Dancy II, "(Un)doing Hegemony in Education: Disrupting School-to-Prison Pipelines for Black Males," *Equity and Excellence in Education* 47, no. 4 (2014): 476–493, https://doi.org/10.1080/10665684.2014.959271; Erica Meiners, *Right to Be Hostile: Schools, Prisons, and the Making of Public Enemies* (New York: Routledge, 2007); Damon Sojoyner, *First Strike: Educational Enclosures in Black Los Angeles* (Minneapolis: University of Minnesota Press, 2016); Sabina E. Vaught, *Compulsory: Education and the Dispossession of Youth in a Prison School* (Minneapolis: University of Minnesota Press, 2017).

Introduction

A Poetics of Black Appalachia
Sabina Vaught and T. Elon Dancy II

Studying Freedom Struggles in Pittsburgh

A study of the struggles against carcerality and for freedom is a study of relationships as they take shape in place. In many ways, then, it is a study of place, of the ways in which place mediates and is mediated by temporal, political, material, cultural, and ideological relational forces.[1] How does the place called *Appalachia* invite us into particular questions about the relationships that form, resist, and refuse school-prison relations? How are freedom and carcerality dynamically constituted and practiced in place?

Appalachia stands as among the most mysterious, reviled, misunderstood, sensationalized, and fetishized regions in the troubled mainstream american imagination. Mobilized as a fixed referent for the devastating interplay of stock whiteness, rurality, and extraction labor, fictive Appalachia provides that imagination with the (always tentative) reassurance that its fears about itself—who it really is, who it will be—are tidily enclosed by geographic boundaries: boundaries that map concocted deviance, abject precarity, and the fruits of a national violence.[2] Dominance always needs somewhere to put its otherness, excesses, surpluses—its human detritus[3]—to contain it, both in the flesh and in the fantasy.

Regions of Appalachia have been viciously economically and geographically primed to be such a place. As scholar and activist Judah Schept writes,

The prison, and increasingly the jail, have expanded in the region as strategic attempts to manage the crises of coal's decline.... Extraction practices and industry decline have created several conditions for which the prison serves as a putative solution. First, the extreme strip-mining process known as mountaintop removal (MTR) has created vast planes of flat land following extraction. Coal industry advocates and prison boosters alike argue that flat land is at a premium in a region characterized by mountains and that such topography positions the region well for prison-building.... Second, the recent decline of production has resulted in the loss of receipts from the Coal Severance Tax, a once-reliable source of revenue for coal-producing counties. Because the tax is adjusted to production levels, the significant drop in production has led to municipal budget crises.[4]

What better place than a region the powerful, the moderately powerful, and the aspirational imagine as a reassuring container, a natural enclosure, for the state and corporate collaborators to build prison projects?[5] What better place than one deformed by capitalist ecocidal terrorism? Where better than the derelict, the divested, the make-believe? For certain, the architects of the Prison Industrial Complex (PIC) find many sites, regions, and conditions to be appealing for its projects. The logics of carcerality afford brutal creative capacity. However, prison projects are commonly paraded as a local venture: a tailored remedy and a personalized boon.[6] Where that fatuous localization of carceral statecraft meets actual people and place, dialectic apertures of struggle form.[7] Through these places and people, we can observe, study, and engage the potent relational dynamism that is the messy, unromantic richness of local knowledge, organizing, and histories.

"Put Me in My Place"

Our decision to dedicate this volume to freedom questions related to education and carcerality in Pittsburgh surfaced contradictory, derivative imaginings (and also total lack thereof) of place and its relations. In fact, when Elon sent Sabina the link to the University Press of Kentucky

"Appalachian Futures" series during a phone conversation, she asked, a little incredulous, "Wait, Pittsburgh is in Appalachia?"
After this interaction, she reflected to Elon,

> After living in the city for eight months, I quickly confirmed my location by a Wikipedia page. What I understood as a labor town, a star on the constellation of the Underground Railroad, a site of industrial excesses and philanthropic consolidations of power, a land and rivers originally in the care and protection of Indigenous peoples,[8] a town forged in coal, steel, and prisons, a hub of the Great Migration, a Black town, a racist sports town, and so much more, is also the largest urban center in a region I lazily imagined as devoid of urbanity. The moment quite literally put me in my place. One of the many gifts of being put in my place is the opportunity to think through how I did and did not arrive here and how that journey might map onto the larger currents of ideology and materiality that shape innately tethered carceral-educational systems and the related struggles for freedom. I began to wonder: How is it that the largest city, or the most densely populated area, is not the *de facto* capital of this corridor region? Does Appalachia have a spatially and culturally distributed capital, center, or heart that might be a radical model for reimagining state-determined regions and our mimicry of them? Given the deep american attachment to urban and rural as trite and desolate racial signifiers, is this a region that both enshrines racialized allocations of urban and rural and simultaneously contradicts them? What is the specific cultural, political relationship to place when it cuts across and in some cases rebuffs state territories without the use of nationalistic or counter-nationalistic identification and also through racial and economic dialectics?

Understanding Pittsburgh as urban Appalachia, as Black Appalachia, will help us just begin to examine these provocations.

What if Pittsburgh is a forgotten place in Appalachia, among the places that have "been absorbed into the gulag yet exceed them"?[9]

Pittsburgh as urban, as Black Appalachia, complicates that absorption. How do we ask questions in ways that challenge adopted presumptions about urban, rural, and the gulag? About Blackness and Appalachia? How do we ask questions about a place made illegible to the forgotten places of Appalachia? The prevailing connections of urban and rural Appalachia, of Black and white Appalachia, express not only through who is incarcerated and where, or even how educational systems (as districts and as endeavors) interact across geographically near but imaginatively divergent spaces. These connections also express through the struggle against them and the struggle beyond them—that for freedom. In the pages that follow, the Black Appalachian struggles for freedom in a convoluted context of carcerality surface historical, contemporary, and possible future connections as well as fissures with which we must contend.

From King Coal to Carcerality

Thoughtful attentions to complex connections between urban and rural, incarceration and education, emerge from the region within which Pittsburgh is nested. Delineating the abolitionist roots of central Appalachia, Judah Schept writes, "If the history and operations of the coal industry set the conditions of possibility for the rise of a carceral political economy to take shape in the region, it is equally true that the history of resistance to the coal industry has helped to shape opposition to the prisons today. Appalachian organizing against the coal industry is a history of struggling for life and democracy and for the abolition of the practices that precluded both."[10]

Moreover, people of such places experience firsthand that prisons not only fail to bring economic remedy to decimated economies but also, as a dimension of organized abandonment, deliberately sustain penal archipelagos across the region's most economically destitute areas. Such experience can index the ideological grifting of the PIC and foment radical movements that exceed the local.

In "Appalachia v. the Carceral State," Adler-Bell[11] highlights the efforts of multiple rural organizers resisting carceral-educational expansion. Of white rural Kentucky organizer Tom Sexton, Adler-Bell writes, "Many of Sexton's friends had been radicalized by the Black Lives Matter movement, which had forced a profound reckoning over race and punishment in America. As they saw it, the state built prisons as a way of recruiting the rural white working class into the economy of racist mass incarceration. And this group wasn't willing to be recruited. By their lights, the moral calculus was straightforward: If you won't stand against injustice when it could benefit you, what good is your commitment to justice?"[12]

When a local school district adopted a prison-jobs curriculum before ground was even broken on a proposed maximum-security prison in an eastern Kentucky county, local journalist Sylvia Ryerson asked, "What kind of school-to-prison pipeline are we creating for young people here in the mountains?"[13] People in the rural region fighting against expanding carcerality are making connections among generational political and corporate corruption; vast ecocide in the form of mountaintop mining, flatland cleanup, and slurry pond runoff as sites and contexts for prison construction and the subsequent ill health of the people incarcerated and in paid prison labor positions; fossil fuel economies, fracking, and the poisoning of children's bodies; profound educational divestment; the lie of prisons as investment in rural economic zones; and the continuum of abjectly extractive capitalist projects, linking coal to incarceration; among others.[14]

These connections consider shared impacts and their divergent specificities, yet they also maintain urban-rural, Black-white mappings of systems and their rebuttal—some of which are quite real and others of which are constructed by consent to dominant imagination as a result of starkly imposed divisions. In other words, they identify common cause and begin to identify dialogic resistance. But what relational dynamism buried by layers of purposeful forgetting might surface ways of thinking that stretch these connections beyond eastern Kentucky or rural West Virginia? How does Pittsburgh, as Appalachia, help us think more deeply about prisons, schools, and the principles and praxes of freedom struggles that remap our notions of this region and so invigorate new possible coalitions?

Metallurgies and Histories

The carceral conditions, practices, and consequences enacted and resisted in what is understood as the rural Appalachian region near Pittsburgh are connected to and live in Pittsburgh and its very immediate surrounds as well.[15] And they have sweeping historical tentacles.

Black life in Appalachia is foundational in the study of Black history in what is called north america. In fact, the first issue of the *Journal of Negro History*, published in 1916, included an essay on freedom and slavery in Appalachia by the journal's founder, Carter G. Woodson.[16] Woodson observed that in white geographic sensibilities, Appalachia was once configured as the region where East met West, as the boundary of *the West* in what is known as the United States—at first extending beyond the Blue Ridge Mountains, later beyond the Allegheny Mountains, and down into the South. This characterization of the zone before the "wilderness" had profound and permanent impacts on racialized social organization. Since this landmark essay in which Woodson offered a map of regional political struggles, historical scholarship on Black Appalachia has focused on several regions encompassing West Virginia, Tennessee, Kentucky, and Georgia, with attention to Appalachian dependence on slavery (slavery existed in every Appalachian county south of the Mason-Dixon line, and slave markets existed in Virginia, Tennessee, and Kentucky, although any gathering of people signaled a potential "sale"),[17] the significance of slavery in building extractive industries that extend into the present, and the longue durée of Black community education struggles that emerged from the period of enslavement in the region.

The labor of enslaved people fueled Appalachia's industrial landscape across agricultural, rail, mining, and other dimensions. In his analysis of slavery's proliferation in southwest Virginia, Kenneth Noe noted several ways slavery was "a source of great economy."[18] Beyond matters of direct sale, Black people as property were also used as collateral to obtain loans or were hired out and loaned to others. Regarding agricultural labor, Black people were made to tend several crops, herd livestock, construct buildings and fences, make bricks and shingles, and perform every kind of household industry labor. Enslaved people were made essential to the mine economy, every other industrial operation, and the needs of private homes and hotels. In particular, slavery powered the rail economy in Appalachia. Black people constructed railroads, including as blacksmiths, carpenters, mechanics, freight hands, and brakemen. In fact, the railroad accumulated so many Black people during the period of enslavement that other companies experienced difficulty finding any for their businesses. Western Virginia is also the site of the Kanawha salt industry, which Stealey argued was one of the most significant manufacturing operations in antebellum Appalachia.[19] Since the War of 1812, Kanawha manufacturers relied primarily on an enslaved workforce and quickly expanded as slavers flocked to the area for capitalist expansion through proprietor and lessor agreements.[20] In short, in spite of the contemporary dominant imaginary of Appalachia as having emerged from and still featured by stock white rurality and a kind of deviant anti-modernity, the region has vast industrial roots tethered as principally to the system of chattel slavery, and so the labor of Black people, as any other region.

And yet the relations of slavery that shaped industrial Appalachia of course exceeded the labor relations that ostensibly defined it. "What can be done to a captive body?" asks Sexton. "Anything whatsoever," he replies.[21] The slavery project is not about a loss that people experience but the structural imposition of denial/loss of peoplehood altogether. Hence, slavery relations in Appalachia as elsewhere encompassed not only labor or social and economic functions but also larger existential and psychological formations of antiblackness and racial hierarchy. These relational formations worked (and continue to work) to incessantly bind Black people to the position and condition of the unthought;[22] unvisible;[23] and historically, revolutionarily unthinkable,[24] meaning that through their unthinkability as human, Black people's capacity for rebellion and freedom was impossible in the imbecilic imagination of structured antiblackness: a structure of inherent unfreedom. It is this same violent structure that asserts the tireless reproduction of Appalachia devoid of Blackness and its freedom struggles—African Indigenous ontologies that well preceded the savage social order.[25]

This antiblack relational context of unthinkability is nowhere more evident than in the examples of resistance that ground the freedom struggles we encounter in this book—struggles drawn from the histories of Black Appalachia. Appalachia is, of course, a site of Black rebellion and fugitive experiments against domination that ranged from overtly organized insurrection to individual resistance. In Drake's essay,

Sophia Ward, who had been chattel enslaved in Clay County, Kentucky, remembers,

> I wuz a slave nineteen yeahs and nine months, but somehow or nuther I didn't belong to a real mean set of people. The white folks said I was the meanest nigger that ever wuz. One day my mistress Lydia called for me to come in the house, but no, I wouldn't go. She walks out and says she gwaine make me go. So she take and drags me into the house. Then I grab that white woman when she turn her back, and shook her until she begged for mercy. When the master comes in, I was given a terrible beating with a whip but I didn't care for I gave that mistress a good 'un too.[26]

Ward's individual action illustrates a refusal sensibility that permeates Black Appalachian freedom struggles and highlights the vital centrality of the quotidian, mundane, often unregistered acts of rebellion against the quotidian, mundane, and often unregistered practices of antiblack violence—a rebellion that emerges across the chapters of this book.

While the southern backcountry areas of Appalachia were sites of resistance like that narrated by Sophia Ward, they were also sites of "antislavery" movements: a term referring to a position against chattel slavery but endorsing subjugated modes of Black being—a maintenance of the racial hierarchy of antiblackness, merely without formal systems of chattel enslavement.[27]

These regions were then contentious, complex, and dangerous cartographies across which an abolitionist geography was mapped. The Underground Railroad—popularly known as a project of "secret emancipation" organized through a moral "defiance of national laws on the grounds that they were unjust and oppressive"[28]—was built and configured in this Appalachian terrain. Indeed, historians trace Pennsylvania as the birthplace of the name *Underground Railroad*. "The origin of the name Underground Railroad," writes Williams, "came into use first among the slave-hunters in the neighborhood of Columbia, in Lancaster County, Pennsylvania. The pursuers seem to have had little difficulty in tracking slaves as far as Columbia, but beyond that point all track of them was lost. The slave owners are said to have declared that there must be an underground railroad somewhere."[29]

Pittsburgh developed into a part of Black Appalachia as both a portal toward escape in the long journey toward freedom and an urban locus of human hunting. While two pathways on the Underground Railroad ended in Pittsburgh, the city was also a setting of fugitive trek to Canada following passage of the Fugitive Slave Act of 1850.[30] Notably, Black people were rarely captured by chattel slave catchers *after* leaving Pittsburgh.[31] Yet, as an indication of Pittsburgh's danger to Black people, when the Fugitive Slave Act was signed and activated on September 18, 1850, over two hundred armed and organized fugitives quickly departed Pittsburgh. The newspapers expressed the mood of the city's white residents after the news—not a general public conviction to protect fugitives but rather surprise that a large number of fugitive slaves had inhabited the city at all.[32] Months after the passage of the act, Woodson, a Black man, was ordered by the court returned to his Kentucky "owner" in chains. The *Post* printed, "The case was determined without the slightest effort being made to resist the law of the land ... We think the result of this case will show that the citizens of Pittsburgh are not disposed to follow the example of the fanatics ... in a treasonable opposition to the law of the land."[33]

The sentiment held firm years later when Black people were prevented from trying to liberate an enslaved girl. The *Post* wrote indignantly, "The character of this city should not be stained, nor its business injured by negro mobs. Its business has suffered severely enough from other causes within the last year, without adding the curse and disgrace of negro riots. We hope that the next riot of the kind will be met with plenty of well charged revolvers in ready and resolute hands."[34]

Black resistance strategies in Pittsburgh, therefore, reflect Black knowledge of Pittsburgh as a site of danger and struggle. Specifically, Pittsburgh's white liberal class carved itself onto the map by asserting Black freedom as fanaticism and Black freedom struggle as worthy of vigilante assassination. We wonder in this volume how this history recomposes and reenacts itself in contemporary Pittsburgh.

We see the recomposition of hunting and capturing in discursive politics evident today, be they in city welcome centers or museums or universities, through which Pittsburgh participates in neoliberal absolution via a redemptive story of the Underground Railroad. While we know several factors facilitated the Underground Railroad to northern and Appalachian locations, we reject an analysis of "the North" or northern Appalachia as sites against slavery. This frame frequently becomes a discursive strategy to absolve the state and its allied antiblack citizenry through silencing historical narratives[35] of individual white saviors and deodorized antiblack politics. However, in conveying the actual conditions of sociality as the so-called civil war ramped up, Du Bois[36] quotes Frederick Douglass, who said, "The South was fighting to take slavery out of the Union, and the North fighting to keep it in the Union."[37] Pittsburgh's history is squarely within this dynamic. Years after Du Bois, Malcolm X's Black geographic mapping in "the ballot or the bullet" is strikingly conversant: "If you're black, you were born in jail, in the North as well as the South. Stop talking about the South. Long as you south of the Canadian border, you south."[38] These historical frames against false northern morality help to further clarify Pittsburgh's location in a Black Appalachian geography.

Welded Histories of Labor, Carcerality, and Education

While Pittsburgh may not be *the* capital of Appalachia, it is *a* capital of carceral history in the so-called United States. As Angela Davis details in *Are Prisons Obsolete?*, "The first full-fledged effort to create a panopticon prison was in the United States. The Western State Penitentiary in Pittsburgh, based on a revised architectural model of the panopticon, opened in 1826. But the penitentiary had already made its appearance in the United States. Pennsylvania's Walnut Street Jail housed the first state penitentiary in the United States, when a portion of the jail was converted in 1790 from a detention facility to an institution housing convicts whose prison sentences simultaneously became punishment and occasions for penitence and reform."[39]

Prison projects have been reciprocally foundational to labor exploitation (and so, of course, slavery) in the United States and so were primed in their aim to both hold captive and exploit labor to be configured centrally in Black american social organization after the formal end of chattel slavery. The resistance to slavery and labor exploitation is entangled with incarceration at their origins such that these are catalogs of foundationally Black experiences and movements.

Over a century after this early prison experiment described by Davis, Pittsburgh continued as a site of labor exploitation and resistance, forged in the furnace of race and gender alliances, divergences, and battles. "At General Motors," writes James Boggs, "local union after local union, *with the Pittsburgh local in the lead*, refused to go back to work until their local grievances had been settled, the International simply brought all dissident local officers to Detroit, where, together with management, it whipped them into line."[40] And yet, as with most labor struggles, Pittsburgh's partially radical labor encountered the capitulation of local union leadership to corporate leadership and central union leadership. These alliances resulted in disregard for the humanizing, relational demands of workers and privileged benefits or resources that actually furthered and protected the carceral features of labor—surveillance, punishment, bodily harm, and more. Such relations resonate across the city today, shaping the carceral conditions and anticarceral movements in contemporary Pittsburgh and responding to Boggs's question of what would happen as a result of these alliances.

What would happen would be hastened by the patriarchal proclivities suffered by the moderate, or cooperative, labor leadership in Pittsburgh. These proclivities promoted assault on labor freedom struggles, provided complicit support for surplus, and so welcomed carceral expansion, not only as caging of surplus humans or new labor for unemployed forces along vectors of race and gender but also in the re-authorship of geographic, political, racial, and gender divides that sustain carcerality. Gender as an inveterate index of Pittsburgh's carceral-labor conditions is evidenced at every turn.

Late nineteenth- and early twentieth-century Pittsburgh was home to cigar and then electric companies among so many others that exploited mostly white immigrant women laborers as a deliberate component of their fruitful expansion into an economically impoverished region. These urban Appalachian women wound coil shortly after giving birth to children and well before their bodies were healed or they were able to care for their newborns. They toiled under low-wage, unsafe, and exhausting conditions often at menial tasks, which made precarious the well-being of entire families and communities. And yet the women—exploited and exhausted—organized in washrooms, engaged in political education in cafeterias, and formed prototypical labor collectives.[41]

Pittsburgh's power dynamics, which we might better understand as Appalachian and urban, worked relentlessly against the promise of cross-racial women's organizing in the twentieth century. Additionally, the patriarchal, racially supremacist, carceral tendencies of union men frustrated antiracist, feminist coalitional efforts. In *Union Women: Forging Feminism in the United Steelworkers of America*, Mary Margaret Fonow highlights Pittsburgh as a cauldron for the alchemical struggles for race and gender freedom within labor organizing:

> Pittsburgh ... could not provide women Steelworkers in the region with the political opportunity structures or mobilizing networks necessary to build a feminist presence within the union. ... First, the rank-and-file insurgents had not been as successful in electing candidates in the Pittsburgh area, so there was little support for women's committees or the formation of district-wide women's caucuses. The districts located in and around Pittsburgh were under the watchful eye of the International located in downtown Pittsburgh, and their leadership was careful not to rock the boat. Second, within Pittsburgh's municipal government, there were few public resources available for civil rights or women's rights projects and for organized labor. Women Steelworkers and activists did forge some ties with the local organizations of the women's movement in Pittsburgh, but Pennsylvania had already ratified the ERA, so the women's movement was not as mobilized [as elsewhere]. ... White activists, calling themselves "industrialized" radicals, moved to the region to build a more progressive labor movement. However, they did not encounter the same conditions as their counterparts in the Calumet region where women activists were successful because of the strength, diversity, and configuration of alliances among social

movements, and the mobilization of several social-movement organizations.[42]

In fact, it was just outside Pittsburgh proper, in a so-called rural region, where cross-racial coalitional organizing thrived among women. Pittsburgh itself was claimed as a territory for racial violence, hierarchy, white so-called radicalism, and apartheid. In light of the histories of Pittsburgh, it is no accident that the state and federal prisons that run to cage state-identified women are located hundreds of miles' and hours' travel distance outside the city. This dislocation is not only a product of the corruptions and exploitations enumerated above. It is also a feature of the targeted race-gender-class work of carcerality: To remove the peoples of cities from the map. To remove Black people, Brown people. This removal speaks to part of what we are asking in this volume. How are the peoples of Pittsburgh not only subject to vast carceral, corporate, ecocidal systems that codify fictive rural-urban or Black-white or feminist-masculinist dimensions of life—important questions in their own right—but also how are the peoples of Pittsburgh and its immediate surroundings involved in complex Appalachian freedom struggles that illuminate the possibilities across this geographic region? Pittsburgh's freedom struggles are not restricted to trite notions of the city versus the country. Instead, they are moored in the entangled repressions and resistances that pervade the entire region, from labor to ecocide.

If Appalachia has long served as the stronghold of rural otherness in the dominant racial imaginary, Pittsburgh's purchase on mainstream racial fantasy has been similarly reductive but perhaps in some ways more accurate. Labor helped secure that. Labor is the proverbial double-edged sword. Access to it, organizing around it, and reward for it drive other conditions of life in the capitalist United States. It is an original and ongoing source of racial and gender control, violent and exclusionary but also creative, communal, and radical. And Pittsburgh's blades are ground to diamond-sharp edges.

American accumulation of Black people into Appalachian industrial capitalism—particularly reinforced through lumber, railroad, and coal-mining businesses and the labor demands of World War I—is widely known as *the great migration* as it resulted in massive relocation of Black people escaping the terrors of the Deep South. Coal companies launched aggressive "recruitment" campaigns, emphasizing a better quality of life. Black kinship—both familial and chosen—additionally powered the relocation as coal miners, for instance, would visit the South to recruit toward better job opportunities. Southern West Virginia became colloquially known by Black people as a place where "money grew on trees,"[43] where antiblack lynchings were fewer, education opportunities were understood as greater, and voting thought to be easier. Yet the migration framework is complicated by the counterinsurgent trappings of the Deep South like debt peonage, manufactured by slavers and employers to industrialize slavery's afterlife. Some Black people's "migration" from the beginning was more of an escape from the Deep South's horrific Jim Crow formulations. This fugitive necessity resulted from the sustained terror of losing loved ones who would be put at risk by a foiled design. The accumulation project also divided families as young adults relocated further north despite the objection of family elders.

On arrival in West Virginia, the terrain of Black life was, too, paved with rocky, "upsouth" Appalachian repressions, which Black people resisted in a variety of ways. Trotter[44] details how the Black population expansion in West Virginia during the late nineteenth and early twentieth centuries paralleled the expansion of the coal industry, doubling from 1880 to 1910 and again by 1930. However, Trotter argues that in spite of their numbers and contribution to industry, Black West Virginians encountered political roadblocking. Yet Black people undertook ongoing, strategic alliances and organized for the right to vote and serve on juries. The desire for institutional and political access and justice continued to shape many Black societies, social clubs, and churches.

Families were shaped by coal mining, such that many Black fathers taught sons through an apprenticeship model, building coal-mining futures against a backdrop of white supremacist racial hierarchy. Under what is known as the Great Depression of 1930, Black people were disproportionately affected by the hard times of unemployment and carceral institutional practices. And when technological advancement changed the way coal mining operationalized, Black people were disproportionately fired, much less likely to find alternative employment and dealing with repression across every facet of life.[45] That same recruitment campaign of the late 1800s that had once promised a better life revealed its insidious, undergirding truths—antiblack political agendas formed in restaurants, hotels, pools, schools, and hospitals—forcing new transitions for Black people in West Virginia or propelling relocation elsewhere. While these many forces of racial terror, migration, labor, family organization, and right shaped rural Black life, as they followed people into Pittsburgh, they expressed themselves through particularities of that urban context.

Pittsburgh's labor history reflects these transformations. Foner[46] documents that by 1917, only two unions in the city of Pittsburgh admitted Black laborers. In describing the stark, systemic "hardships and social struggles of urban black workers," in the postwar United States, Trotter[47] writes that white Democratic politicians catered to white labor in Pittsburgh so that of thousands of laborers in the city, "in 1964, Pittsburgh recorded only one black apprentice bricklayer, operating engineer, and lather; two sheet-metal workers; three painters; and four carpenters."[48] While organized labor (including the obviously carceral, such as police) has long been racist in character and practice, Pittsburgh's organized labor helped define Pittsburgh as a supremacist industrial city and contributed to conditions of living that permeated the entire area. Those conditions, anchored in part in extreme white, masculinist labor power, have been visible over time in the labor force of public K-12 educators in Pittsburgh. As white teachers are among the largest labor force, we wonder about the conditions for educational labor in Pittsburgh that are relevant not only to its certain role as an industrial city home to robber barons but also to Appalachia in its complexity.

Part of that complexity is that, through various forces over time, people migrated to Pittsburgh. We are particularly interested in Black Pittsburgh, and while we have talked about some of the forces of Black migration, we are most interested in how Black people live in Pittsburgh. We borrow this sensibility in part from those historians of Black migration who point us to the interrelations of migration, labor, and social life formations[49] and in part from the contributors to this book whose stories and analyses are a gravitational pull into the focus on Black life in Pittsburgh. Pittsburgh is perhaps uniquely shot through with stories forgotten in the larger narrative of Black life—stories forgotten in a forgotten place.[50] How do Black people construct liberatory social life in this brutal city? How do Black people draw on and build long practices of freedom and organize those around education and against carcerality? How does place shape and get shaped by this freedom struggle? As Jessica Klanderud has written in her rich study of the socio-spatial formations of the twentieth-century Hill District, *Struggle for the Street: Social Networks and the Struggle for Civil Rights in Pittsburgh,*

> The streets of the Hill District of Pittsburgh, Pennsylvania, and other neighborhoods where African Americans lived and worked were not fixed lines of geography that divided the residents of the city, white from Black. Instead, they formed the arteries that moved goods, people, and importantly, ideas in and out of the neighborhood. Street spaces within the Hill District allowed residents to create Black-controlled public spaces to build and work through their political, economic, cultural, and gendered ideas of proper usage and to push back against the forces that created ghettos and instead allowed them to create a neighborhood . . . they formed their own social networks of information and ideas in segregated neighborhoods as they created their own city within the larger urban space. The streets provided a public space for the formation and transmission of ideas throughout the African American community of Pittsburgh. These streets were sites of struggle and cultural development. It was through those struggles and across class lines that African Americans in Pittsburgh formed a neighborhood and a movement.[51]

Like Klanderud, we are interested in Black space, Black placemaking. How do the land, the classroom, the home school, the street, and elsewhere shape and get shaped through the freedom struggles we read about?

We wonder in the pages that follow about the freedom work of educators in public schools and other organizational and community contexts. Pittsburgh also has a deep-well history of freedom labor, evidenced by the organizing work of Black laborers themselves, the long and powerful run of the Black-owned *Pittsburgh Courier*, the uninterrupted work of creative freedom-makers from August Wilson to contributors to this volume, and the collective efforts of educators, among so many others. How are these Appalachian? How do they help us locate Appalachia, reimagine its possibilities, and unearth potent connections?

This book is organized into five sections drawn from bell hooks's *Appalachian Elegy:*[52] returning to sacred places; sometimes falling rain / carries memories of betrayal; renegades roam here; fierce grief shadows me; listen little sister / angels make their hope here. Each section is introduced by a brief narrative and is shaped by contributions from artists, poets, community organizers, young activists, and more. We invited contributors to this volume to narrate their stories and bring to bear their analyses. The resultant volume is therefore a complex text: authors have divergent ideas about Blackness, about carcerality and its relationship to education, and about racial formation and power. Contributors map different Black Pittsburghs. Our intention in convening these contributions, and in organizing them in the poetics of Black Appalachia, is to contribute to the conversations about Black freedom work in urban Appalachia. We do not aim for the ideas across this volume to represent a cohesive stance or politic, a radical or liberal perspective or practice. Rather, together they form a universe of stories of how people understand their context and commitments, of how people make place.

Gilmore asks of forgotten places, "How do they set and fulfill agendas for life-affirming social change?"[53] The people and pages of this book ask that very thing. How do Black freedom struggles in Pittsburgh, forgotten as Appalachia, share old knowledge and offer new agendas for life and freedom-living in Appalachia? We invite readers to connect in this way: to look for productive contradictions, nuances, political tensions, affect, and all the possibilities those obtain. This is a volume meant to spark the questions motivated by a shared commitment to freedom-living.

Notes

1. Ujju Aggarwal, *Unsettling Choice: Race, Rights, and the Partitioning of Public Education*. (Minneapolis: University of Minnesota Press, 2024); Ruth Wilson Gilmore, *Golden Gulag: Prisons, Surplus, Crisis, and Opposition in Globalizing California* (Berkeley: University of California Press, 2007); Katherine McKittrick, *Demonic Grounds: Black Women and the Cartographies of Struggle* (Minneapolis: University of Minnesota Press, 2006).
2. Cedric Robinson, *The Terms of Order: Political Science and the Myth of Leadership* (Chapel Hill: The University of North Carolina Press, 2016).
3. Angela Davis, *Freedom Is a Constant Struggle: Ferguson, Palestine, and the Foundations of a Movement* (Chicago: Haymarket Books, 2016).
4. Judah Schept, "Planning Prisons and Imagining Abolition in Appalachia," in *The Routledge International Handbook of Penal Abolition*, ed. Michael Coyle and David Scott (New York: Routledge, 2021), 387.
5. Sojoyner, *First Strike*; Clyde Adrian Woods, *Development Arrested: The Blues and Plantation Power in the Mississippi Delta* (New York: Verso, 2017).
6. Gilmore, *Golden Gulag*.
7. Robin D. G. Kelley, *Freedom Dreams: The Black Radical Imagination* (Boston: Beacon Press, 2002); Dylan Rodriguez, *Forced Passages: Imprisoned Radical Intellectuals and the US Prison Regime* (Minneapolis: University of Minnesota Press, 2005).
8. And also notably a place where many express confusion or the inability to determine which Native nations were or are here, an absence of certainty that often results in deleting any reference to peoples and reifying the need for a certainty that may not be a feature of this place.
9. Ruth Wilson Gilmore, "Forgotten Places and the Seeds of Grassroots Planning," in *Engaging Contradictions: Theory, Politics, and Methods of Activist Scholarship*, ed. C. R. Hale (Berkeley: University of California Press, 2008), 31–61.
10. Schept, "Planning Prisons," 388.
11. Sam Adler-Bell, "Appalachia vs. the Carceral State," *New Republic*, November 25, 2019, https://newrepublic.com/article/155660/appalachia-coal-mining-mountaintop-removal-prison-fight.
12. Adler-Bell, "Appalachia vs. the Carceral State," para. 4.
13. Kate Jenkins, "How Federal Prisoners Might Become Appalachia's New 'Black Gold,'" *Scalawag*, January 27, 2017, https://scalawagmagazine.org/2017/01/how-federal-prisoners-might-become-appalachias-new-black-gold/, para. 1.
14. Gwynn Guilford, "The 100-Year Capitalist Experiment That Keeps Appalachia Poor, Sick, and Stuck on Coal," *Quartz*, December 30, 2017, https://qz.com/1167671/the-100-year-capitalist-experiment-that-keeps-appalachia-poor-sick-and-stuck-on-coal/; Judah Schept and Sylvia Ryerson, "Building Prisons in Appalachia: The Region Deserves Better," *Boston Review*, April 27, 2018, https://bostonreview.net/articles/prisons-are-not-future-appalachia-deserves/; Panagioti Tsolkas, "Mass Incarceration vs. Rural Appalachia," *Earth Island Journal*, August 24, 2015, https://www.earthisland.org/journal/index.php/articles/entry/mass_incarceration_vs._rural_appalachia/.

15. Mike Ludwig, "Evidence of Fracking Chemicals Found in Bodies of Pennsylvania Children," Truthout, March 23, 2021, https://truthout.org/articles/evidence-of-fracking-chemicals-found-in-bodies-of-pennsylvania-children/.

16. John C. Inscoe, ed., *Appalachians and Race: The Mountain South from Slavery to Segregation* (Lexington: University Press of Kentucky, 2001).

17. Richard Drake, "Slavery and Anti-slavery in Appalachia," in *Appalachians and Race: The Mountain South from Slavery to Segregation*, ed. John C. Inscoe (Lexington: University Press of Kentucky, 2001).

18. Kenneth W. Noe, "'A Source of Great Economy': The Railroad and Slavery's Expansion in Southwest Virginia, 1850–1860," in *Appalachians and Race: The Mountain South from Slavery to Segregation*, ed. John C. Inscoe (Lexington: University Press of Kentucky, 2001), 111.

19. John E. Stealey III, "Slavery in the Kanawha Salt Industry," in *Appalachians and Race: The Mountain South from Slavery to Segregation*, ed. John C. Inscoe (Lexington: University Press of Kentucky, 2001).

20. Ibid.

21. Jared Sexton, "The Vel of Slavery: Tracking the Figure of the Unsovereign," *Critical Sociology* (2014): 591.

22. Saidiya V. Hartman and Frank B. Wilderson III, "The Position of the Unthought," *Qui Parle* 13, no. 2 (2003): 183–201.

23. McKittrick, *Demonic Grounds*.

24. Michel-Rolph Trouillot, *Silencing the Past: Power and the Production of History* (Boston: Beacon Press, 2015).

25. Cedric Robinson, *Black Marxism, The Making of the Black Radical Tradition* (London: Zed Books, 1983).

26. Drake, "Slavery and Anti-slavery," 18.

27. Ibid.

28. Irene E. Williams, "The Operation of the Fugitive Slave Law in Western Pennsylvania from 1850 to 1860," *Western Pennsylvania Historical Magazine* 4 (1921): 150.

29. Ibid., 151.

30. The Fugitive Slave Act of 1850 required that fugitive enslaved people be returned to enslavers even if they were harboring in a free state. This act doubled down on the earlier Fugitive Slave Act by adding penalties and punishments for state and local noncompliance. See act, https://avalon.law.yale.edu/19th_century/fugitive.asp.

31. Williams, "The Operation of the Fugitive Slave Law."

32. Ibid.

33. Ibid., 154–55.

34. Ibid., 155.

35. Trouillot, *Silencing the Past*.

36. W. E. B. DuBois, *Black Reconstruction: Black Reconstruction in America 1860–1880* (New York: Simon and Schuster, 1999).

37. Ibid., 61.

38. Malcolm X, "The Ballot or the Bullet," April 3, 1964.

39. Angela Davis, *Are Prisons Obsolete?* (New York: Seven Stories Press, 2003), 46–7.

40. James Boggs, *The American Revolution: Pages from a Negro Worker's Notebook*, 2nd ed. (New York: Monthly Review Press, 2009), 26, emphasis added.

41. Emily Martin, *The Woman in the Body: A Cultural Analysis of Reproduction* (Boston: Beacon Press, 2001); University of Pittsburgh Library System, "Pittsburgh Women in Organized Labor @ Pitt Archives: The Early Years," July 29, 2022, https://pitt.libguides.com/pittsburghwomen_organizedlabor/early_history.

42. Mary Margaret Fonow, *Union Women: Forging Feminism in the United Steelworkers of America* (Minneapolis: University of Minnesota Press, 2003), 103.

43. Joe W. Trotter Jr., *African American Workers and the Appalachian Coal Industry* (Morgantown: West Virginia University Press, 2022), 15.

44. Ibid., 15.

45. Ibid.

46. Philip Foner, *Organized Labor and the Black Worker, 1619–1981* (Chicago: Haymarket Press, 2017).

47. Joe W. Trotter Jr., *Workers on Arrival: Black Labor in the Making of America* (Berkeley: University of California Press, 2019).

48. Ibid., 142.

49. Trotter, *African American Workers*; Joe W. Trotter Jr., *Coal, Class, and Color: Blacks in Southern West Virginia, 1915–32* (Morgantown: West Virginia University Press, 2022).

50. Mark Whitaker, *Smoketown: The Untold Story of the Other Great Black Renaissance* (New York: Simon and Schuster, 2019).

51. Jessica Klanderud, *Struggle for the Street: Social Networks and the Struggle for Civil Rights in Pittsburgh* (Chapel Hill: University of North Carolina Press, 2023), 1.

52. bell hooks, *Appalachian Elegy: Poetry and Place* (Lexington: University Press of Kentucky, 2012).

53. Gilmore, "Forgotten Places," 31.

Part 1

"returning to sacred places"

Beginning with *On the Horizon*, we consider "what is next" as also what is past or what has passed. Elegies and futurities invoke discordant origins of place and how those origins shape our relations here: of an Indigenous child's experience of being hunted and relocated as part of the genocidal effort to cement colonialism's merger of militarism and education; of looking east to the sacred start of each new day, of caring for land; of escape; of the passing on of traditions. Contributors in this section point to multiple horizons, mapping a complex terrain of relations and possibility. What relations refuse carceral schooling, enact or mediate migrations big and small, and reclaim practices of return home? What are the relations to place: to rivers that must be crossed, that both restrict and liberate Black life; to land in which Indigeneity is everywhere and yet formally erased; to earth and plots and farms that are the sites of Black self-determination struggles? We invite you to enter with curiosity and to leave with questions deepened by stories of and in place.

Sabina Vaught

On the Horizon

Morgan Overton

On the Horizon is a mixed-media piece representing that moment when you are on the precipice of a new chapter in life—marking a breakthrough coming your way. The figure appears eyes closed and content as they face a new "horizon," with a sun and its rays dominating the other half of the portrait. This piece of art serves as a reminder to find peace and reassurance in what is next as it is meant to be part of our individual story.

Morgan Overton, *On the Horizon*, 2022

Wawawpewnowat

Jennifer Johnson

A small blurb, published on July 10, 1903, in the Carlisle Indian School newsletter, *The Red Man and Helper*, noted, "Mr. Johnson, of the Sac & Fox Agency, Oklahoma, brought us seven pupils, on his way to attend the Educational Convention in Boston."[1] Johnson was likely attending the National Education Association Conference in Boston, where the fates of Indigenous children were being vigorously discussed. A large segment of the conference programming was held for the Department of Indian Education. It was at this meeting that Richard Henry Pratt, the architect of Carlisle Indian School, proclaimed, "Any expenditure of public money to segregate Indians and to build them up and strengthen their Tribal life is unwarranted because against the best interests of both the Indians and the government."[2] Educators were gathered to discuss themes of the "transfer of Indian children"[3] in the same breath as civilization. It was there that methods of taking Indigenous children were assessed, and I wonder if local school officials discussed how they would sometimes set fire to the prairies to catch Indian children to send to school. Indigenous children were being hunted.[4]

My great-grandfather, Wawawpewnowat, or William Newashe, entered Carlisle Indian School on July 5, 1903, at the young age of thirteen. He traveled to Carlisle Indian School with his younger sister, Maweso, whose English name was Emma, as their parents had passed away, both from consumption. The notice in the newsletter likely heralded their arrival in Carlisle, Pennsylvania.

Wawawpewnowat and Maweso's schooling experiences are meticulously and clinically detailed through student records from Carlisle

Indian School and the Sac & Fox Agency. I recognize that for the Sac & Fox children, like many others who traveled east to Carlisle, the federally sponsored project of Indian boarding schools represented a pattern of forced exile from their homelands. For the Sac & Fox people, this exile was one among many in which our people would be uprooted from the lands they knew intimately. I came to know my great-grandpa through archival records. He had passed long before I was born, so researching his schooling experiences at Carlisle was a way to get to know him, to become familiar with who he was. As a scholar of Indigenous educational histories, I was familiar with Carlisle Indian School and the stories that have emanated from survivors and their descendants. Carlisle is infamously known as a precursor to the proliferation of federally supported boarding schools across the country.

In what is now known as Pennsylvania, the history of the land details how settler demands for land forced a rupture between Indigenous Nations and their homelands. The Susquehannock Nation called the area home for approximately eleven thousand years preceding colonization, and their homelands spanned lush valleys and waterways.[5] The land that the town of Carlisle was developed on was a site eagerly sought after by the Penn family, and through a series of land grants and illegal licenses to land issued by Thomas Penn, the land of the Susquehannock became owned by settlers.[6] A bustling area that was once a site of commerce and Intertribal trade among Nations, the state of Pennsylvania is no longer home to any state or federally recognized Tribes.[7]

Prior to statehood, in 1750, two Quaker men, Anthony Benezet and the enslaver Richard Humphrys, stipulated in their wills that the proceeds from their estates should be utilized to develop a school for Black and Indigenous children. Although the process to develop the school took many years, advocates for education were often met with violent opposition. In May 1838, a violent mob of whites laid siege to and burned the new Pennsylvania Hall, where Quakers were meeting to discuss education for Black youth.[8] Education for Black youth was a threat that enraged the white mob that day, yet advocates persisted in the establishment of a school decades before the Civil War. The development for the African Institute in 1852, later renamed the Institute for Colored Youth, became a site for freedom and refusal as prominent leaders such as Octavius Catto[9] and Fanny Jackson Coppin[10] crafted educational opportunities for Black youth. The school boasted faculty with Ivy League degrees, and it was a flourishing site that was highly supported by the Black community.

Two decades later, in a small community located over a hundred miles west of Philadelphia, plans for the development of a school for Indian children were ramping up. The school, Carlisle Indian School, would represent a wave of genocidal policies that demanded the most precious of Indigenous Nations—Indigenous children. The development of Carlisle was remarkably different from the early beginnings of the African Institute. There was no angry white mob burning down buildings in righteous anger. Rather, the white rage had coalesced over generations into a highly funded military campaign by the US government to exterminate Tribal Nations in order to gain access to land.

Richard Pratt was a military officer who oversaw the imprisonment of Indigenous prisoners of war at Ft. Marion in St. Augustine, Florida.[11] He brought in teachers to provide lessons in English and viewed his efforts as an experiment to "kill the Indian in him, and save the man."[12] Pratt's experience at Ft. Marion led him to petition the US government to develop an educational institution where he could carry out his goals and further his mission. Subsequently, Carlisle Indian School opened its doors in 1879. Landis noted that students were brought to Carlisle "to ensure the cooperation of their resisting parents and grandparents."[13] It was a system of carefully calculated control, inhumane to the families who were no longer able to parent their own children. A little over a decade later, when my great-grandpa arrived at Carlisle, like the Ft. Marion group, he would have had his hair cropped and military-style clothes selected for him to wear. Pratt's ideologies directly influenced school-based policies that sought to forcibly separate him from his language and cultural lifeways as a young Sac & Fox boy. Tethered directly to the Ft. Marion people who were imprisoned in Florida, Carlisle established conditions for carcerality and education in the area. Carlisle's carcerality, sanctioned by the federal government and its agents, gave rise to meticulous control and brutal punishment as discipline. It set the bar for what education could consist of. No longer would religious missions have to masquerade as benevolent organizations to lead students to Christianity. Once the federal government gave the green light to Carlisle and its architects, the conditions for carcerality and education were connected to larger campaigns of war and genocide. The agents were governmental employees, religious organizations, and philanthropic organizations that were all deeply invested in the education of Indigenous children. At the root of it all was access to land. Carcerality, education, and control were synonymous with civilization and colonization.

At Carlisle, Wawawpewnowat and Maweso participated in school outings. William was being trained as a tinner and photographer. Carlisle's policies were to send students to white families within the community to perform labor for them.[14] In exchange, students received small earnings that were promptly turned in to the school superintendent, who would then make decisions on how students could spend their funds. The seizure of student funds and decision-making authority also extended to funds that were held in trust for them at their home agencies. Multiple letters were exchanged among the Sac & Fox agent, the Carlisle School superintendent, and William and Emma regarding the use of their own funds. Government oversight of student funds and determination over how funds were disbursed were additional methods to control students even long after they had left Carlisle. Letters between government agents and school officials indicated they decided where students would live after leaving school. At times, the decision of the agents was that students could not live with their own families. These were early probationary measures enacted to continue to control the lives of Indigenous youth. What this really meant was that after students had completed their education, fulfilled the requirements of the institutions, they were still viewed as incapable, as threats to the establishment, and this warranted another layer of surveillance after they left the school.

To date, I have not found a graduation record for my great-grandpa, and his student files indicate he took leave from the school often, sometimes right after the football season ended. Fear-Segal and Rose found that only 758 out of the over 10,500 students graduated from Carlisle.[15] A significant portion of his school experiences were as an athlete for

Carlisle's football team. An article in the 1911 *New York Times* entitled "Newashe Out of Indian Team" documented, "The Carlisle Indian football team will be handicapped in the game against Lafayette at Easton tomorrow by the absence of Newashe, who has been threatened with an attack of pneumonia."[16] Yet, as Bloom reminds us, for all the highlights and accolades, Carlisle student athletes' performance on the field was viewed by administration as an opportunity to showcase Pratt's civilization efforts.[17]

Although Pratt saw athletics as an opportunity to highlight what he perceived as the success of the school, some student athletes viewed sports as an opportunity. My great-grandfather's participation in football and baseball was undoubtedly important to him as he left Carlisle to pursue a career playing professional baseball. He played for minor leagues in both the United States and Canada before retiring from baseball in the early 1920s, and when he passed away, he was memorialized as a Carlisle athlete in local newspapers.

Intertwined with William's records were those that he shared with his beloved sister, Emma. They shared a strong bond, and while at Carlisle, they relied heavily on each other for support. Emma was a devout student and excelled in the language arts. Her name was frequently mentioned in student publications as she enjoyed an active social calendar. A prolific writer, she shared her Sac & Fox culture in the *Carlisle Arrow*,[18] writing about *The Merman's Prophecy*. At a school such as Carlisle, whose aim was to stamp out any vestiges of students' culture, Emma unwaveringly continued to assert her identity as a Sac & Fox youth.

As a 1912 graduate of Carlisle, Emma had educational goals that did not end once she left Carlisle. She was determined to complete her education and worked hard to achieve her goals. In September 1912, she penned a letter to the Office of Indian Affairs, writing, "I wrote concisely and emphatically pertaining to my desires and it is my hope that you authorities will be able to see me in school by the first of October. It is my determination to get to school and I am going to get there. I hardly have education enough to fulfill my desires to help my tribe and be a credit to it."[19]

Young Emma viewed education as a way to advance the interests of her Sac & Fox people. She very much desired to further her education at a business school in Philadelphia, and she requested funds to do so. On receipt of her letter, the assistant commissioner for Indian Affairs denied her request, stating that although her ambition was commendable, there were no laws in place to enable the office to pay her tuition.[20] Emma had no control over her own funds, and even though she requested the use of her own money, federal bureaucracy hindered her efforts. Furthermore, the agent advised her to pursue educational opportunities by returning to Carlisle to gain instruction in commercial courses because they were free. The juxtaposition of a "free" education in which one was, quite frankly, not free is a stark reminder that the only education afforded to the youth was what the government agents set the parameters for. The conditions for education at Carlisle were industrial, training students to perform duties as laborers. Such is the carceral state; it requires a logic that controls student movement, wielding power and harnessing dreams and ambitions.

Emma responded sharply to his advice, stating, "It is not my desire in the least to return to Carlisle and under no circumstances will I ever be induced to do so. I am through attending those and it has been my desire now for some time to attend a business school."[21] Furthermore, she reasoned, "I have attended Carlisle for the past six years and I know good and well, too well anyway that with all its facilities to advance the Indians, it has not given me what Pierces can and another thing my former teacher has told me time and time again that what I need is competition and I know that she is not mistaken in the least."[22]

She lamented her low pay at the store she was working at and explained, "I know I have tried for positions but because of the deficiency of my education, I have not been granted the opportunity."[23] Emma then stated, "This money that I have has not all duly been from the annuity, but the lease from the lands which I inherit from my father and mother and I know good and well that if they were living it would be their earnest desire to see me making something of myself."[24] Emma was a strong advocate for her education, and it is remarkable that in a school that required that she give up her cultural identity, Emma refused. As Mohawk scholar Audra Simpson reminds us, refusal is the "very deliberate, willful intentional actions that people were making in the face of the expectation that they consent to their own elimination as a people, that they consent to having their land taken, their lives controlled and their stories told for them."[25] As a result of her advocacy and sheer determination, Emma began her business school studies.

At Carlisle, students were exploring ways in which to assert their identities. For my great-grandpa, his identity was very much tied to his athleticism. For Emma, it was through her writings and her education. I often wondered how Carlisle might have affected their identities and lives when they returned to the Sac & Fox Nation. It was important to Emma that she be of service to her Tribal Nation, and William's historical records demonstrate service as well. A few short years after he left Carlisle, he was drafted in World War I. Although Carlisle sought to fully assimilate students and prevent their return to their home communities, both Emma and William did return home. William established his home in the area, where he served on the Sac & Fox Tribal council and maintained membership in a Christian church. Later in life, he helped to establish a service club for the Sac & Fox people as a World War I veteran. His daughter, my grandmother, was named after his sister, Emma.

Over a century after their attendance at Carlisle, in 2021, the Honorable Deb Haaland, the first Indigenous secretary of the Interior, ordered an investigation into the federal boarding school system. On a listening tour in Anadarko, Oklahoma, she remarked, "Federal Indian boarding school policies have touched every Indigenous person. I know some are survivors, some are descendants, but we all carry the trauma in our hearts."[26] As I thought about her remarks, it was true. I do not know of anyone within my family and Indigenous friends who has not been affected by the federal boarding school project. Not a single person. Carlisle and the 408 boarding schools that operated across the United States were concise in their goal to culturally assimilate children.[27] The removal of children like my great-grandpa and his sister far from their homelands was an important component of the US project of appropriating and acquiring Indigenous lands. The Federal Indian Boarding School Initiative Investigative Report affirmed that "the United States established this system as a part of a broader objective to dispossess Indian Tribes, Alaska Native Villages, and the Native Hawaiian community of their territories to support the expansion of the United States."[28] Despite federal policies that targeted their core identities as Indigenous people, students at Carlisle and across other boarding schools resisted. They *refused*. In the Appalachian region, the resistance of early Black educators who defied angry white mobs by providing a thriving educational system for Black students, followed by student refusal at Carlisle, situates the long arc of freedom struggles in schools. Forty-four years after first entering the doors of Carlisle Indian School, my great-grandfather, William Newashe, along with my great-grandmother, Myrtle, were guests on the *Indians for Indians Radio Show*, a popular radio show hosted by his relative, the Sac & Fox chief Don Whistler.[29] On that warm August day in 1949, he served as an announcer for the annual Sac & Fox powwow and invited listeners to come celebrate with them.[30] The deep timbre of his voice traveled across the airwaves as he explained protocol for the camps. After his announcements, he sang along with his relatives and announced the Slow War Dance, Swan and Buffalo songs that were sung by the Sac & Fox singers. Like the drumbeat that remained consistent, so, too, did he. He was home.

Notes

1. "Man-on-the-band-stand," *The Red Man and Helper*, July 10, 1903, https://carlisleindian.dickinson.edu/sites/default/files/docs-publications/RedMan-Helper_v03n46_0.pdf.

2. Irwin Shepard and Charles W. Eliot, "Notes. The National Education Association. Boston, July 6 to 10, 1903," *Elementary School Teacher* 3, no. 10 (June 1903): 737, http://www.jstor.org/stable/992916.

3. Ibid., 738.

4. Indian Pioneer Papers Collection, J. E. Davis Interview, Western History Collections, University of Oklahoma Libraries, Norman, Oklahoma, 1937, https://repository.ou.edu/islandora/object/oku%3A16243?solr_nav%5Bid%5D=4e6f069894110b978c07&solr_nav%5Bpage%5D=0&solr_nav%5Boffset%5D=0&search=%2522J.E.%2520Davis%2522.

5. Christopher J. Bilodeau, "Before Carlisle: The Lower Susquehanna Valley as Contested Native Space," in *Carlisle Indian Industrial School: Indigenous Histories, Memories and Reclamations*, ed. Jacqueline Fear-Segal and Susan D. Rose (Nebraska: University of Nebraska Press, 2016), 65.

6. Ibid.
7. Ibid., 71.
8. Milton M. James, "The Institute for Colored Youth," *Negro History Bulletin* 21, no. 4 (1958): 83, http://www.jstor.org/stable/44213172.
9. Lightning Peter Jay, "Contextualizing Octavius Catto: Studying a Forgotten Hero Who Bridges the Past and Present," *Social Education* 84, no. 6 (2020): 342–47.
10. Linda M. Perkins, "Heed Life's Demands: The Educational Philosophy of Fanny Jackson Coppin," *Journal of Negro Education* 51, no. 3 (1982): 181–90, https://doi.org/10.2307/2294688.
11. Anita Satterlee, "The Carlisle Indian Industrial School," ERIC ED472262 (2002): 4, https://files.eric.ed.gov/fulltext/ED472262.pdf.
12. N. Scott Momaday, "The Stones at Carlisle," in *Carlisle Indian Industrial School: Indigenous Histories, Memories and Reclamations*, ed. Jacqueline Fear-Segal and Susan D. Rose (Nebraska: University of Nebraska Press, 2016), 45.
13. Barbara Landis, "The Names," in *Carlisle Indian Industrial School: Indigenous Histories, Memories and Reclamations*, ed. Jacqueline Fear-Segal and Susan D. Rose (Nebraska: University of Nebraska Press, 2016), 91.
14. Satterlee, "The Carlisle Indian Industrial School," 11; Louellyn White, "White Power and the Performance of Assimilation: Lincoln Institute and Carlisle Indian School," in *Carlisle Indian Industrial School: Indigenous Histories, Memories and Reclamations*, ed. Jacqueline Fear-Segal and Susan D. Rose (Nebraska: University of Nebraska Press, 2016), 108.
15. Jacqueline Fear-Segal and Susan D. Rose, "Introduction," in *Carlisle Indian Industrial School: Indigenous Histories, Memories and Reclamations*, ed. Jacqueline Fear-Segal and Susan D. Rose (Nebraska: University of Nebraska Press, 2016), 2.
16. "Newashe out of Indian Team," *New York Times*, October 28, 1911, https://timesmachine.nytimes.com/timesmachine/1911/10/28/104841153.html?pageNumber=14.
17. John Bloom, "The Imperial Gridiron: Dealing with the Legacy of Carlisle Indian School Sports," in *Carlisle Indian Industrial School: Indigenous Histories, Memories and Reclamations*, ed. Jacqueline Fear-Segal and Susan D. Rose (Nebraska: University of Nebraska Press, 2016), 127.
18. Emma Newashe, "The Merman's Prophecy," *Carlisle Arrow* (December 1912): 1, https://carlisleindian.dickinson.edu/sites/default/files/docs-publications/RedMan_v05n04c.pdf.
19. Emma Newashe, "Correspondence Regarding Business School Enrollment (1912)," Carlisle Indian School, Dickinson College, https://carlisleindian.dickinson.edu/sites/default/files/docs-documents/NARA_RG75_CCF_b026_f13_86716.pdf.
20. Ibid.
21. Ibid.
22. Ibid.
23. Ibid.
24. Ibid.
25. Audra Simpson, "Consent's Revenge," *Cultural Anthropology* 31, no. 3 (2016): 327.

26. Mary Annette Pember, "Road to Healing: Deb Haaland Pledges Boarding School Truths Will Be Uncovered," *Indian Country Today*, July 10, 2022, https://indiancountrytoday.com/news/we-all-carry-the-trauma-in-our-hearts.

27. Bryan Newland, "Federal Indian Boarding School Initiative Investigative Report," May 2022, 4, https://www.bia.gov/sites/default/files/dup/inline-files/bsi_investigative_report_may_2022_508.pdf.

28. Ibid., 3.

29. Lina Ortega, "The Indians for Indians Radio Show," University of Oklahoma Libraries, 2019, https://shareok.org/handle/11244/323802.

30. "Indians for Indians Radio Show," Western History Collections, University of Oklahoma Libraries, August 2, 1949, https://repository.ou.edu/uuid/15b0b12d-eeb9-5cc2-b3ce-545f3803b82b.

Grounded Justice

Unearthing the Birthright of Liberated, Collective Black Environmental Justice Futures in Pittsburgh and Beyond

M. Beatrice Dias, Cassie Quigley, Alyssa Lyon, Ariam Ford, and Ebony Lunsford-Evans

Abstract

When did we begin to see ourselves as apart from the earth and each other? The dissonance in our Earth song resonates within the catastrophic environmental and social devastations we are experiencing across the globe. Most decision-makers look to computing technological innovations to sustain our current way of life. But whose lifestyles are we truly trying to maintain, and at whose expense? And should we even invest in this futile endeavor to sustain an unsustainable way of living? Black knowledge traditions offer us deep insight into how we might rewrite our collective futures in harmony with our environment and each other. This chapter conveys possibilities for environmental justice from the perspectives of three extraordinary Black environmentalists in the Pittsburgh region. Their work is contextualized in our historical roots, grounded in our present socioenvironmental landscape, and branches out to our speculative freedom futures; their stories weave into the rich fabric of Black Appalachian community wisdom and collective power.

Introduction

Think back to your childhood, your memories of growing up, your family stories, and your life events. Everything we do and experience in our lifetime is connected to an environment: a space, a place, a location. Growing up, Ariam Ford only wanted to be in beautiful spaces, places that contrasted the stark and uninhabitable federal penitentiary she visited as a child to see her father. She carries this memory with her in her work at Grounded, a local nonprofit dedicated to land justice in Pittsburgh. Ford tells her team, "Literally everything you do has to happen on a piece of land somewhere, that's why it's so valuable."[1] Her vision is to ensure land value is redistributed in racially equitable ways such that those who were historically and unjustly dispossessed can reclaim their inheritance to this intergenerational wealth. Ebony Lunsford-Evans, or Farmer Girl Eb, is spiritually connected to the land she cultivates through her community-oriented and educational farming practices. Sowing literal and figurative seeds in her childhood neighborhood sprouts possibilities for more fruitful and liberated Black futures: "We're building farmers, we're building healers, we're building bankers. We're going to have a base ready for [the next generation]. Because we're not going to put them in the same situation we're in."[2] Building on the wisdom of her ancestors, her birthright, she is creating holistic, land-connected communities to counter the oppressive socioeconomic systems that were never designed to benefit her or her people. Alyssa Lyon is dedicated to creating healing spaces where Black people can authentically connect with their rich lineage as earth-oriented beings: "I think it's important to help Black folx reimagine themselves in the space of not what they can't do or can't access, but from the power that we intrinsically have."[3] Her work with the Black Environmental Collective is aimed at advancing just solutions that support Black communities' ability to combat environmental threats to their quality of life, food, environment/place, and climate change. As such, she seeks to agitate inequitable social structures and combat environmental injustices so we might rewrite the narrative to uplift Black knowledge traditions, Black thriving, and Black love.

In this chapter, we interweave wisdom that emerged through conversations with Ariam Ford, Ebony Lunsford-Evans, and Alyssa Lyon. The work, stories, and vision of these three remarkable Black environmentalist women in the Pittsburgh region highlight local freedom struggles within an environmental justice context. Grounded in Black radical traditions, their efforts offer us insights into the possibilities for how we might live in relationship with place and people. The ongoing global pandemic, increasingly devastating impacts of climate change, America's intensifying racial reckoning, and proliferating global militarism should give us pause and push us to adapt our ways of being on this earth. Yet our world continues to operate within a framework of what Cedric Robinson referred to as "racial capitalism," which is "dependent on slavery, violence, imperialism, and genocide."[4] If we wish to survive our changing global environment and thrive in freedom futures, we need a new blueprint for how to be in community with our land and one another. The wisdom in this chapter outlines a path for us and offers a freedom song for our collective humanity.

Background and Context

Pittsburgh sits on "land and near the rivers originally in the care and protection of the Adena and Hopewell Nations, and the Monongahela Peoples, and shared over time by many Indigenous Nations."[5] Situated in the northern region of Appalachia, this city of about 300,000 residents[6] has experienced several transformations over the years. Since its colonization by European settlers, Pittsburgh developed into an industrial hub, owing to abundant natural resources and a landscape conducive to extracting and transporting the land's riches. This industrialization also led to detrimental environmental consequences, with pollution clouding the lives of Pittsburgh residents. After the steel industry's collapse, the Carnegie, Frick, and Mellon empires (among others) emerged as educational institutions, museums, parks, libraries, and scientific and technological bases; these establishments encompass much of the contemporary structure of the city.[7] While dominant narratives of Pittsburgh often focus on its industrial history, sports traditions, and research and educational enterprises, this land is also a site of freedom struggles, from serving as a stop in the Underground Railroad to labor movements and uprisings for civil rights and racial justice. Black knowledge traditions, resistance, and resilience have shaped much of Pittsburgh's rich social and cultural landscape. Yet the city is one of the most inhospitable places to live if you are Black and more so if you are a Black woman, with unforgivable mortality rates, adverse educational and economic outcomes,[8] and environmental racism.[9] It is in the midst of this complex and rich historical context, on this sliver of Appalachian land, that the stories of the three Black women featured in this chapter emerge.

Black Women Freedom Fighting for the Land

As a lifelong resident of Pittsburgh, Ebony Lunsford-Evans has a relationship to this land that is deeply rooted and intergenerational. She holds multiple identities in this region as daughter, wife, mother, descendant, ancestor, entrepreneur, farmer, educator, leader, land steward, and community builder. Her journey as a business owner and community organizer is a spiritual walk for her. She had walked a different path before, toward an academic career, but was denied that future due to financial hurdles she could not surpass. This setback was devastating at that time, and she turned to her spirituality to guide her path. It was at this moment that she felt called to connect more deeply with her ancestral heritage: "As a Black woman, why am I in this situation? People who look like me were the first to walk this earth. How did we lose the sun, the rain, the moon, the stars, the mountains, as a person who looks like me?" Following these questions led her to research her heritage and learn more about how her plight as a Black woman walking this earth had taken this turn. Her findings propelled her to take action and move away from anger and blame toward doing something different: "I knew that I wanted to help create community. The first thing that God led me to was to feed my community." Although she had no prior experience with farming or growing, she felt that this knowledge was a part of her lineage, and so it must be accessible to her; with this in mind, she began to teach herself how to cultivate the land: "This is what my ancestors did—they lived in relationship with the land. This is my birthright."

On arriving in Pittsburgh from New York City, Alyssa Lyon noticed differences in the labor landscape for Black people, who appeared to be more heavily employed in the service sector in Pittsburgh compared with New York City. She made a strategic move to environmentalism and sustainability because those spaces in Pittsburgh were primarily occupied by white people. This move has been fruitful and has connected her dual passions for building community and supporting people to a more holistic purpose: "We keep taking these bite-sized chunks of what's wrong with Black communities and trying to solve them. And I think we purposely ignore that they're all connected. For example, it doesn't make sense to tackle air, water, and land separately or in some kind of order." As director of the Black Environmental Collective, she works with local leaders to agitate for environmental justice in Pittsburgh's Black communities, which have historically been, and continue to be, disproportionately impacted by the hazards of pollution. The Collective is a part of a Black think-and-do tank concerned with eliminating barriers for overburdened and underresourced communities. They fill a void within the predominantly white Pittsburgh environmental movement and take a comprehensive approach to tackling the multiple, interrelated factors that affect the health of a community, including food access, climate change, and environmental concerns (i.e., water, air, and land pollution): "We're here to bring Black folx into the mix and also serve as a safe space. We don't get a lot of space as Black folx to sit, to breathe, to collect our thoughts because I think we're always in a state of urgency. So how do we allow people in the Collective to imagine a new world, to imagine access to green life, to reconnect to our roots? We come from an earth-oriented people, so how do we reconnect ourselves, take back what's ours?" Alyssa lives in these questions, and this propels her freedom struggles.

Ariam Ford directs Grounded Strategies, which works to improve the social, economic, and environmental health of distressed and transitional communities by building capacity to reclaim vacant and underutilized land. Grounded Strategies was founded in 2007, based on a thesis project of Carnegie Mellon University students who investigated repurposing the underutilized resource of vacant land that Pittsburgh has in quantity and concentration. Between 1950 and 2000, the city lost two-thirds of its population, and this decline has led to an accumulation of unoccupied, uncultivated, and unattended land: "This is what happens when you have all this leftover space where people aren't anymore. They tore things down and now the land is vacant." Ariam recognizes that in the United States, land is the number one way to generate and pass down wealth intergenerationally: "So, without land, in the current status of how our system works, you really have no lifelong capital movement as far as wealth building. We see this as an opportunity to, overnight, create a 'landed class' in Pittsburgh's Black and Brown neighborhoods, using vacant land." Ariam is fighting for land justice and to reclaim the dignity and honor of people who were unjustly dispossessed of their earth inheritance.

Ebony, Alyssa, and Ariam are continuing a legacy of freedom fighting and land stewardship in Black Appalachia; they have answered the call of their ancestors to join an intergenerational freedom song in harmony with the earth and are making a blueprint forward.

Purpose in Struggle

Ebony, Alyssa, and Ariam are motivated to help shape a different narrative—from surviving to thriving—for those who, like them, live on the margins of institutional power. This is the *why* that drives their collective justice work. As Black women walking this earth, they understand their connection to place and land. Ebony embodies this wisdom in her work as a farmer, entrepreneur, community leader, and advocate for environmental justice: "Before we were slaves, we were farmers. Schools only talk about slavery and not about the wisdoms we held about land and growing that are a part of our legacy. My purpose is to move with the understanding that it is our birthright to grow healthy foods and change the social determinants of our health."

Alyssa fights for equal access to thriving. She works to translate the language of oppressive systems so that communities of color can wield their inherent power to agitate for change. Her love for Black people propelled her to take this journey into environmental justice work and fight against systemic oppression: "I need to start rewriting the narrative and unlearning these things about myself and my people in order for us to be in a successful place. I want us to get away from the narrative that Black women have to be superheroes and Black people have to have superpowers in order to see success. I know foundationally that our people are resilient (for lack of a better term), and we have the ability to succeed. But resilience doesn't mean you have to struggle every day." So she works on building a community of Black love and Black power, to focus on healing, to write their own story of resistance, to reclaim their inheritance as land-connected people, and to affirm their right to thrive.

Ariam's great-grandparents lived on the same land they were once enslaved on. After Reconstruction, the land was divided, and her family members built a life there. They are also buried there. The house was eventually foreclosed and flipped into a rental vacation house, glossing over and depreciating the blood, sweat, tears, and joy that were poured into the land over generations. This was her mother's home—where she was born and grew up—and she can never go back there except as a transient renter of the land her family toiled over many years to cultivate. In an eerie echo of this tragic land story, Ariam's grandmother's house became vacant after her grandparents and uncle, who lived there, passed away. However, this time her mother was able to stop the foreclosure by paying a steep price. This is another home that has so much meaning and value to her family and their lineage: "It's now condemned and vacant, and the animals have it, but there's this piece of land a quarter mile from the Chesapeake Bay, where I learned to swim and crab, that has immense value. Now it just sits there. We were able to save it from land loss, from a predatory loan that my grandfather took out. But now none of us have the capital to do anything with it." Her family's history, in relationship to land and space, drives Ariam's work.

Collective Struggle

"My house is black from all the soot and the dirt from the plant just down the street. Our children can barely walk up and down the sidewalk. We get air-quality alerts all the time." This is the stark environmental reality that Alyssa contends with in the predominantly Black Pittsburgh neighborhood where she lives. She is determined to recenter the priorities of Black people in a city that is becoming increasingly white-, green-, electric-car-, and windmill-washed but not focused on urgent issues concerning Black communities. In her capacity as director for the Black Environmental Collective, Alyssa aims to work with the knowledge of Black communities to influence political and regional outcomes and to push a new and shared agenda. Moving into the sustainability field opened her eyes to how everything is connected and rooted in systems that are set up for neighborhoods like hers to constantly fail: "We're not requiring, not making it mandatory, for systemic change. I think we're the ones constantly getting run into the ground, dying from fatigue, dying from heart conditions, dying from just being burnt out." She looks around at the glaring contrasts between adjacent neighborhoods, where a predominantly white and commercial area hosts green spaces, whereas the predominantly Black and residential locale next door is plagued with brownfields: "We should all be infuriated by the juxtaposition!" Alyssa understands that we need a collective effort to confront these systemic injustices from multiple fronts—those working within the system and those working from the outside. She wants us all to feel behooved to become co-conspirators (not just allies) in agitating the inequitable system: "We need people to walk with us into the fight." Collective action ensures that individuals and specific groups do not have to bear the full burden of getting our communities what they need and should have: "We deserve equal access to prosperity. Just let us have the things that we need in order to thrive. America is the land of pulling people up, and no one can answer the question of 'why don't you want to see Black folx succeed?' No one has an answer because it doesn't make sense."

Ariam's childhood experience of visiting her father in prison expanded her view of what constitutes one's environment, which for her includes both built and natural spaces or all the different places one has to engage with throughout a life. Her initial goal in life was to always be in nice spaces, and her approach was to follow the path of successful white men who are predominantly celebrated in US media and infrastructure. College exposed her to more diverse people and material. These encounters helped her realize that her access to resources or lack thereof was not primarily due to anything she did as an individual but were instead results of an inequitable system. So she changed course and now pursues collective justice for Black and Brown communities who are disproportionately subjected to living in hazardous and unpleasant spaces: "For me, environmental justice is about the access to the things you have to create the place where you live. This is similar to bird nesting—what material do you have to build your nest?" In order to achieve this form of justice, we need to alter the core resources available to people, and land access plays a significant role in this equation. Ariam's group, Grounded, is focused on changing the way people view land: "Land is inheritance—these are places that people worked hard and long to create." She reflects back on her own family's struggles with land ownership; it is unbearable for her to imagine devaluing all of that history into a meager amount that property is sold for during a sheriff's sale. The history attached to a piece of land is not accounted for in the current structure of property assessments. Grounded aims to quantify the value of labor and love that were poured into a place and also reconcile the racial injustices that led to these lands becoming vacant and thereby valued less. Ariam understands that the language of this capitalist economy is numerical, and so their approach is analytical and quantitative. In essence, they are translating historical, racially based land injustices into numbers in order to challenge the land devaluation calculus. This formulation paves the way for a more equitable redistribution of land wealth. It is also a radical shift from Grounded's initial efforts to beautify and convert vacant lots into biofuel sources: "We realized we were just helping people make land look nice, but it never belonged to them, and they didn't get to keep any of the value generated." Their new directive is to maximize ownership and access to these unoccupied land parcels, with and for the communities who live in these undervalued neighborhoods: "How can we continue to beautify the land and improve the urban ecology and also make sure that in doing so we know that that sweat equity ends up in the hands of people who have been living with this environmental injustice?"

Ebony works directly with the earth. She recalls, while growing up, hearing the message that she should not get dirty and being taught that the dirt can harm us. She has had to unlearn notions of what type of work she should be doing: "We have to unlearn what we've been told.

There was life before slavery that links us to our roots of environmentalism. Our relationship is with the dirt. Our relationship is with the land." Making, watching, feeling, and experiencing her first avocado sprout brought everything together for her: "I felt it through the ground, through my body. It jolted my whole life. It was amazing." That moment gave her the drive to create and move away from blame. In 2019, she started Out of the End, an initiative to build sustainability, equity, and livability as foundations for Black and Brown communities within the Greater Pittsburgh area. She wanted to counter the harmful and limited stories she and other Black people are told about themselves: "We're going to create our own story that needs to be told." Ebony realized that there is not enough information or technology available to trace back her lineage and find out the depth of Black wisdom and connections to the land across the world. So she looks within herself and toward her community for the tools she needs to do her earth-honoring and life-sustaining work.

Looking back at history, Ebony reflects on how much of the local infrastructure in Black neighborhoods was destroyed since the end of the Reconstruction era. For example, there were over 130 Black-owned banks operating in the United States between the end of the Reconstruction era and the beginning of the Great Depression; however, that number was down to eighteen in 2020.[10] She understands this loss on a personal level: "Even with me doing all this, building a business and creating community, I can't walk into one bank and get no help. My money's sitting there in all these banks, and I can't walk into one of them and get not one bit of help at all." In spite of the unparalleled contributions Black people have made to build the wealth of this nation, Black customers are still more likely to be denied a loan or credit from a bank or financial institution.[11] Similar to the banking industry, today there is only one remaining Black-owned hospital nationwide, none in Pittsburgh:[12] "We, as people of this hue, own no hospitals, no healing centers, but we are the sickest." Fundamentally, Ebony understands that the path to freedom is through building holistic communities. This includes establishing interconnected agricultural, financial, and health structures within and through individuals and groups in the neighborhood: "I am doing the work that it takes to build community."

Freedom Dreams for Black Futures in Pittsburgh

I think the future is going to be some kind of replication of what Black people knew, which is building community and sustainability within ourselves. Not just sustainability, not just resilience, but thrival. —Alyssa

A future where we are getting back into position and knowing who we are—a place where we are creating one sound. —Ebony

I imagine a world where we have solved all the basic problems that cause people to struggle so that we can start solving bigger problems and making better art and understanding more about life and our whole purpose—it's not just to live and die at the same job. —Ariam

Ebony's freedom dream includes Black and Brown communities thriving and leading: "Being in position to help one another, understanding that it is hard work, and controlling our futures by getting into position." She recognizes that our healing has to be prioritized for this vision to come to fruition. This restorative work must be collaborative and built in solidarity with one another. In her practice, she is making an effort to connect with those who are Black but come from different language traditions: "It's really important for us to recognize our shared lineage and try to learn from each other." Ebony's life work pushes against assimilation so that we can enrich our lives with the multitude of languages, cultures, and knowledge traditions, especially those stemming from the African continent. She is starting by connecting with immigrant communities here in Pittsburgh: "We will find a way to create one sound."

Ariam believes we are approaching a tipping point of collective consciousness that resonates with the Renaissance period, a time of great upheaval. In moving through this portal of change, we will encounter many challenges and difficulties: "Because Black people have had to struggle for so long, we're ready! With the knowledge that history has to teach us, we're going to be able to leave this renaissance and lead that way through to the new world and take all the people, even those dragging their feet behind, and make sure they'll be able to eat in the climate crisis. But I'm not worried about changing their minds anymore. I'm going to let them eat when we get there, but I'm not going to struggle on the way there."

With this passion, Ariam imagines freedom futures where people can function beyond basic survival without struggling and build out their dreams for the world. To her, freedom is the ability to choose your own fate and location in life and express who you are in the world, without fear or doubt. And this dream coalesces through community building: "When different people's expressions mingle amongst each other, then you have ingenuity and innovation and progress."

Alyssa recognizes that the fight for freedom futures requires long-term thinking and cultural shifts: "We're engaging in mindset work. We're engaging in generational work. So we have to agitate the system, not just for today but truly for the minds of future generations." She calls to mind the work of the Black Panthers, who created their own systems for food, education, protection, and so forth. Building on their model, we can work toward securing the resources we need to create our own political agenda and liberated destinies. In doing so, we will need to let go of the current, racial-capitalism[13] operating system of the United States and the world and build a different way of being by reaching back toward Black knowledge traditions, community orientation, and earth connectedness: "I think success is learning to operate less from a place of trauma and more from a place of peace, and a place of understanding, and a place of healing—absolute healing for the Black community. I think that we deserve it; I think it's been a long time coming. And so I want success from a place of healing for Black folx."

We are called to engage in a freedom struggle for our collective, earth-oriented, liberated, environmental justice futures. We can begin this journey in our small corner of Appalachia with Ebony, Alyssa, and Ariam and join with other pockets of transformative environmental activism across the globe to heal, to grow, to thrive, and to care for the land and each other.

Notes

1. Personal communication between co-authors.
2. Ibid.
3. Ibid.
4. Robin D. G. Kelley, "What Did Cedric Robinson Mean by Racial Capitalism?" *Boston Review*, January 12, 2017, https://www.bostonreview.net/articles/robin-d-g-kelley-introduction-race-capitalism-justice/.
5. Sabina Vaught, personal communication, 2021.
6. "Quick Facts, Pittsburgh City, Pennsylvania," US Census Bureau, 2022, https://www.census.gov/quickfacts/fact/table/pittsburghcitypennsylvania/POP010220.
7. "Pittsburgh," *Britannica*, July 25, 2023, https://www.britannica.com/place/Pittsburgh.
8. Brentin Mock, "Pittsburgh: A 'Most Livable' City, but Not for Black Women," Bloomberg, September 20, 2019, https://www.bloomberg.com/news/articles/2019-09-20/how-pittsburgh-fails-black-women-in-6-charts.
9. Kristina Marusic, "Environmental Injustice in Pittsburgh: Poor, Minority Neighborhoods See Higher Rates of Deaths from Air Pollution," June 12, 2020, https://www.ehn.org/environmental-injustice-pittsburgh-air-pollution-2646169635/particle-1.
10. Kristen Broady, Mac McComas, and Amine Ouazad, "An Analysis of Financial Institutions in Black-Majority Communities: Black Borrowers and Depositors Face Considerable Challenges in Accessing Banking Services," *Brookings*, November 2, 2021, https://www.brookings.edu/articles/an-analysis-of-financial-institutions-in-black-majority-communities-black-borrowers-and-depositors-face-considerable-challenges-in-accessing-banking-services/.
11. Ibid.
12. "Black History Month: A Medical Perspective: Hospitals," Duke University, October 20, 2022, https://guides.mclibrary.duke.edu/blackhistorymonth/hospitals.
13. H. L. T. Quan, ed., *Cedric J. Robinson: On Racial Capitalism, Black Internationalism, and Cultures of Resistance* (London: Pluto Press, 2019).

Liberation Is Yet to Come

An Interview

S. L. Akines, Win Nunley, and Robin-Renee Allbritton

S. L. Akines *is a PhD candidate in the department of history at Carnegie Mellon University, where her studies center the history of the Black radical tradition in education. She has been a home educator since 2008.*

Win Nunley: Could you please tell us a little bit about yourself, a little introduction and your history and your own formal and informal schooling?

S. L. Akines: My name's Stacey Akines, and I actually moved to Pittsburgh about ten or eleven years ago. And so I've had a variety of schooling because my parents were military. I was born in Hawaii, and the first school I went to was Aiea Elementary, which is on the island, but that was kindergarten. But by the time the first grade came around, we moved. And so I did some schooling in North Carolina near Camp Lejeune military marine base. And then I ended up, by the second grade, being schooled in Bessemer, Alabama, which is right outside Birmingham.

And I still changed schools a lot. Because when I first moved to Alabama, my grandmother, she never liked public schools, so she put us in a Catholic school, even though she lived across the street from the public school. And so I went to Catholic school for a couple years, and then my mom was not liking that because she went to Catholic school her whole entire life. And so when my mom came down from North Carolina, she put us in public schools.

I ended up going to fourteen different schools in twelve years. So it was very hop, skip, and jumping because my last two years of high school, I went off to a boarding school in Mobile, Alabama. So that's my background. And then, of course, I went to college, bachelor's degree, master's degree, and now I'm going working toward a PhD.

WN: Awesome. You're home educating your child. Does any of that have to do with your upbringing and your grandmother's views on schooling?

SLA: Yeah, I never really considered that until now, but my grandmother was born in 1937, so she was born during Jim Crow. And so by the time my mother was born twenty years later in '57, schools were legally supposed to be integrating. And so the Catholic schools were already integrated, for the most part, at the time that my mom entered school. She didn't want my mom going through that, being bused.

And it's surprising because that's not the normal narrative. My grandmother wanted something more settled, more calm, where she knew the teachers. And those Catholic schools at that time had a tradition. She went to St. Francis—that's still located in Bessemer—and it was a Black Catholic school at that time. Most of the kids that went there were African American, Black, and so she liked that. And so yeah, just having a settled environment, knowing what my children's curriculum would be, definitely influenced [my decision to homeschool] and her views because I was kind of raised by my grandmother.

WN: In what ways have you experienced connections between schooling and carcerality?

SLA: One of my reasons for moving out of Alabama is because charter schools at that time [weren't] legal in Alabama. And so I was hearing so much about charter schools in the Black community when I moved here. Charter schools were public, they were free, and they were the way to go. And so I was, like, I need to move to a state that has charter schools.

That wasn't my only reason, but that was one of my reasons. And so when I got here, I put my son in a charter school and thought everything would be okay, and I was pretty much satisfied with it until around the third and fourth grade. My first experience really was him getting in trouble, getting sent into the office. And then you get warning, warning; then the suspension starts. So by the fourth grade, he had become known as a troublemaker. And so that was a rough year for him, and it really came all to a head when he was in his art class, and something happened between him and another student. And then that student's cousin said, "Leave my cousin alone." And so it was two on one. It became a physical confrontation at that point. And the art teacher, who was a petite white woman, was scared, and she called security on him.

I had never experienced security being called on myself in school, but my son being in the fourth grade, it was . . . You didn't see security really until high school back in my day. But the security for me, as a mom, that was eye-opening because I had always read about it, seen it, but then when it happens to you, and for my son, a security guard at that time was no different from a police officer because of the way they were dressed and the stature that they have—and remember, he's a fourth grader. So he ended up getting suspended, and it just so happened that the suspension happened for five days, and the sixth day, when he was to return, was the last day of school. But he had gotten suspended before in school, so it was kind of like that in itself was the end.

It was just perfect timing. I didn't send him back to school for the last day, but it was kind of like that summer I had a chance to let it stew. And I was like, she called security, and that was her reaction. And I said, now he'll enter into the fifth grade with all this history and paperwork. And I wasn't sure that I wanted it. And he was actually on the honor roll every single time. He was an honor roll student. And so I didn't want his paper trail to affect him, his learning, or his views about learning because he still had a positive view. At that point, he didn't like art. And even to this day, he doesn't like art in that traditional sense that the schooling frames it as, but he loves to learn about hip-hop and other kinds of art.

And I just wonder sometimes why he never latched on to art. But we'll never know. But for me, that was the first time I said it's real, and it can happen to me and anyone. And so I took a drastic move, and after he got suspended that last time, he never returned to being enrolled in a public school.

WN: What has been some of your most valued work toward freedom in this context?

SLA: My most valued work is just being able to spend time in the formative years, like the young developing years of my children's life, and being able to experience and grow with them, watching them grow, experiencing things with them, shaping their views of things. So that's how I view my work, my service. And I do view it as I'm serving my children, but they also return the service and the investment in everything immediately. So that's, I think, my most important and valued, as far as my value. Valued work is actually being able to serve my children.

WN: How does homeschooling fit into the struggle for liberation and your personal struggle for liberation as well?

SLA: As far as liberation is concerned, we're, right now, as a community—and when I say *community*, I just mean those in the struggle, those who are oppressed, those who feel they're oppressed—that we're not liberated yet. So we're struggling for it. And so when I think of liberation, I think of future. And I think there is no future without the youth, without children. So me home educating my children in itself contributes to the future. And we have that intent of liberation. We have the goals of liberation, the objective of liberation, and so they can learn about "what do you think liberation is?".

And to me, just having the notion, or seed planted, that you are not liberated because it takes a long time, a lot of experiences to figure out "wait a minute, we need to be liberated." That in itself is a contribution:

giving the youth the notion that liberation is yet to come. And using experiences, your own as a parent, as an education facilitator's experiences, and the experiences that they can read in biographies or autobiographies of people before them struggling for liberation, and letting them know "you're the future. We're not liberated yet, but you're the future." Liberation can only come in the future. It can't come in the past. And we are in the present right now, looking forward to liberation.

WN: How would you define *liberation*?

SLA: I think liberation is like a shapeshifter. That's how I look at it. So it manifests itself in different contexts or different ways depending on the context. It just doesn't have really a fixed definition. But as far as homeschooling, as far as home education, it's incomplete; freedom, liberation, all these practices that we're attaining, it's incomplete. So again, it goes back to before, when I said the goal is liberation, but we try ourself, we try our best to express it, express liberation, express freedom as just being, simply being.

So, for example, I use the limited freedom that home education affords me, to be, become, and engage in what I believe to be a mother. So that's one who cares for, guides, and passes on familial and cultural assets or traditions and cultural traditions. It can accomplish so much: linguistic traditions, philosophical traditions, religious traditions. But just being and becoming and being able to become something that I feel is a part of expressing liberation or expressing freedom or striving towards liberation regarding the kids or my children.

Freedom also facilitates being so they can be children. Just being a child is a form of liberation for Black folk. It's a form of liberation. Being allowed to be a child, being allowed to become an adult. We cannot take Black children becoming young adults and becoming adults for granted. A lot of us don't make it. We do not make it to see adulthood. And just engaging in their local and global surroundings is an act of liberation, just being able to understand there is a world outside of the United States.

WN: So what do you think a fully free world would look like in your own eyes?

SLA: I think a fully free world . . . I don't know. But in the homeschooling context, freedom in schooling is home education. Because schooling is a relatively new phenomenon. Masses of children gathering in one place for eight to ten hours a day is institutionalization. It's not freedom. It's unfreedom because it's kind of like, yeah, you had a freedom for your parents to choose for you to go there, but it's still, when you get there, it's unfree.

Just imagine if every parent in the world engaged with their children, was able to pass down traditions, Indigenous knowledges, what would the world look like? This is my worldview. If Indigenous people were allowed to pass along their languages, what would the United States look like? What would it sound like? What would it be? Where would it go? What would it become? Would the United States exist in a free world? Would the United States even exist?

So this is my idea of freedom in education, free to pass along those invaluable things, traditions, culture, languages, practices that we don't have time to pass down when families are separated or children are separated from their communities, from their Indigeneity, from wherever they're coming from when they go to school.

WN: So liberation and freedom is the goal. How does homeschooling fit into that? Do you believe that homeschooling would still be a thing in a free world?

SLA: I think the concept of homeschooling or home education would not exist in a free world because homeschooling did not exist before schooling. The terms did not exist before schooling. So although children were educated at home, technically, it didn't exist. I think that just these concepts, in a free world, wouldn't exist. Children would be free to be children. They would still learn. There would still be traditions passed along, but automatically the terminology would change. You would start again, switch learning—schooling, education might even go to the wayside. But "look what I learned today, Mom" or Dad or whomever, cousin, neighbor; this is what you learn. You learn to possibly milk a cow or possibly explore the internet.

You learned that today. You weren't schooled in it. You weren't educated in it. There might not have been any formal class. And I think, too, learning would be more informal than formal. You still would have formal learning because you still need people to know how to perform heart surgery, for example. You just don't need someone walking off the street, observing a couple heart surgeries, or even five years of heart surgeries, and then saying, "Yeah, I'm a doctor; I perform surgery."

WN: So what are your feelings about political education?

SLA: I think that a Black home education is inherently political. Specifically my role as a home education supervisor, where we facilitate (and I say *we*, because it's more than just me, but the state labels me as *the*—there has to be a home education supervisor—but we facilitate) international, Indigenous, familial knowledges. And I think that in itself is engaging in political education. For example, when my youngest child recounts his dreams and we spend the entire day trying to have fun with that, trying to interpret it, imagine what would've happened if it continued on and continued on, even being able to ask the next day, "Did you pick it up or not?"

But I think that's political; daring to dream, having the time to dream, having the awareness to recall a dream, having the space to narrate or put that dream into action is political. And that's just an example in so many ways, not saying that children that are not home educated cannot dream and put their dreams into action, but I'm saying in the school time being able to discuss it and have someone there to engage with them about it and dream with them, pick that dream up. That's something that is, again, Indigenous. We know that other cultures outside of the schooling culture take dreams very seriously. And so I just wanted to use that as an example of something that's political education that people might not even think is political: a dream. But we know that so many people—Martin Luther King—had a dream. Daring to dream, daring to imagine. So many scholars have taken just the imagination as being something that can turn political.

WN: So I have a pretty broad question here, but what do you think counts as an education?

SLA: As far as my situation, being the Black situation, I think political education is an education. It's a requirement of education. And so not only just dreaming but passing on down the tradition of realizing that you're in a specific situation, that you're in an oppressive situation, that in itself is an education. And getting that education young and as early as possible is one step in future liberation. The longer you wait to actually realize and become educated, politically educated, being in a Black situation, the further out you extend liberation, your liberation, communal liberation. And so political education is just knowing the situation you're in, the situation that people like you were in before you, and daring to dream of a situation other than that what you're in. And I think that's my definition of education. And in another time or another space, it may be something different. But specifically to me and mine, that is definitely what education is.

WN: In what ways does Pittsburgh's geography impact your perception of freedom?

SLA: I think Pittsburgh in general, because it's known for its three rivers, it feels so free because a river can take you anywhere that you want to go. So as far as being a home educator, you can use those rivers for economy, nature, all types and forms of education and just their Indigenous meanings. The significance to the Indigenous people who were here and still are here, but it also creates unfreedom or a restriction because to cross a river can be a big thing. It can isolate you.

And so I think it's a big contrast. It can go either way, depending on what you're trying to do, because when it comes to information, when it comes to traditions, you have to find a way if you want to attain some types of knowledge or pass on; you have to find a way to get it out, get it down these rivers, get it across the river. And that sometimes can be hard in Pittsburgh. It can be hard. It can separate you from, even though you might be four miles from a library, it might separate you an hour, depending on the time of day. So that's the way it contributes. It allows for vast amounts of freedom, but it also does constrict.

Part 2

"sometimes falling rain / carries memories of betrayal"

How might "falling rain" describe both the totalizing environments of terror and the lifegiving of insurgents who rupture, track, and refuse? How might our memories serve as guiding text for how we might study over time as essential to charting a course for the future? Carceral systems represent a recomposition of conquest and enslavement, in both their implementation and their impact. How do the pieces in this section illustrate these mirrored/reflective experiences—focusing on deliberate and systemic carcerality within spaces in Appalachia? As advocate and activist Amber Thompson notes in her interview, "Everything is carceral," and further, referencing the space of philanthropy and pitting communities against each other for resources, "These are Black people that are suffering and white people, specifically white men, who have some kind of class status benefiting from it."

Lori Delale-O'Connor and T. Elon Dancy II

The Burgh

Cue Perry

When discussing urban Appalachia, I feel a perfect representation is the city of Pittsburgh. A perfect visual representation.

Cue Perry, *The Burgh*, 2022

The Effects of a Black Child's Education

Breanna Ewell

Breanna Ewell is a first-year student at Indiana University of Pennsylvania, studying sociology and communications/media.

When I was a young child, my mother and myself just moved more toward the center of Mckees Rocks, PA. So my school district was considered Sto-Rox. When I was eleven or twelve—preteen age—I transferred to Urban Pathways, which is a middle and high school. It's in downtown Pittsburgh, PA. Sto-Rox is my district school, but my mom did not want me to go there because my mom didn't think that the school was serious enough. They had a school band, sports, but they were not serious about academics. So my mom applied to the Northside Urban Pathways Charter School.

What I learned from the transfer was that the academics were different. And Urban Pathways was all African American. Sto-Rox had mostly white and African American students that were in the McKees Rocks district. Urban Pathways didn't have any field trips or events. We had cheerleaders and basketball, but there was no band or football games or dances. The building was too small for that. Sto-Rox had field trips and different activities, and they are big on sports. I think if we had a band I would have learned to play an instrument. All we had were academics, and the other school had all the sports and activities. Urban Pathways had a Black Student Union and the Lighthouse team, which is basically a student council. You had to apply to those things and do an interview in order for the staff to accept you. Also at Urban Pathways, high schoolers had the opportunity to be a part of the National Honors Society. To be a part of the organization, I had to write an essay, do an application, do community service, get two recommendation letters, and pass the interview.

What I really learned, and what I wrote about for my senior project, was how the education system in Pittsburgh is broken. Why did I have to switch schools? The question is: Shouldn't a child still receive the best education possible even though one attends their community school? The schools in the city of Pittsburgh consist of private, public, charter, and a small portion of homeschool co-ops and networks. Each school is very different from the other ones as far as policies, protocol, codes of conduct, education system, etc. For instance, in my community, my school (Sto-Rox) is labeled as delayed education. Once I transferred schools for middle school, I would try to relate my education to other people in my community, but they would respond, "We didn't learn that yet." Did that mean their education was held back?

The majority of schools in Pittsburgh consist of mostly teachers who are white. This means that in a lot of schools within the Pittsburgh area, disparity exists, which has a big impact for students who are African American. For example, for students who are Black, it can be uncomfortable if a white teacher teaches the school subject of Black history. In this case, it is not only a very touchy subject, but sometimes it allows a student to question, "Is the teacher teaching our history correctly?" or "Why is a white teacher teaching African American studies when they are not the same race as I am?" It tends to make students feel uncomfortable and sometimes infuriated.

There is also a funding problem, especially with Black students. We need to be exposed to something that every student does not get. I researched different schools in comparison to mine: Perry, Carrick, Sci-Tech. These schools were partnered with the University of Pittsburgh and Community College of Allegheny County. Those students could take college classes for credits like cosmetology, culinary, wood workshop and have chances to experience something new and possibly find their passion. Schools that are considered low-income need more partnerships with other organizations and colleges. Not every school in Pittsburgh or around the city in home districts gives opportunities that could help a child reach their success.

My own personal experiences with engaging in Pittsburgh schools have been very different. Sto-Rox was very open, educated, and active. It was a very diverse community, which allowed me to engage with races other than my own. Within my grade, we interacted and created friendships. A student can still continue to attend their home school district and have a chance to grow and create new bonds with people around their community. However, many schools in different communities do not have strong academics. So the system is set up where Black students lose a piece of their education or lose something important.

Emerge

Morgan Overton

Emerge is an oil painting created after cases of police violence against Black individuals in 2020. As a response to the murders of Breonna Taylor, George Floyd, Ahmaud Arbery, and countless lives lost to racism, this piece reflects the heaviness I felt as a Black woman, in addition

Morgan Overton, *Emerge*, 2020

to sorrow felt at large. The piece features a Black woman, who emerges through a hectic background of pixelations, smudges of her natural hair, and erasure of her mouth. Through history, the Black community has been subject to systemic means of oppression to erase our humanity, our voices, and the features of our ancestors. However, our resilience has been strong enough to emerge through it and reclaim our rightful place on earth.

We're Going to Figure It Out

Reflections from an Interview

Amber Thompson, Cadence Spruill, and Chetachukwu U. Agwoeme

Amber Thompson is an equity service designer who works with businesses to de-bias organizational infrastructures and implement systemic changes. Amber is also a Black radical mother who resides in Pittsburgh and has advocated for disenfranchised and underserved populations since she was a young girl.

On Motherhood

I'm actually from Johnstown. It's still Appalachia, an hour and a half east, northeast of Pittsburgh. I moved [to Pittsburgh] to go to school. I went to Point Park for undergrad, and I ended up getting pregnant my last semester and had to drop out of school with three classes left, which lingered for seven years following that. And during that time, my daughter was diagnosed with epilepsy. Becoming a parent of a child with a disability added an additional layer. I was prepared for it because of my background. I've always been part of social work.

I worked a lot with kids in my early years of my career, and the moment I became a mother of a child with a disability, then everything just got twenty thousand times harder than just being a Black woman in Pittsburgh trying to finish school and work, and I was playing volleyball 'til now I'm a mom with a child with a lot of severe needs. And I would say seven years after that, to be very honest, a lot of my memory is—probably because I had a lot of trauma—my memory is very vague, but the majority of that time, it was literally just advocating for my daughter's mental health, her physical health, her education, her social health, and to the point that by year seven I started to breathe. And now I can confidently say, "Oh, who am I?" I'm an activist. I'm an advocate. I'm still a mother. I'm also a caregiver to my mother, who is getting sicker. So I'm just a Black woman out here in the world trying to change it.

On Community

Well, a lot of my work is actually defining community. So with whom it is, I work from the theory of marginalization. The more marginalized people are, the more apt that is where my work is going to be. And to be more specific, it's going to be Black and Brown people at all intersections. That's where I'm focused at. I believe I use intersectionality as a framework. I build Black femme queer theory in all of my analyses, all of my language. So I'm really focused on Black and Brown marginalized people.

But I understand where the resources and where access needs to be built. So I do have those internal relations. But again, with people who center Black and Brown people. Always. I have very low tolerance for conversations that I feel like I have to explain that.

On Activism

In my activist work, I like to support organizers. I like to support advocates. I'm really good at capacity building, organization development, and, really, strategy. So my activism is either that inside-outside game where I'm on the inside as a consultant, but I'm on the outside as an advocate in helping to build those strategies to connect that bridge between the haves and have-nots. That's my whole work. That's what I'm creating a platform right now, a tech platform, to create a predictive analysis for oppression. It started in education. Mainly that's where I worked at first, and then once my daughter started to go to school, it had to be. It's the only place I don't consult because I won't make money. There's no nice way of saying these people are not the best people. It's solely working education, working around children with disabilities, people with disabilities. But it has moved into tech because I see when we're talking about not using the master's tools to dismantle the master's house—Audre Lorde—I'm looking at this as technology isn't a master's tool. And I'm looking at it as how can we take this to dismantle that house?

So where my activism is, it's on the ground. I believe we should be moving to a place where it's decentralized, there's no figureheads, no one person to point to. My activism will be in education as long as my daughter's in school. I need to be able to help build the capacity of our organizers.

On Philanthropy

This region is led by white men or men in general because there's so much misogynoir. I don't even want to excuse Black men from the conversation because I've dealt with more from Black men negatively than any demographic in this region. But there's no process or no way for us to communicate our needs and the folks who are responsible to do that, to be held accountable in doing so. And everyone would say, "Oh, that happens everywhere." No, here they're actually funded to do that.

That I think is uniquely different than other regions—that our philanthropy is pumped into oppressing communities and pitting communities against communities. Pitting Bloomfield against Lawrenceville. Pitting the Hill District against Hazelwood. That is literally what's happened, and these are Black people that are suffering and white people, specifically white men, who have some kind of class status benefiting from it.

On Technology

I think technology is one of those tools where we have gatekeeping and barriers going on. But a prime example is one of my friends. He played basketball D1—was not going to go to college unless he got a scholarship. His parents couldn't afford it; he had no ambitions to go to college, but he had a background in hacking. He got access to computers, going to the community, to his neighborhood community play space through high school. Technology is something that if you're exposed to it, you own that. You can own your space. You can own parts of your Black web or your web and the Web3. That's decentralized. I do understand how technology is used through the actual utility of it. I do understand who owns the utilities of that, but there's a level of organizing that social media is doing. There's a level of organizing the dark web is doing. There's a level of change that we own as people that the upper echelons don't. And I don't think we are leveraging that. I think the people who want to kill us are leveraging it much better. This is not the master's tool. The master can shut off the internet, of course, but the master's not going to do that because that would be shutting off their lifeline. Although, that is how white people work.

On Tech Surveillance

So a lot of my work is assessing or evaluating or monitoring programming or impact for companies. And in regard to algorithms, there's a whole organization called Algorithm Justice League. They're really focused on technology that impacts facial recognition, things like that. But there's technology that monitors and surveils people in the education space. There's technology that monitors and surveils people in the, what is it called? I want to say *fire safety*. But really, people who are working in community development, who are looking, monitoring, scanning underground. These automated cars, these self-driving cars, they're surveilling people. We are being surveilled from so much technology. There's no data sovereignty. We don't know what data they have of ours. We're not authorizing them to take it.

On Carcerality

Everything is punitive if you're poor. So that's why it's not intentional because you did something wrong; it is literally just living and existing in a world where you are not privileged. Everything is carceral. And everything in the tech space. I feel like I am a conspiracy theorist because I really have to break down how everything impacts Black people. How everything impacts poor people. How everything impacts people with disabilities. Because yeah, I'm not looking at carceral as being in jail. I feel like carcerality is being poor. The struggle that I'm having just because I'm poor, I do feel like I'm being punished constantly. That's why I went to college. Now I'm being punished for going to college. It's definitely an absolute system, and everyone who is not privileged is punished. But we're all impacted by this. And that, when we talk about Appalachia, growing up in a super-poor town and still seeing my mother, who had an education and a master's degree; my grandfather, the first Black man to get a bachelor's from St. Francis University, having multiple PhDs, and we're poorer than poor white people that I grew up with, that's carcerality. I think about my upbringing constantly, and even in the relationship I'm in now, my family, me, we have way more education, way more knowledge than the white folks that we're around. And we have way less. Way less. And access to way less. Again, every day I wake up. You don't have to be in jail to feel like you're in.

On Abolition

I do believe in abolishing everything. I also believe that in between where we're at and where that is, there has to be some kind of staggering or some kind of tiered or scaffolding approach. We should be trying to figure out how systematically we're building into that system and unbuild it, and build into a reparative system, into a therapeutic system, into a communal system. That's how I feel about it.

I think what abolition taught me is . . . just like how I said, the process of analyzing or evaluating what's wrong to repair or change it. And we're not going to get a new system unless we are intentionally trying to abolish what we know doesn't work. I think that's what abolition taught me, is like, "Okay, if this doesn't work, then we need something new." But a lot of people don't follow that.

So my community, I guess more recently, our mayor's a progressive. Our city council is pretty progressive. So in a very literal sense, our local community is trying to process defunding the police. And defunding the police is a public safety issue, right? It's not only the police. Our fire department had a Red Lives Matter flag. I've never even seen that.

The funny thing about that is just no one has ever said *defund the fire department*.

I think we should abolish the education system. The school has to change, and I say *school* in the context of a building that everyone goes to, and everything under the guise of education has to change. And freedom for me would be having options to educate my child and it not be in a building but also those options extended to other children because if I could have a community of kids, of other like-minded parents or some intentionality to foster that, this would be better.

On Criminalizing Children

They have police there in my daughter's school. She had the police called on her in fifth grade. She was nonverbal. She's very strong, and she's very big for her age. She was hugging the van driver, and they called the police on her. They tried to put a police intervention in her IEP (Individualized Education Program). Their first response to what happened was "We need to add this police intervention to her IEP." They criminalized her hug. They also criminalized other behaviors, her needing sensory input—so her acting out, like rolling on the floor. Those are things that she would be sent to sit in the office for, and then they'd stop. She needed sensory input. She needed to exercise. And this was all within her first kindergarten year.

On Community Policing

Well, I went to a community meeting and got the police called on me. That was in the city of Pittsburgh, in Homewood. So community meetings is where carcerality exists. There are police. Sometimes they have security. They called the police.

Fox Chapel—during the pandemic, they had a meeting around masks. Someone running for public office basically had a group of white angry parents "heil Hitler" at a school board meeting about masks. When you talk about police, in our region, they want to consolidate police. That school district, the police in that school district that would be policing me if they consolidate without any equitable metrics or any care to the community. So we're not consolidating until they have that plan. I don't want "heil Hitler" policing my neighborhood, policing my child. My community got a bunch of Black kids. No. Black people let Black people be oppressed in their face very openly in this region. It's, again, not like a lot of different cities. In many cities, Black people are fighting for Black people. My colleagues in Philly who are organizers, one of them (a Black Indigenous woman) was called the N word in an organizing meeting with Black people at the meeting, and they ain't say nothing. The school district and all of our legislative bodies is the Blackest in this city. The Blackest. When we talk about systemic issues or we talk about representation, people always have this false sense of "if we replace the white people with Black people, it will be better." No, we have . . . I think Baltimore is a prime example too. Baltimore has all Black. They got a Black DA, Black mayor, Black police chief. But this region, though, Black people infantilize Black people. That means they look at them like children. They look at them like animals. They don't think they can make their own decisions. I think there's a massive amount of eugenics built into all of our institutions, especially Carnegie Mellon University, where it's like everything is designed to blame us for our problems in this region. Black people are not champions of Black people.

I may not be from Pittsburgh, per se. I'm from Johnstown. It's very similar. Same thing, same Black people. Everything is an individual blame. People don't understand systemic or structural issues in this region to be able to effectively communicate what's happened. It's easy to say, "You're doing this, so that's why this is wrong." The blame is on the person instead of the system in this region, again, because the money is pumped to protect the system versus protecting the people. I was on a call with a whole bunch of people, and a man started to talk crazy to me, and I got muted when it was my turn to get crazy. It was a Black man talking crazy to me, and it was a Black woman who muted me.

On Black Appalachia

I think Black people in this region have a different type of perseverance and resilience that does not exist anywhere else, to be very honest. A lot of my colleagues who are building very radical or changing things are from this region because if you can fix it here, you can fix it anywhere else in this country. When it's the worst place in America for Black women—it's literally the worst place in America for Black women—you can fix it here, you can fix it for any person in the country.

What I process about urban Appalachia is that I never thought about it like that. I do think there is class solidarity. If you give poor white people options or you show them different, they'll do it. They will come. They will work. We could be together. And that's the thing. People are, "Well, have you done it?" "Yes, yes, I have." I've organized white folks in blue-collar spaces in this city in districts that I was told not to work with, not to organize with. And why? Who are the people that you read about? Class solidarity. We need class solidarity, and we need our classes to understand race. They're not going to understand that unless there are people who understand race talking to them.

That's why I said I think people in Appalachia are the most persevering people, most resilient because we're not going to ever go without. We'll always find a way. And I do think that there is something to be said about Black communities or Brown communities in Appalachia. We're going to figure it out. And if that means we all come in together and live under one house on one piece of land, they're going to do it, and we are going to figure it out. Left and lost is not a thing because we never had.

Pittsburgh does not care about Black people. They don't care. But Black people, we're going to figure it out. Always and forever.

On Political Education

I think, at the most basic level, political education is understanding who makes decisions or who is in power. I think political education is understanding your geography or your location and the politics and where you're at.

A lot of my classes were in the community. All my professors were in the community, and we weren't in classrooms. We were in the work and with people that we should be in community with defining our communities before we go into that work. I do think there's a lot of intentionality around who would be teaching. And always I think it should be someone who's participated in it but also someone who is willing. I think also in these communities, elders have a hard time listening to younger folks, so they also have to be in a position or a place to be able to say, "Okay, maybe it's different for you now." And be able to process that as well. If you're coming into the classroom, you have to be able to take those kids out of that classroom and connect them to the work that you're teaching them about.

On Freedom

What does it mean to be free in your community? Free in my community would be having a roof over my head and food in my belly and not having to rely on my labor. I do understand that that is a very limited thing, but I'm still in the process of envisioning what freedom looks like and what liberation looks like or feels like. I want to contribute to the world as I am and where I see fit, and I don't want to have to work. And if I don't have to work, there are a lot of other things I wouldn't have to do, like go to college. I could learn with my community, and we could use our resources in the land as we see fit. That is freedom to me. Women entered the workforce the moment Black women were brought to America, but there were working women in Europe, so I'm tired. I don't want to work. I want to live. I want to have fun. I want to go swim in a stream or river and eat some watermelon out of my yard. That is what I want to do.

Excerpts from Slow Walking in Circles: The Struggle to Improve African American Student Achievement in the Pittsburgh Public Schools

A report of the Equity Advisory Panel (EAP), October 2020

Anthony B. Mitchell, James B. Stewart, Wanda Henderson, and Tamanika Howze

Standardized tests [are] "the new lynching tool" for the aspirations of African Americans.

—Dr. Barbara Sizemore

This section contains excerpts from a document that emerged from deep and collective study. The original 111-page report, published in October 2020, includes extensive data from Pittsburgh and its public schools. For inclusion in this volume, we retained portions of the scholarly basis of the project as well as the action agenda.

Introduction

In the late 1980s, educational researcher and activist Dr. Barbara Sizemore declared that standardized tests in the United States would become a national mechanism for racially segregating high achievers from low achievers in US schools. Dr. Sizemore believed standardized tests were racially biased and advocated for educational reform. In *Walking in Circles: The Black Struggle for School Reform*,[1] Sizemore powerfully and prophetically forecasted the educational achievement perils that African Americans and historically oppressed groups in the United States would face in the twenty-first century.

This investigation presents this critical story from the viewpoints and experiences of reformers. Consequently, this document aims to inform and enlighten a broad spectrum of readers (e.g., parents, community and civic leaders, educational leaders, advocacy groups, researchers, and policymakers) who engage in educational advocacy and reform. Its title is an adaptation of Sizemore's classic study. Indeed, much of Dr. Sizemore's leadership centered on confronting inequities and disparities in US schools and institutions. The Advocates' efforts over the last twenty-five years built on the foundations established by Sizemore. Hence, it is not an overstatement to conceptualize the struggles begun by the Advocates as an opening salvo in what would become a twenty-first-century civil rights struggle. It is a struggle for educational justice in public schools in the United States. This struggle is a paradigmatic example of the advocacy required to address what Ladson-Billings describes as "the education debt."[2]

The origins of the Advocates date back to the late 1980s, when the African American community's dissatisfaction with the district's school-community climate and concern that the district was failing to educate African American students intensified. In the early 1980s, Pittsburgh Public Schools (PPS) established a School Improvement Program (SIP) to develop and pilot school improvement strategies in several low-achieving African American schools. The African American community's concerns heightened when the SIP's "authoritarian-centered" model did not contain the appropriate culturally relevant frameworks and strategies for accelerating academic achievement among African American students. During this period, African American PPS administrator Dr. Lou Venson's outreach to the African American community catalyzed concerns about PPS's equity policies and educational practices. Dr. Venson directed the SIP from 1981 to 1989 and deeply understood the inadequacies of the SIP model and PPS system. Subsequently, in 1987, the Advocates, a community-based group of concerned parents, activists, and educators, mobilized and organized to represent the African American community's concerns about allegations of unfair treatment of African American students and disturbing educational achievement disparities. In the early 1990s, these concerns escalated when parents and community stakeholders questioned the district's institutional policies and practices and commitment to providing quality education for African American students.

EAP Mission and Action Agenda

The process leading to the Conciliation Agreement began with the establishment of the Equity Advisory Panel (EAP) in 2006. Since then, the EAP's significant goals and objectives have focused on catalyzing radical institutional reform and investment in the lives of African American children. We believe that confronting the educational debt is necessary to liberate African Americans from ineffective leadership, incompetent teachers, curriculum oppression, and union policies and practices that undermine the academic success of far too many African American students. Thus, the focus of the EAP includes a host of strategies to ensure that the PPS and the PHRC maintain accountability for implementing the Conciliation Agreement and raising the academic achievement of African American students. The previous section documented two core elements of the EAP's strategy (i.e., aggressive advocacy for organizational commitment and equitable policies and practices) and engagement with the PHRC to seek assertive oversight of district compliance with the Conciliation Agreement. In our efforts, we continue to consistently review data provided by PPS and required by the terms of the Conciliation Agreement. We also continue to independently monitor learning outcomes and provide recommendations for in-service professional development programming for administration and faculty, as well as for consultants to conduct external evaluations. Last, we rigorously advocate for adopting a Culturally Relevant Education (CRE) curriculum and engaging the African American community by disseminating information to garner support for the systematic implementation of the Conciliation Agreement.

Data Review

The EAP, in collaboration with the PHRC and the district's equity officer, routinely monitors data and standardized testing performance by race, ethnicity, and socioeconomic status. One of the shortcomings of the original compliance agreement was the failure to require the district to disaggregate the data by gender. This oversight is problematic because African American male students exhibit disproportionately poorer outcomes than other demographic groups on some measures. Fortunately, the most recent incarnation of the Conciliation Agreement mandates the disaggregation of data by gender.

Independent Monitoring of Learning Outcomes

In a 2007 workshop with administrators, the EAP introduced a "report card" exercise where PPS personnel assigned grades to themselves based on their performance in implementing the EAP recommendations. Among these individuals, the most common self-assessment ratings were D and F. This finding, though not a surprise to the EAP, validated the EAP's concerns and analysis that the PPS was not committing the appropriate leadership and resources (financial and staff) for addressing the achievement gap and Consent Decree. In 2010, the EAP again used the concept of a report card to condense data reporting, facilitating a more focused examination of disparities. As noted previously, the typical meetings between the EAP and district personnel involved the review of numerous and voluminous data reports that left limited time for in-depth analysis and response. Unfortunately, PPS was unwilling to provide the data in the proposed format unless this report format could substitute for the more extensive format required by the Conciliation Agreement.

In addition to suggesting more useful reporting processes, the EAP has provided detailed feedback to the PPS and the PHRC regarding program design and monitoring progress. For example, the EAP provided detailed feedback regarding the district's 2013 submission to the PHRC regarding its diversity initiatives.

Professional Development and External Evaluation Recommendations

The EAP has repeatedly submitted recommendations to PPS regarding potential consultants to provide in-service professional development programming for personnel and external evaluations of the district's equity efforts. Regrettably, the district has consistently ignored these recommendations. Instead, PPS hired expensive consultants whose educational philosophy aligned closely with the district. Local foundations often underwrote the extensive funds expended on these consultants. The precedent for dismissing EAP recommendations and championing consultants who reinforced the district's preexisting biases occurred in May 2010, when PPS unilaterally cosponsored a presentation by Dr. Ronald Ferguson focusing on the achievement gap.

In contrast to the EAP, Ferguson's approach minimized the significance of cultural dissonance as a significant contributor to the achievement gap. The Courageous Conversations initiative is another example. Glenn E. Singleton founded Courageous Conversation in 1992 to provide racial equity education and training to governments and organizations. Local foundations have supported several other consultants unilaterally chosen by PPS, including the Council of Great City Schools, the National Council on Teacher Quality, and Drs. Pedro Noguera and Denise Collier. During the Memorandum of Understanding (MOU) process, at various points, these organizations and consultants have conducted climate and culture studies and facilitated professional development training. Unfortunately, few benefits resulted from these efforts, and in some cases, PPS did not make final reports available to the EAP or disseminate them publicly.

The EAP has had no access to funds to implement its professional development and external evaluation proposals and lacks the authority to obtain commitments from PPS personnel to participate in non-district workshops. Efforts to modify the legal status of the Advocates to facilitate the solicitation of external funding to support educational reform efforts have been unsuccessful. Although less than desirable, the EAP's resource challenges have not been insurmountable as the panel's passion and will to achieve results for the Advocates and African American community are immeasurable. Consequently, among EAP members, the question "And how are the children today?" is the inspiring opening charge that EAP members state to the administration to demand accountability for the success of all students.

Culturally Responsive Education

The EAP's first significant recommendation advocated for systemwide implementation of CRE. The basic theory of CRE asserts that culture is central to student learning and embodies a professional, political, ethical, and ideological disposition.[3] Gloria Ladson-Billings states, "It is an approach that empowers students intellectually, socially, emotionally, and politically by using cultural referents to impart knowledge, skills and attitudes."[4] During all three PPS administrations that this analysis examines, philosophical differences and debates occurred regarding the merits of CRE as a culturally relevant educational philosophy and teaching and learning curricular strategy to address the racial achievement gap. Since 2006, the EAP has recommended several nationally recognized scholars and experts on CRE and Afrocentric education to the PPS, yet the only success to date has been the agreement with the district to engage the services of Dr. Molefi Asante to train administrators, teachers, and staff. Dr. Molefi Kete Asante, one of the foremost scholars and experts on Afrocentricity, consulted with a select group of administrators and teachers during the 2016–2017 school year. Unfortunately, Dr. Asante signed the contract during the transition between the second and third administrations. However, the incoming administration was much less supportive of Asante's ideological and pedagogical frameworks for instructional leadership and curriculum infusion. Consequently, despite the EAP's adamant support and request to the new administration that PPS continue Dr. Asante's work and expand it to other schools in the district, PPS terminated his contract in 2017. This questionable decision understandably disappointed the EAP and raised doubt regarding the new administration's commitment to the agreement and transformative school reform. Dr. Asante described his assessment of his brief, disappointing experience in PPS in his book *Revolutionary Pedagogy*, where he noted the pervasive tendency of new superintendents to remove programs instituted by their predecessors. He also suggested that the district is a low-performance system that engages in the multibillion-dollar "high-stakes testing" industry at the expense of infusing transformative culture and pedagogy that motivates students to learn.[5]

Community Outreach

The Advocates and the EAP have tried various approaches to inform the community about the circumstances faced by African American students and its efforts to address these problems. In July 2008, the Advocates hosted a community meeting to explore strategies vis-à-vis the Conciliation Agreement. Similarly, in October 2008, the EAP sponsored a community forum titled "CRISIS: The Education of African American Students in the Pittsburgh Public Schools" at the East Liberty Branch of the Carnegie Library system. In January 2009, the EAP issued a three-page "Newsletter Report." Unfortunately, because the EAP had to rely on PPS staff to produce and distribute this document, it was impossible to continue producing this potentially valuable outreach effort. In 2010 and 2014, Dr. James B. Stewart, the first chair of the EAP, penned two op-ed articles assessing efforts to reduce educational disparities in PPS. The first, written in 2010, "Let's Stop Walking in Circles, It's Time to Close the Achievement Gap between Black and White Students," describes both historical and (then) contemporary efforts to reduce the achievement and opportunity gaps. It also cited the PHRC's and EAP's role in challenging PPS to remedy ninety-four problems over five years (2006–2011) and monitor compliance. In 2014, Dr. Stewart, responding to only marginal progress in African American academic achievement, penned a second editorial, "Still Walking in Circles: Let's Rededicate Ourselves to Closing Achievement/Opportunity Gaps between White and Black Students." This article also highlighted the support of the Gates Foundation to improve teacher assessment, the introduction of Courageous

Conversations workshops on race relations, and the creation of the We Promise program to increase support for the academic performance of African American males. Both articles referenced the late Dr. Barbara Sizemore's path-breaking study "Walking in Circles: The Black Struggle for School Reform" and identified numerous urban reform issues. In each edition, Dr. Stewart noted the district's lack of leadership for developing an equity office, limited board support, and lack of policies promoting equity.

Aside from these specific efforts, the EAP has been unable to mount and sustain an effective communication and outreach campaign. As a result, it has proven to be challenging to mobilize community support for the work of the EAP. In contrast, the A+ Schools initiative successfully holds PPS accountable by educating and organizing supporters of reform efforts. A+ Schools Pittsburgh is an independent community organization that advocates for equity and excellence in Pittsburgh Public Schools. Each year, A+ produces reports to PPS and the public on all students' academic performance and achievement. The present chair of the EAP, Wanda Henderson, did present a statement on behalf of the Advocates at a student rally sponsored by A+ Schools on May 15, 2012.

Despite the limited success of its outreach efforts, the EAP has consistently challenged the PPS regarding its flawed parental policies and practices. In the first MOU, the EAP consistently criticized the following:

(a) ineffectiveness of the district's communications to parents as not parent-friendly in language and style,
(b) lack of a culturally responsive parent engagement philosophy,
(c) failure to build relationships with high-risk parents and families in schools in neighborhoods that had the highest rates of educational failure, poverty, and crime, and,
(d) ineffectiveness in informing parents about the Pennsylvania Department of Education oversight and policies relating to standardized exams and the No Child Left Behind Law of 2002.

These concerns require schools to inform and educate parents about the Keystone Exams[6] and the Every Student Succeeds Act Parent and Family Engagement Provisions.

In the first and second administrations, the EAP's communication concerns challenged the district to improve parent communications. In addition, during the second administration, in August 2014, Dr. Huberta Jackson-Lowman, an Advocate founder and complainant, keynoted a parent conference at the DoubleTree Hotel. In the third administration, the EAP advocated for PPS to contract with the Association of Black Psychologists (ABPsi), led by Dr. Jackson-Lowman, to implement its culturally responsive "community-university model" for parent empowerment. Still today, parent engagement and empowerment remain a major EAP priority and are frequently advocated for by EAP panel members during MOU proceedings.

A Luta Continua! (The Struggle Continues)

Ladson-Billings identifies three significant factors that impact educational leaders' challenges addressing the education debt: (a) the impact the debt has on present education progress, (b) the value of understanding the debt in relation to past education research findings, and (c) the potential for forging a better educational future.[9] Subsequent developments suggest the continuing relevance of the central question of whether PPS will continue to "slow walk in circles" or partner genuinely with the EAP and develop and implement a viable strategy to ameliorate the persisting racial achievement gap and other manifestations of racial inequity. PPS has unveiled a new draft equity plan that will hopefully significantly alter the district's historical inability to reduce disparities. It also has more openness to implementing best practices—particularly, the concept of community schools. It is encouraging that the teachers' union is not resisting this effort, although it involves a significant transformation of past policies and practices.

The EAP continues to advocate for radical institutional reform including implementing systematic CRE strategies to address the increasing racial and cultural diversity within the city of Pittsburgh and the region. The EAP's annual reviews with the district and PHRC continue to document numerous factors within PPS institutional climate and operational systems that contribute to inequities and stratifications in achievement across race, ethnicity, gender, and class. The EAP's investigations have also identified alarming safety trends in some of Pittsburgh's African American neighborhoods and communities—trends that impact students' and parents' safety and emotional well-being. The EAP contends that this problem negatively impacts the Pittsburgh region's future and diminishes parents' involvement, positive engagement, and community support for PPS. The EAP believes that transformational leadership, starting with the board of education, the superintendent, and central office administration, is imperative for modeling the vision, values, and competencies necessary to strategically address achievement gaps and create partnerships with all appropriate stakeholders. We believe that these steps are essential to move PPS and the region toward a more positive and inclusive trajectory. Effective leadership to address achievement gaps requires systemwide accountability for implementing institutional equity and culturally responsive strategies to improve teaching and learning.

The EAP is actively continuing its monitoring role and advocacy for policies that will ameliorate long-standing disparities experienced by African American students. In 2022, the EAP and PPS board and administration, with support from the Pittsburgh Black Elected Officials Coalition, agreed to extend the Conciliation Agreement for an additional five years. This analysis demonstrates that any significant improvement in reducing disparities requires advocacy, leadership, governance, funding, and innovation focused on the systematic transformation of an archaic system. The time is long overdue for PPS to address the education debt! If not now, then when?

The cry of the ghetto is being heard by a nation with its fingers in its ears.
—Barbara Sizemore

EAP members 2006–present:
Chairs: Dr. James B. Stewart and Wanda Henderson (Advocate/EAP)
Panelists: Mark Conner,* Dr. Larry E. Davis,* Celeta Hickman,* Dr. Regina Holley, Kirk Holbrook,* Tamanika Howze (Advocate/EAP), Dr. Anthony B. Mitchell, Maria Searcy,* and Will Thompkins
*Former EAP member

Notes

1. Barbara Sizemore, *Walking in Circles: The Black Struggle for School Reform* (Chicago: Third World Press, 2008).
2. Gloria Ladson-Billings, "From the Achievement Gap to the Education Debt: Understanding Achievement in U.S. Schools," *Educational Researcher* 35, no. 7 (2006).
3. Tyrone C. Howard, *Why Race and Culture Matter in Schools: Closing the Achievement Gap in America's Classrooms* (New York: Teachers College Press, 2010).
4. Gloria Ladson-Billings, "Toward a Theory of Culturally Relevant Pedagogy," *American Educational Research Journal* 32, no. 3 (1995): 465–91.
5. Molefi Kete Asante, *Revolutionary Pedagogy: Primer for Teachers of Black Children* (New York: Universal Write Publications, 2017).
6. The Keystone Exams are administered to all Pennsylvania eleventh-grade students in Algebra I, biology, and literature and are required for high school graduation. https://www.education.pa.gov/K-12/Assessment%20and%20Accountability/Keystones/Pages/default.aspx.

Caste, Carcerality, and Educational Inequity

A Call to Restore Liberating Educational Opportunities for Black Pittsburgh

Esohe Osai and Sean Means

The greatest threat to a caste system is not lower-caste failure, which, in a caste system, is expected and perhaps even counted upon, but lower-caste success, which is not. Achievement by those in the lowest caste goes against the script handed down to us all. It undermines the core assumptions upon which a caste system is constructed and to which the identities of people on all rungs of the hierarchy are linked.[1]

In 1979, Dr. Harry Clark, a Black educator and jazz musician, founded Pittsburgh Creative and Performing Arts School (CAPA)—the first public arts magnet high school in Western Pennsylvania. Located in Homewood, a Black neighborhood on the far east end of Pittsburgh, the school was destined to become a space of educational excellence. Uniquely, CAPA connected culture, creativity, and academics, supporting deep learning and engagement.[2] The presence of CAPA within the context of this particular neighborhood was reminiscent of the Black Renaissance era and waves of cultural, artistic, and intellectual renewal in Black sections of cities over many decades in the United States. Notably, Homewood had already produced artists such as Erroll Garner, Mary Lou Williams, and Billy Strayhorn, all of whom exuded Black creative genius in the mid-twentieth century. In keeping with that legacy of Black excellence, historical records of CAPA paint a picture of a thriving educational space that nurtured both talent and educational potentiality.

Through the '90s, CAPA existed as a "rose in concrete," surviving through turbulent times for Black Pittsburgh, which was experiencing the aftereffects of caste-like policies (e.g., restrictive housing covenants) that further hyper-segregated and isolated the Black community. In Homewood, that looked like increased community traumas and challenges associated with urban poverty. Despite that reality, CAPA thrived in Homewood as a magnet school that invited young people to a culture of high academic expectations while providing space for artistic expression. With a Black founding principal and Black artists and educators, CAPA spoke to the inherent greatness of Blackness in Homewood. However, in 1998, the Pittsburgh school board voted 7–2 to move the school from Homewood to downtown Pittsburgh. According to the opposing board members, also two of three Black people on board, the decision to move the school was made without consideration of how the change would affect Homewood and without any input from community members.[3]

Relocating CAPA, which went on to become a nationally ranked Blue Ribbon school and the "crown jewel" of the Pittsburgh Public School District, speaks to the manifestation of anti-Blackness in public schooling. In a district that is predominantly Black, the school now has a student population that is 62 percent white and accepts students who apply from outside of the district. The move from a Black neighborhood has implications for how we see educational divestment—from communities and individuals—as part and parcel of the prison industrial system. This chapter unveils how policies in our educational system communicate caste-like expectation of Black nonachievement through the removal of opportunity. We begin with a brief description of racial caste and its connections to carcerality while detailing the social conditions, including schooling, of the Black community in Pittsburgh. Centering the experience of one of the authors, we then provide a micro-level focus on the impacts of the message of expected nonachievement for Black students and their teachers. We conclude the chapter by highlighting the efforts of the Justice Scholars Institute, a program initiated to restore pathways of educational excellence and thriving in schools that serve Black youth in Pittsburgh broadly and specifically within the Homewood neighborhood.

Caste, Carcerality, and Racism in Pittsburgh

Isabel Wilkerson describes caste as "the . . . *withholding of* respect, status, honor, attention, privileges, resources, benefit of the doubt, and human kindness to someone on the basis of their perceived rank or standing in the hierarchy."[4] In the United States, caste is race-specific. Black people have been systematically denied opportunity through concerted and ingrained efforts to restrict access to fundamental rights and means of livelihood. The effects of this caste are linked to Black suffering as practices and policies *withhold* what is fundamental and necessary to Black humanity. This results in the confinement and entrapment of Black bodies, which is carceral.

Castro and Magna suggest that carcerality operates as a form of social control pervasive across all aspects of life. They say that "carcerality makes an overreliance on punishment a logical, necessary, and ostensibly just means to achieve a particular . . . racist social order."[5] The desired social order reflects a caste system and suggests that carceral practices and policies have racist implications. For example, the move of CAPA from Homewood had racialized consequences, intended or not. Similarly, as you will read in the student story below, being kicked out of a magnet school and sent back to a neighborhood school is a racialized experience that has implications for Black academic identities. Caste presents itself through messages suggesting that educational achievement is not feasible for students who identify as Black and who, in the Pittsburgh context, are often living in segregated, low-income communities.[6] The messages align with a carceral logic that seeks to take away Black freedom and restrict, confine, and suppress opportunities to learn and advance in desired educational pursuits.[7,8]

The caste system and resultant carceral realities have a long history in Pittsburgh and many other urban centers in the United States. History tells the story of Black people moving to this industrialized city during the Great Migration, seeking the so-called American dream. However, as happened across this country, they were met with discriminatory housing policies, illegal school segregation practices, and limited opportunities to benefit from growing economic opportunities. Almost a century later, Black suffering among Pittsburgh residents continues to manifest itself. A 2019 report ranked Pittsburgh as the worst city for Black people across several indicators, including health, income, employment, and educational outcomes.[9] Though many US cities had similar stories of anti-Black policies, the effects have been particularly detrimental to the livelihood and well-being of Black communities in the urban Appalachia context of Pittsburgh, Pennsylvania.

Pennsylvania ranks among the worst states related to inequities for students across racial and income groups.[10] Specifically, Pennsylvania is the second worst state in the United States when measuring the opportunity gap between Black and white students and between poor and nonpoor students. For example, Black and Latinx students in the state are less likely to attend schools that offer advanced courses and more likely to have inexperienced teachers. In Pittsburgh, racial and economic segregation overlap considerably, leading to a high proportion of Black neighborhoods that are also high-poverty. The story of Pittsburgh is a story of deeply entrenched inequities. This racially unjust history continues to plague Black communities by denying access and opportunity, ultimately disrupting equitable learning opportunities for Black children. The effect of this reality is a caste system, clearly seen in the public school system.

Pittsburgh Public Schools (PPS) has failed to provide an adequate education for Black students. In 1992, this failure received heightened attention from the Black community, who formed Advocates for African American Students in the Pittsburgh Public Schools, led by scholar-activist and educator Dr. Barbara Sizemore.[11] This community group initiated a class-action lawsuit against the PPS board for the persistent failure to meet the educational needs of Black students in the district. The complaint named "excessive suspensions and harsh discipline, distribution of class grades, exclusion from certain special programs and . . . a large, racially identifiable academic achievement gap between African American and white students"[12] in violation of the Pennsylvania Human Relations Act (PHRA). In 2006, PPS made a conciliation agreement that included ninety-four action steps to improve the educational conditions of Black students; however, the terms are still yet to be realized despite multiple extensions.[13] Incremental changes have occurred, including creating an equity office within the district, forming a volunteer equity advisory panel made up of community-based volunteers, and, most recently, soliciting an external equity audit. Nevertheless, decades of effort have not yet led to substantive changes in educational prospects for Black families in Pittsburgh.

The challenges highlighted by this thirty-year lawsuit are not surprising given that the schooling system in our racial state aims to ensure the educational "failure" of the lower caste. The departure of CAPA from a Black community to a rebranded school that serves mostly non-Black students speaks of the subtle racial caste that excludes opportunity for many Black and "underclass" youth. Consequently, most Black children in the city are locked into a schooling system that precludes them from opportunities to gain access to skillsets required to pursue college and career aspirations. These racialized realities become more evident when we look into our schools and hear the behind-the-scenes stories of students' experiences. For that, we return to Homewood and visit a classroom in the neighborhood's public high school, Pittsburgh Westinghouse. The firsthand account that follows is written by Sean Means, a Black male teacher with over ten years of experience teaching and serving in Homewood.

Sean Means's Story

The bell rings, and the class follows the regular rituals and routines, taking seats and writing their warm-up as we prepare to engage in the day's activity. Most students have started, but one student, Travis, seems disengaged in the process and has yet to begin. I walk over to his desk, quietly ask how he is doing, and request he start the warm-up. He ignores me and begins to play on his phone. I give him a moment, then try to redirect him again. This time, he starts to yell at me, finishing his phrase with "I'm not one of these fucking coach kids. I'm *gifted*!"

Throughout that year, I would try to work with Travis, but each time he would remind me that he had come from a magnet school for gifted students and that he wanted no part of this nonmagnet space represented by our students, our staff, or our school's culture. Travis had inculcated the expected message of the caste system that Black neighborhoods, with Black schools, are not spaces of educational achievement. And thus, he felt like being forced here was like being sentenced. Being pushed out of the magnet and back into his designed-to-fail neighborhood school, he believed he didn't have to listen to school staff because he felt being at the school was punishment enough. I took it as "what more can you do to me?" The child was hurt and angry, cast out from a school most consider "better" since it was a magnet school. A place where white families sent their children. A place where parents with college degrees, options, and wealth send their children. A place where Apple technology, extravagant trips, and overall infrastructure were the standard. A place where rules, regulations, and memorandums of understanding (MOUs) keep certain students in and filter out those who do not meet that standard. Not a space where he could be provided the scaffolds and support needed to achieve, even as a Black youth in a world that probably often felt antagonistic. Instead, Travis's dismissal felt like a judgment against him as he felt he was banished to a space of "nonachievement." He fell victim to the racial caste expectations that society pushed on him. The party line would be "we're sending him to a more supportive environment," but he knew he'd been punished. How do we change a narrative with such a policy in place?

Recounting my experience with Travis, who had recently been sent from a magnet school back to us, his neighborhood school, is one of my most vivid recollections of how educational policy plays out in the classroom. The story of Travis is one instance, but I have too many to count over the years. Students from magnet schools explain that they are constantly threatened with "if you don't comply, we'll send you back to your home school." Under immense pressure to maintain their own learning environment, school leaders often follow through on that threat, justifying the decision that it was done "for the greater good." The example shows that stigmas stick, and educational standards—and, more importantly, expectations—are altered based on the race, privilege, and socioeconomic status of students and their families. The dismissal of Black students from magnets communicates a message of exclusion and punishment, as opposed to belonging and support. Notably, in the 1970s, when the district first started magnet schools, they included a policy that would maintain a racial balance in the schools to ensure Black students could gain entry to these specialized spaces. The policy was eventually done away with, and now we have a district with a 33 percent white student population yet with a relocated and reconfigured CAPA where 62 percent of the student body is white.

Let me be honest. I've felt angry about this practice of moving students from magnets to their neighborhood schools since I stepped foot in Pittsburgh as an educator. Our protection of the privileged was out in the open, a covert operation that was far from a secret. During my years at our school, we have had over ten principals, and state and district-level initiatives move in and out like a revolving door. Leading education scholars, consultants from a religious organization, and a West Coast public charter school, along with their consultants, have come to PPS to help us reimagine urban education. Consultants specializing in school improvement strolled in, telling teachers, "All you have to do is believe." These meritocratic and heart-nudging consultants came and got people all fired up but were gone in the middle of the night. They did not turn anything around. Nothing. To be fair, I do not claim to have the answers; I just know you can't keep a caste and expect great things. Even though South Africa has done away with Apartheid on paper, the prioritization of the privileges is still common practice. Pittsburgh is no different.

When engaging in courageous conversations, some of my opinions are cast off and seen as cynical or unproductive. The assumption is that I don't care about, much less love, my students. Nothing could be further from the truth. I often receive pushback from outsiders, "allies," and district leadership who ask me about why we have the current racially inequitable system in the school district. I usually respond with the following: the policies connected to the racial caste, the lack of autonomy provided to school-based administration, and the one-way transfer of students. Most importantly, I ask them, "Where do you send *your* children?" This is often met with them stumbling over their words; eventually I get usual talking points. When we say we have high standards for all students, do we mean it? Should I have ever expected the "allies" to be in the trenches with us? The most left of liberals, who proudly place Black Lives Matter signs in their yards? How could none of them find their way to putting their child in a place where for once they would be the minority? I unapologetically believe in integration. In my opinion, the best learning can occur when all sides are willing to consistently engage with people from communities different than our own. So it has disappointed me when those who have options continue to make the same decisions. Their active participation in the current process hoards access to engaging learning environments predominantly for white students in a district of mostly Black students. Despite these challenges, I have been proud to be a part of a program that has made me hopeful about what we can do to invest in the most educationally marginalized students in our district—the Justice Scholars Institute.

Justice Scholars Institute—Restoring Education Liberation in Black Communities

As Martin Luther King Jr. noted in 1964, the efforts to oppress Black communities, since the times of slavery, are enacted through the deprivation of an adequate education.[14] King's observation speaks to the caste system and suggests that it is intricately connected to education inequities in the United States. In the twenty-first century, sadly, that story has not changed very much. In fact, the situation has worsened to the degree that our nation has developed a prison industrial complex directly connected to systemic failures in urban education.[15] The prison industrial complex thrives on the educational marginalization of Black students who attempt to navigate insufficient schooling systems that provide them with less-qualified teachers, nonculturally responsive curriculum, zero-tolerance policies that criminalize youth, standardized tests that are racially biased, and fewer courses that are intended to prepare students postsecondary education. Black students are given the short end of the stick with these inequities in our system and then expected to find viable and sustainable pathways into adulthood. Instead, they often end up leaving school bored, miseducated, and underprepared for life. School districts across the United States are complicit and thus must be intentional about disrupting systemic inequity and inequality through strategic innovations that challenge the status quo. As Harper notes, schools of education are also complicit in their failure to effectively train teachers and provide supports to local school districts.[15] In response, the Justice Scholars Institute (JSI), a college preparatory program, was established in 2016 as a partnership between the University of Pittsburgh and Westinghouse Academy in Homewood. The first author, a Black woman, founded the program as a response to her engagements in the neighborhood as a community-engaged scholar. Through listening to students, teachers, and community members, a specific need emerged for college preparatory learning experiences and engagement with ideas that would address systemic and pervasive social inequalities through a social justice lens.

A primary component of JSI is providing college-credit-bearing courses through the University of Pittsburgh's College in High School (CHS) program. The opportunity to earn college credits supports completing a college degree, especially for low- and middle-achieving high school students.[16,17] National data reveals that Black students are less likely to earn college credits in high school because they often attend segregated schools with few advanced course-taking opportunities.[18] Leveraging the resources of an accredited dual enrollment program, JSI can help to scaffold teachers and students into the expectations of a college learning environment, allowing students a better opportunity for a successful transition into postsecondary education. In addition to the advanced courses, JSI provides educational enhancement opportunities, including college preparatory workshops, out-of-school time justice-focused youth development opportunities, training in justice-focused research, and teacher professional development.

Since its founding, JSI has expanded to serve three neighborhood schools where most of the district's Black, low-income students attend school (adding Pittsburgh Milliones and Perry Traditional Academy in the Hill District and Perry North, respectively). Over the past few decades, these three schools have seen few students graduate, enroll in postsecondary education, and complete a college degree within six years. This reality does not speak to any incapability in the students; instead, it speaks to a broader system that has excluded Black students from the type of learning experiences that can lead to success in postsecondary education. Acknowledging the inherent educational potentiality of Black students, JSI intends to create spaces for deep engagement and learning that can support students' postsecondary aspirations. Since the beginning, JSI has grown from one teacher to nine teachers (including Sean Means) across the three schools. Those teachers teach seven CHS courses, including African American History, African American Literature, and Intro to Statistics.

JSI has systematically built components that create opportunities and expectations that can lead to success in postsecondary for Black students. Importantly, our work is a *rebuild* project because we recognize that Black achievement is not new in our communities. The history of Black educational excellence is evident when you enter Westinghouse Academy and see a wall of fame filled with Black people who earned college degrees and work as professionals in education, medicine, civil rights, arts, and entertainment, among other fields. However, due to the emergence of a deeply entrenched prison industrial system, which has marginalized Black communities and dehumanized Black youth, we are working to rebuild the pathways to educational advancement that once existed in our communities.

JSI has created a space for Black (re)imagining and (re)visioning in the name of freedom.[19,20] What we are clear about in our work in service of Black humanity is that "the pursuit of education in service of transcending Black unfreedom has never successfully absolved that suffering but has more so been a meaningful way of existing in spite of it."[21] Despite our Pittsburgh-specific caste system reality, we are confident that Black children in this city can achieve their desired academic and professional aspirations. Thus, we continue in our labor of love, working against a recalcitrant caste system, promoting liberation through educational opportunity and access for students in Pittsburgh's Black communities.

Acknowledgments

The authors would like to thank Dr. Shanyce Campbell for her thoughtful contributions to various iterations of this chapter and for her commitment to supporting the Justice Scholars Institute. We would also like to thank Megan Hanlon for her archival research.

Notes

1. Isabel Wilkerson, *Caste: The Origins of our Discontents* (New York: Random House, 2020), 224.
2. Adam Winsler, Taylor V. Gara, Alenamie Alegrado, Sonia Castro, and Tanya Tavassolie, "Selection into, and Academic Benefits from, Arts-Related Courses in Middle School among Low-Income, Ethnically Diverse Youth," *Psychology of Aesthetics, Creativity, and the Arts* 14, no. 4 (2020): 415.
3. Carmen J. Lee, "Downtown Move for CAPA Ok'd," *Pittsburgh Post-Gazette*. October 29, 1998.
4. Wilkerson, *Caste*, 70, emphasis added.
5. Erin L. Castro and Sydney Magana, "Enhancing the Carceral State: Criminal/ized History Questions in College Admissions," *Journal of College Student Development* 61, no. 6 (2020): 816.
6. Marc V. Levine, "The State of Black Milwaukee in National Perspective: Racial Inequality in the Nation's 50 Largest Metropolitan Areas. In 65 Charts and Tables," *Center for Economic Development Publications* 56 (2020), https://dc.uwm.edu/ced_pubs/56.
7. Damien M. Sojoyner, "Black Radicals Make for Bad Citizens: Undoing the Myth of the School to Prison Pipeline," *Berkeley Review of Education* 4, no. 2 (2013): 241–63.
8. Shaun R. Harper, "Black People vs. Educational Culprits Engaged in Our Systemic Mass Incarceration in the United States of America," *Peabody Journal of Education* 96, no. 5 (2021): 582–87.
9. Junia Howell, Sara Goodkind, Leah H. Jacobs, Dominique Branson, and Liz Miller, "Pittsburgh's Inequality across Gender and Race," 2019, https://pittsburghpa.gov/gec/reports-policy.
10. Sara Schneider, "After Three Decades, Pittsburgh School District Renews Agreement to Work toward Racial Justice," 90.5 WESA Pittsburgh NPR News Station, August 25, 2022, https://www.wesa.fm/education/2022-08-25/after-three-decades-pittsburgh-school-district-renews-agreement-to-work-toward-racial-justice.
11. For more information on this work, see chapter in this book by the Equity Advisory Panel.
12. Barbara Sizemore, *Walking in Circles: The Black Struggle for School Reform* (Chicago: Third World Press, 2008).
13. Schneider, "After Three Decades."
14. Rev. Martin Luther King Jr., "Education and Equality," *Equity & Excellence in Education* 2, no. 3 (1964): 12–13, https://doi.org/10.1080/0020486640020303.

15. Harper, "Black People vs. Educational Culprits."

16. Nina Thomas, Stephanie Marken, Lucinda Gray, and Laurie Lewis, "Dual Credit and Exam-Based Courses in US Public High Schools: 2010–11. First Look," NCES 2013-001, National Center for Education Statistics, 2013, https://eric.ed.gov/?id=ED539697.

17. Melinda Mechur Karp and Katherine L. Hughes, "Study: Dual Enrollment Can Benefit a Broad Range of Students," *Techniques: Connecting Education and Careers (J1)* 83, no. 7 (2008): 14–17.

18. Junia Howell and Alannah Caisey, "What We Need Is Education: Differentiating the Mechanisms Contributing to Persistent Racial Inequality of Education," *Phylon* 56, no. 1 (2019): 58–80.

19. Kelley, *Freedom Dreams*.

20. Cynthia Dillard, *The Spirit of Our Work: Black Women Teachers (Re)member* (Boston: Beacon Press, 2021).

21. Jarvis R. Givens, "Literate Slave, Fugitive Slave: A Note on the Ethical Dilemma of Black Education," in *The Future Is Black: Afropessimism, Fugitivity, and Radical Hope in Education*, ed. Carl A. Grant, Ashley N. Woodson, and Michael J. Dumas (New York: Routledge, 2020), 24.

Part 3

"renegades roam here"

In the face of the counterinsurgent carcerality that dominates schools and other spaces in Pittsburgh, people continue to push back. They resist. Children recognize unfair and oppressive practices in their schools and communities, and they fight for their individuality and autonomy in big and small ways. Caregivers experience the same systems they went through seeking to continue harm on their children, and they both teach their children to navigate these systems and advocate for change. Activists and artists experience censure and respond by changing narratives and teaching young people to do the same through hip-hop, poetry, and visual arts.

In this section, we focus on Black caregivers', activists', and children's resistance to the systems violently antagonistic to their existence. From a visual depiction of "The System" to a *belligerent* teacher asking, "Why not?," the pieces in this section have in common a shared struggle toward self-determination in the face of systemic impact. They illustrate the violent operation of police and policing in schools while highlighting "renegade" responses, acts of opposition and self-determination. As you engage with the works in this section, we ask you to consider the following: How are schools foregrounded as carceral spaces across these narratives? What are different approaches to resistance, and how might they work in concert with each other? And finally, how might the questions and acts of resistance and self-determination be considered across the times, spaces, and lived experiences represented in these pieces (and yet undetermined futures)?

Lori Delale-O'Connor

Taj Poscé, *The System*, 2021

The System

Taj Poscé

In the creation of this work, I really wanted to use a form of abstraction to shine a bright light on the systematic issue of the school-to-prison pipeline. In a sense the painting is fairly literal, where in the top section is the depiction of pipes running directly to and through a plot of space that represents the school grounds and into another section of bars (prison bars) in the lower part of the painting. In its simplicity, this painting also shows a complex interconnectivity, weaving, and interlocking of the school system and the prison system—both of which are being loomed over by these casting white clouds, which representationally could be the larger powers that be: the governance looming over this system and allowing it to happen with no real resolutions. Overpolicing in schools; budgets being allocated poorly; the lack of real resources, recreation, mentorship, and trade. All of the simple solutions, bound up by the clouds, casting gray shadows over the corruption.

Bridging Perspectives

Criminology, Education, and Lived Experiences with Children from Pittsburgh Sentenced to Death by Incarceration

J. Z. Bennett and Christy L. McGuire

In this chapter we present a dialogue between two Black men raised in Pittsburgh. Through an exploration of their lived experiences of being sentenced to life without parole as children (what we will refer to in this chapter as *death by incarceration*), we bridge the intricate interplay between the domains of criminology and education. The Pittsburgh region of Pennsylvania is the second largest metro area in the state, with many individuals serving juvenile life without parole (JLWOP) sentences, the majority of whom are Black. The prominence of the JLWOP population in urban Appalachia highlights the degree to which the prison industrial complex[1] is permeating Appalachian communities. While we understand the carceral organization of society means young people have to navigate multiple vectors of repression, we were most interested in the role of formal schooling in these men's experiences of carcerality and perhaps in their anticarceral sensibilities or efforts. This account details the ways that two people envision educating for freedom despite the repressive efforts of school and prison.

A criminologist, Bennett invited the two Pittsburgh-based men formerly incarcerated for life to share their experiences with him and education researcher Martez Files in a public dialogue at the 2022 Center for Urban Education Summer Educator Forum (CUESEF).[2] James

Hough and Ricky Olds—ages forty-eight and fifty-eight at the time of the public discussion—had been sentenced to death by incarceration at ages seventeen and fourteen, respectively. During the forum, they shared narrative accounts of their schooling experiences in urban Appalachia from before, during, and after their years of incarceration.³ As we came to understand, however, their sentencing began long before their "criminal" offense—before cops and courts. It originated in part from their schooling experiences, in the classroom.⁴

Early Childhood Schooling Experiences

Bennett and Files began the conversation by asking James and Ricky about their schooling experiences. James, who attended Frick Elementary located in Oakland near the University of Pittsburgh, responded to the question "How would you describe your schooling experiences growing up?":

> I was recognized as a prodigy as a child artistically, and I was given different opportunities throughout my young childhood to develop that talent. Thankfully I did. And I was able to thank God because that's been one of the major saving graces throughout my life . . . it [gave] me my first foot in the water that art is something outside of myself. And that I could experience it in a larger world. And it offered another glimpse into possibility. But, as all these stories have a similar theme or similar events, I ended up succumbing to the environment.

James was recognized as an artistic prodigy in elementary school and received free classes at the Carnegie Museum of Art. Despite some isolated positive learning experiences both in and out of school, his overall experiences as a gifted and brilliant Black boy led to him choosing to leave the system in tenth grade, when he was attending Schenley High School in North Oakland. Ricky, who attended Mary Junkin Cowley Elementary School on Pittsburgh's North Side, also highlighted the reality of how being intelligent can complicate the classroom space for Black children. He stated, "School was tricky, you know why? Because

I was kinda smart . . . like I said, I was able to get good grades without even trying. I used to like to read. I just picked that up. My mother always bought us books, and so I had a pretty decent vocabulary from reading a lot."

Ricky described how his mother was providing an educational context for her brilliant son outside of educational institutions. Education was a familial practice, which is part of the Black Radical Tradition.[5] He continued, "I felt funny, like I had to dumb down to try to fit in. You couldn't express yourself. They expected certain things, especially from little Black kids, but at the time I didn't get that because I was Black . . . so I was always in trouble, and they would always be like, 'He's very smart, but he has no discipline.' It's the labels they put on you when you just don't follow the rule, when you're independent. These would be positive things today, but then they was a problem."

Ricky continued to express himself and did not give up or give in to pressures to conform. He also decided to leave school by the tenth grade after attending Latimer Junior High School on the North Side. Despite having some very positive schooling experiences and excelling academically, he was still labeled as problematic by his teachers. Both James and Ricky were gifted, smart, and insightful children who experienced counterinsurgent attacks of schooling on Black intelligence, Black creativity, and Black life.[6] Indeed, their stories point to the ways in which antiblackness in Pittsburgh worked through schools to discipline individual, family, and community intelligence.

Relationships between Schooling and Prison/Carcerality

Ricky and James also valued education while recognizing that it was not a safety net. As they reflected on their educational experiences, both expressed the difficulty in understanding how education could help them transcend their circumstances. James, who spent twenty-six years in prison, replied to the prompt "Can you talk about how growing up in the Pittsburgh area shaped your experiences inside of school?":

> Fortunately I was very good in school, but I want to say I didn't see the value in education. Even today, I really can't understand why I didn't because I respect education. All throughout my life, I've educated myself; when I did have the opportunity to go to Villanova at SCI Graterford, I took that opportunity, and I excelled. So I always had a tremendous respect for learning and education, but the school system at the time, you had to really propel yourself. The environment wasn't a safety net, you know what I mean? You know, educationally.

Although James says he did not appreciate *schooling*, he always valued *education*. One reason many people do not see a difference between education and schooling is because they are situated in systems that are programmed for Black institutional failure.[7] Ricky emphasized how social institutions—or systems—are designed so that some will win, while others will fail, especially schooling and prison. Ricky, who served thirty-eight years in prison, said, "I do believe that the whole system that we have is founded on something that could never foster and promote justice to begin with; it never was designed to." His insight into the deliberate design of educational institutions resonates with scholars who have documented the historical purposes of schooling to enclose, punish, marginalize, and otherwise repress Black students and people.[8] He elaborated, "So we need systems created by people today who perceive a different reality than their ancestors saw and cause them to create those systems. We need different systems today. And that's why we can't continue in our education system to rely on the same old cons, and your same old Freuds, and your same old Maslow's hierarchy of needs."

Ricky astutely observed that outdated Western perceptions are relied on to narrate a genealogy of education, which predetermines outcomes in children's schooling experiences. Moreover, he revealed the role of deep study (often outside formal schooling) that is central to the Black radical tradition.[9] He has studied Freud and Maslow and was able to issue thoughtful critiques of their repressive frameworks. This is particularly striking as Maslow's hierarchy of needs is often adopted unthinkingly to make paternalistic, benevolent claims about people who are impoverished or are in some other way marginalized. Yet we know radical study and thought emerge from sites of hunger, unfreedom, and so forth. Additionally, Ricky expressed the praxis of the Black radical tradition: imagining and planning a free future.[10] When invited to consider that "extensive research has documented that most youth of color are often criminalized and viewed in a dehumanizing manner before they are formally processed in the criminal justice system. How did you come to understand the relationships between schooling and prison or carcerality?" Ricky responded by describing how this sorting mechanism operates:

> First of all, life in America immediately creates in one group this sense of inferiority and it begins in the education system. You cannot condition one group in a society to feel inferior without, at the same time, conditioning the other group to feel superior. Though they may not personally feel that they feel superior to somebody else, you can't help it because that's how you see in this system from two different ends of the polarity scale.
>
> It became clear to me that these systems, schools, these people, if they didn't try to make me feel lesser, then they just assumed I was lesser than, and they always assume that I couldn't speak for myself... I didn't know what was best for me, and I resented that. So I just felt like, you know what? There's got to be more. This can't be it.

Although Ricky and James detailed how schools can be sites of exclusion and violence through racist hierarchies and ideologies, they both expressed hope for a better future and a free world and described how they continue to build and create a more livable and lovable world for themselves and others.

Freedom Dreams: Beyond Carcerality to Visions of Liberation

In the spirit of Robin Kelley's work *Freedom Dreams: The Black Radical Imagination*,[11] we concluded our conversation by asking Ricky and

James to freedom dream about a world beyond prison. Three years following his incarceration, James described his ideas about freedom and how he embraces freedom in his work as an artist in the community.

> So to me, freedom is definitely critical in the work that I do now, artistically, but also in a sense of freedom to engage with the community, freedom to interact with people in different places, whether it be art-related or not. To me, that freedom is essential in accomplishing goals like community development, activism, and my own personal artistic practice.
>
> I'm currently an artist participating in the Carnegie International 58th edition in Pittsburgh. I'm doing a mural inside the community known as the Hill District, the home of August Wilson. And I chose to do that mural here for a particular reason. The model that I use to produce this mural is a community-based model, where we bring the community in, and we have meetings about what visually the community wants to see. And from there, that mural develops and not so much on its own, but it's those ideas that the community has are channeled through me as the artist. And I use myself as a vessel that they can artistically speak through.
>
> As an artist, a lot of my practice, not so much conceptually but internally, is centered around freedom and centered around making choices that only I can make. Making choices that I believe in and being free to make those choices.

Here James articulated an important way he practices freedom:[12] creating art with and for his community and serving as a channel or conduit between himself and the world. He is an actor in a collective movement for freedom through artistic expression, decision-making, and collaboration. Ricky, who had been in the community for five years following his incarceration at the time of the plenary session, underscored how choices are important to freedom and elaborated on how he envisioned freedom in contrast to when he was incarcerated. In response to the questions "How is your current work aligned with your vision of freedom? When you dream about what's possible for vulnerable youth, what ideas come to mind? What can we build, create, develop, or innovate to make this world more livable and lovable for them?" he stated:

> First of all, I personally believe that most people today are not free, just given a few sets of choices, and they choose one or the other. Personally, when I got out, I had a job, but I decided I wanted to go back to school. The parole person was like, "Well, you're overreaching. We don't really like school. You need to work." So I went back to school against his recommendation, and we had a big fight about it, and I was almost in violation, but then we had to look at the rules and say, well, college is workforce development, so there's no punishment to be had.
>
> So I went back [to school]. I felt like I was in prison in terms of all these young people now, and they're in this learning environment supposedly, but many times, I felt in conflict with maybe the professor. . . . I told all the students, no matter what they say, you have to evaluate it. You have to see how it works in your life, in your own belief system. You already have, but you hide it because you want to fit in. You want good grades, and you want to earn a decent living.
>
> I feel like we all have to understand that we have gifts and talents that many times the education system does not bring out. So we need the freedom to believe in ourselves. We need the freedom to understand that we're capable of anything we desire, and if this universe can give you the desire, it can also give you the means to fulfill it. That's something I learned, and so that's what I consider freedom.

Despite carceral attempts to limit or control his choices, Ricky actively pursued a formal education while also mentoring younger students to think critically about what they were being taught. He described the ways in which gaining freedom through education requires an intentional, anticarceral struggle. When asked to imagine a world beyond prison, James and Ricky presented visions of liberation that included the importance of incorporating freedom in all aspects of our lives. They remind us that we must first freedom dream before we can build, create, develop, and innovate a world that is more livable and lovable for children, especially Black children in urban Appalachia.

Conclusion

The conversation with Ricky and James—two Black men from urban Appalachia sentenced to death by incarceration as children—highlights the ways in which schools serve as sites of these sentences. Both men lost decades of their lives to unjust systems that ensnared them when they were still children. Long before their first encounters with cops and courts, their experiences in classrooms played critical roles in imposing a racist hierarchy through exclusion and violence. Specifically, their schooling experiences in Pittsburgh speak to the complexities of the classroom in the school-lifetime incarceration nexus. Ultimately, we need more critical dialogue among education researchers, criminologists, and the nearly twelve thousand individuals in the United States sentenced to life as children that deeply examines the long-term impacts of practices in schools that give way to sentencing primarily Black children to be condemned to die in prison. Pittsburgh, the city of bridges, is an apt place to bridge these perspectives on schools and carcerality through lived experiences in urban Appalachia.[13]

Notes

1. Mike Davis, "Hell Factories in the Field," *Nation* 260, no. 7 (1995): 20.

2. CUESEF is a national conference hosted by the Center for Urban Education (CUE) in the University of Pittsburgh School of Education.

3. Quotes in this manuscript were primarily taken from their words in the CUESEF interview and supplemented with individual interviews Bennett conducted for his dissertation (J. Z. Bennett, "Life after Life: A Narrative Review of Incarceration and Reentry Experiences of Children Sentenced to Life without Parole in Pennsylvania" [Unpublished diss., Temple University, 2022]).

4. Edward Fergus and J. Z. Bennett, "Introduction: Masculinity and Boyhood Constructions in the School-to-Prison Pipeline," *Boyhood Studies* 11, no. 2 (2018): 1–16.

5. Lasana Kazembe, "'Listen to the Blood': DuBois, Cultural Memory, and the Black Radical Tradition in Education," *Socialism and Democracy* 32, no. 3 (2018): 146–63.

6. Sojoyner, "Black Radicals Make for Bad Citizens"; Vaught, *Compulsory*.

7. Mwalimu J. Shujaa, *Too Much Schooling, Too Little Education: A Paradox of Black Life in White Societies* (Trenton, NJ: Africa World Press, 1994).

8. Chrissy Anderson-Zavala et al., "Fierce Urgency of Now: Building Movements to End the Prison Industrial Complex in Our Schools," *Multicultural Perspectives* 19, no. 3 (2017): 151–54, https://doi.org/10.1080/15210960.2017.1331743; Erica Meiners, *For the Children? Protecting Innocence in a Carceral State* (Minneapolis: University of Minnesota Press, 2016).

9. Robin D. G. Kelley, "Black Study, Black Struggle," *Boston Review*, March 1, 2016, https://www.bostonreview.net/forum/robin-kelley-black-struggle-campus-protest/.

10. Robin D. G. Kelley, *Freedom Dreams: The Black Radical Imagination*, 20th anniversary ed. (Boston: Beacon Press, 2022).

11. Kelley, *Freedom Dreams*.

12. bell hooks, *Teaching to Transgress: Education as a Practice of Freedom* (New York: Routledge, 1994).

13. The authors would like to thank Dr. Martez Files, who was instrumental in codeveloping the interview protocol questions for the plenary session at the 2022 CUESEF gathering, which made this book chapter possible. We also would like to give a special thank-you to James Hough and Ricky Olds for sharing stories of their schooling experiences in urban Appalachia.

A Lost Soul in Someone's Body

Briayelle Gaines

Briayelle is a senior at West Mifflin Area High School. She plans to attend college to study criminal justice and criminology. She is driven, adventurous, and diligent.

I really enjoy going to school and learning new things, and usually the day goes by fast without a problem except for this one day. Everyone's mood was just off, and there were a lot of fights happening and drama going around. But it all cooled down by the time everyone was leaving to go to tech.

On my way to the bus I was having a conversation with my sister about the events that were occurring that day, and this girl was behind us and had overheard us talking and had asked us if we were talking about her. I responded with "nobody is talking about you," and she said, "Don't get smart, bitch." And I said, "Watch your mouth and who you're talking to." And then my sister and I proceeded to get on the bus.

The tension was very high on the bus, and you could tell. Now, before this incident, I did know this girl, and we were actually really good friends, but I didn't like the fact that she always used to walk over my sister, being that they were in the same grade at the time. I was sixteen in the tenth grade, and my sister was seventeen in the eleventh grade. But my sister is more of an introvert; she really stays to herself and doesn't say anything to anybody unless they say something to her. So, growing up, I was always defending my sister even though I was the little sister. And my mom always saw that as a problem.

The bus ride was awkward for the other people, and you could tell. I would say ten minutes into the bus ride, the girl was just tagging on the problem, so I said, "You're still talking about the problem for what?" And she was like, "Do you want to fight?" And I said, "It's whatever." But she continued to talk and sit down with her boyfriend. And then the next thing you know, her boyfriend said, "I would rather you fight her in front of me than not in front of me." So she stood up, and we proceeded to fight while the bus was moving. The fight only lasted for about one minute.

The bus driver called the West Mifflin Police, being that we were in the West Mifflin area. But the protocol is she was supposed to call the school police and turn the bus back around to go back to the school. The police didn't arrive to the bus until twenty minutes later, and by that time, the fight was already over, and everyone was already calmed down, and we were all just ready to be at Steel Center. The first police who came on the bus was a female, but I don't think she was on call because she just came on the bus, asked who was fighting, and nobody responded, so she left. And then it took another 5–10 minutes for the other police to come.

Then the next policeman came on the bus, and he talked to the bus driver before he came to the back. Then he came to the back and came straight to me and asked what my name was. And I asked him why he was only talking to me, and he responded with "The bus driver pointed you out." And I proceeded to ask if she pointed anyone else out, and he didn't respond. When he got on the bus, you can tell he was a little uptight. He appeared to be about six foot five and a good 270 pounds; he was more on the heavy side. At the time, I believe I was fifteen and not even 100 pounds. He then asked me what my name was again, and I just looked at him. And then he told me to get off the bus. So I grabbed my book bag and was trying to get off the bus, but there was another policeman in front of me, so I was walking at a steady pace, and he didn't like that, so he started jabbing me in my back. I told him multiple times, "Don't touch me. Don't touch me. Don't touch me." But he just kept jabbing me, so I pushed my elbow back and pushed his hands off of me.

Then the next thing I know, I'm turned around in a seat, and my nose is bleeding. Everything happened so fast. I remember screaming in pain while he had my face against the window and had my arm twisted behind my back. I kept telling him, "You're hurting me. You're hurting me." It's like he didn't care or hear me. Then the next thing I know, both police were on me. The bigger one had his knee in my back, and the other was pulling on me. I remember one of them pulling my hair and wrapping my braids around his hands and yanking my head back and forth and back and forth multiple times. It felt like my head was going to be dislocated from my body. I remember everyone screaming and trying to help me, saying, "Let her go, let her go."

He ended up putting handcuffs on me. They weren't that tight when he put them on, but that wasn't my main concern at the moment. They put me in the back of the cop car, and I just sat there for about twelve minutes. I asked to talk to my sister so she could call my mom. That twelve minutes felt like the longest twelve minutes in my life. My brain was completely empty. I didn't even know what just happened; all I knew was that I was in pain, and I just wanted my mother. I was in disbelief that something like this would happen to me. You see this shit on TV and different shows and stuff, but when it actually happens to you, it's like "did that actually happen?"

During that time, I wasn't sure how to process everything. I felt stuck in time, like I had to keep reliving that day. Every cop car, every blue light, every siren triggered me, and I went through a point in time where the presence of men in general made me feel uncomfortable and less of a human. They eventually got the girl off the bus and put her in another cop car. When the officer who arrested me came back to the car, the first thing he did was try to give me a napkin to clean up my face, and I told him, "I'm not doing anything, and nobody is touching me without my mother being present because I'm a minor." And he still tried to get my face cleaned up; he called the paramedics, and when they came, I simply told them the same thing I told the officer. And they tried to encourage me to just clean it up so I can look more presentable. He finally got in touch with my mother, and they talked. Not sure what was said, but all I heard was my mother saying that she'll be there.

During the car ride, I did in fact let the officer know that the handcuffs were not tight and that they kept falling off, so at that point I just took them off and sat them on the seat next to me. When I told him, he didn't respond. He ended up taking me to Jefferson Hospital. Once I got there, he was explaining what happened to the nurses outside, and he told them I was a "safety hazard" because my cuffs kept falling off. They proceeded to put me on a bed with my arms and legs strapped down and explain to me that it was for my safety and the safety of others around me. I felt like an untamed animal.

He called my mother again because I refused to let anyone touch me or communicate with me. When he hung up on the phone, I remember him saying, "I already know how this is going to go." From there on, I lost all respect and any kind of sympathy for that man. My mom did eventually come, and I remember her yelling at them for discharging me before she got there because, once again, I was minor, and they needed her permission. I remember my mother looking at me like she didn't recognize me. I remember hearing my baby brother crying in his stroller in the back seat of her car. They eventually cleaned me up with my mother's permission. Me and my mom talked briefly, and I just wanted her to hold me and comfort me and tell me everything was going to be okay. When she first arrived, we couldn't even talk to each other because the officers were rushing us out the door.

They end up taking me to a station. They fingerprinted me, made me take the string out of my pants, took multiple pictures of me, and put me in a jail cell. It was late December, so it was snowing really bad, and it was freezing outside. It was even colder inside the cell at this moment, and I felt more like an animal than a human. I didn't have any shoes; all I had was a sweatshirt and sweatpants, and not to mention I didn't eat. I was in that cell for about seven hours. I remember I had to use the bathroom, and it took nearly twenty minutes for me just to get someone's attention so they could let me use the bathroom. They did let me use the bathroom in another cell. I remember feeling gross and like I was being watched. I looked around, and there was a camera. At this point, I just felt numb physically and mentally. Eventually I just fell asleep because I had nothing else to do but stare at a wall.

When they had all the paperwork they needed, they put me in another police car and drove me to Shuman. When I got there, they took my height, made me get butt-ass naked, made me bend over and cough and take a shower in front of someone. They put me in Gate G because of my last name. When I got there, it was about dinner time, but I couldn't eat; I couldn't sleep nor use the restroom. I couldn't do anything. I was stuck. It felt like I was a lost soul in someone's body.

When I was walking to my gate, I remember walking past the other gates, and the boys were running up and staring at me, whistling at me, saying things like "nice tits." It felt gross to be in my body, and I felt ashamed. I did meet some other girls in my gate. I talked and listened to them—they told me and explained why they were in there. And at this point, it made me grateful and appreciative for the things that I have and the support of my family because I realized that some people don't have it as good as me. There was this one girl who was in there because her parents just didn't want her, and they wouldn't come get her, so she was stuck in there. I felt bad because I wanted to help her but couldn't. I was just as mentally and physically stuck as she was. I believe I was in there for two nights. Like I said before, I didn't eat or sleep. When I did receive food, the other girls were begging for it, and I felt bad, so I let them have all my food. They seemed like they needed it more than I did.

My lawyer finally met up with me, and we talked about everything, and he said that he was getting me out. And he indeed did get me out. After that, I had to do another hearing with the head of the Shuman detention.[1] He let me off on house arrest and told me that was his "Christmas gift" from him to me and I should be thankful that's all the cop did to me because being that I'm Black, I should already know how they treat us. This stuck with me because he was Black and made me feel like I failed my community. Once again, I realized how fucked up the system is and people are, regardless of their race or gender.

I was on house arrest for about four months, and around this time COVID-19 just hit, so everything was shut down regardless. With COVID-19 being a huge thing at the time, they kept pushing my court date back and back until a full year passed. Each time my court date would approach, my family and I would get excited, just for them to push it back to a later date. We continuously had to jump through hoops that entire year. I did end up getting off of the anklet and ended up on probation for a couple of months. Everything was so hectic. I did end up going to therapy, and I did physical therapy for my neck, my spine, and my major concussions. I did anger management classes. I did a lot, and I was just exhausted with the whole situation and wanted it all to be over and to just forget about everyone and everything. I was tired of being looked at like a troubled teenager who did something for attention. The whole incident was all over the news, and everyone heard about it. I could feel the stares. But long story short, stuff happens for a reason, and you can learn from it, or you can keep dwelling on it. I decided to take my experience and let others hear about it to let them know that they're not alone and it's okay to speak up. I'm going to school for criminal justice, and I'm going to learn more about the system. I'm going to make a change in my own life and maybe in others'.

Note

1. Shuman Juvenile Detention Center is in Pittsburgh, Pennsylvania. It was closed in September 2021, though plans are being made to reopen it in 2024.

Black Caregivers' Educational Strategies to Avoid and Disrupt Potential Pathways toward Criminal (In)justice

Lori Delale-O'Connor, James P. Huguley, and Ming-Te Wang

> *My dad tells me, and my mom tells me, if a cop sees me and they start asking questions, keep my hands away from my pockets so they don't think I'm reaching for a weapon; don't talk back; do everything they say.*
>
> —Black child living in Pittsburgh, PA

Threats of violence toward Black children are real and omnipresent, and as Black caregivers consider their children's education and socialization, the possibility of harm at the hands of both educators and police looms large.[1] Black caregivers incorporate their concerns about verbal harassment, physical violence, incarceration, and even death into the ways they navigate opportunities and expectations around educating their children.[2] In this chapter, we draw from our prior conceptualization of *racialized compensatory cultivation*[3]—the processes by which Black caregivers support their children to both develop their interests and mitigate harmful contexts—to discuss the ways Black caregivers may connect their in- and out-of-school educational strategies to the avoidance and disruption of harm, violence, and incarceration for their children. We further note the ways these strategies may silence and constrain Black children for what caregivers deem the sake of their physical safety.

While this work builds on numerous bodies of academic research, narratives of lived experience, and artistic accounts of Black life, the data we examine come directly from interviews and focus groups with Black caregivers (twenty-seven parents and one grandparent) and their children (twenty-six adolescents in middle school) living in Pittsburgh, PA. We recruited families purposely to meet an overarching study goal of talking with caregivers and children who could provide detailed information on how Black caregivers support the educational outcomes of their middle school children. Caregiver focus groups and interviews centered on general parenting practices, issues of race—including heritage, pride, and discrimination—and parents' engagement with their children's education and schooling. Child focus groups and interviews addressed comparable topics from the child's point of view.

Data analysis demonstrated that Black caregivers were acutely aware of the ways subjective disciplinary practices by their children's teachers and administrators, as well as potential interactions with police, disparately impacted their Black children's likelihood of experiencing violence at the hands of these adults and/or being pushed toward the legal system. They saw it as their job to address these hazards through practices that connected to both in- and out-of-school learning opportunities—focusing on engaging these opportunities as safety mechanisms. We begin with both caregivers' and youths' own words to illustrate these points and make the connections of police and potential carceral aspects of school to Black caregivers' practices of racialized compensatory cultivation. Then we connect their statements to the framework of racialized compensatory cultivation.

Keeping Children Busy and "Out of Trouble"

Caregivers felt the free, outdoor play in the neighborhood environment was unsafe, with some comparing this to their own experiences growing up.

> **Caregiver 1:** Can you see, can you see your kids outside and know that they gonna be safe now? You know?

Caregiver 2: That's true.

Caregiver 1: It's just so hard because we were, we was so, we went since we got home and did our homework, we was outside playin'! These kids don't.

Caregiver 2: Until the street lights came on! It's just, it's just, it's just sad that they just can't play like they used to.

So some Black caregivers deliberately sought out out-of-school activities to keep their children safe and out of "trouble."

Mom: Do y'all keep y'all kids busy whereas they don't get into a lot of things? Like he's, my son he's playin', he played basketball, he played football, or he's down the street at [elementary school] on Monday, here Tuesday, Wednesday . . . just to keep him active so he doesn't get into the streets.

Grandmother: You know, I keep him—I keep him busy all the way through the summer so he don't have time to get into too much (trouble) because we'll be running to practice or running to swimming, but it takes a lot. I'm glad I'm retired (because) as a parent because [laughter] I'm on the go. My car's got thousands of miles, here to there, taking him there, getting him to different places.

The activities that families involved their children in as out-of-school enrichment served another purpose: keeping them busy and safe—and "off the streets," where caregivers noted the possibility of harm at the hands of both peers and the police.

Fears of Racist Police

Black youth were also acutely aware of the potential for violence at the hands of police, as one child noted when asked what he worried about most.

> **Interviewer:** What do you worry about most as a middle school student? What do you think? What do you do about those worries?
>
> **Child:** Getting killed.

In a focus group discussion, children noted a similar perspective but shifted conversation toward the role of police:

> **Child 1:** Kids and grownups have been dying.
>
> **Child 2:** Our friends and family have been dying.
>
> **Child 3:** Yeah, like the white policemen be, um, fighting the girls in school and punching the boys in their necks. And they be unconscious or something or whatever you wanna call that.

Preparing Children for Police Encounters

More explicitly, Black caregivers were preparing their children for the direct interactions with police that they expected they would have. These directives were framed with the goal of humanizing a Black child in the eyes of police by constraining their behavior, with a focus on demonstrating that the young person is not a threat and, further, that they are respectable and worthy.

> **Caregiver:** I make sure that paperwork on the vehicle is always together. It's always a fresh copy of it. It's always readily available to him in that arm rest or whatever. And I tell him that he needs to be responsible in terms of your word choice that he uses. I tell him, you're educated, you're articulate, so that what you— you're handling business at that point. This is not an informal conversation. If he asks you questions about "Where you going? Where you're coming from?" answer those questions. You know, "yes sir, no sir, yes ma'am, no ma'am." Different things like that. Use eye contact so that you're conveying truly who you are.

You're not pretending to be someone else—because he is an educated Black male.

Caregiver: And especially in regards to the police, I tell him, if you even have an encounter with police, which will happen, I'm sure—I think he's already had one encounter, he's told me. I explain to him that when you're dealing with the police, you have to always let them take your hands out of your pocket to see you're not holding anything. You can't talk to them with slang, or like you would with your friends on the street, because they've already got a negative view of you . . . when it comes to a Black boy, their trigger finger is really itchy. And it's sad. And it's not—I don't say that because you see it on the news, hear about it on the news. I've seen it. I've experienced it throughout my life.

Caregiver: But I've told my kids if they have to do a buck dance in order to get out of it, that's what they need to do. They said, "Mom, what's a buck dance?" All right, we're gonna have to watch an old movie [laughs]. But you know if you have to be humble, say, "Sir, I'm sorry, sir." Just use the *sir* word because I think that is imperative. And I've told other kids, some of their friends, your main thing is you want to stay alive. I don't want to have to go to protests because you're dead, so you say what you need to do and be as cooperative as possible. Be uber apologetic or whatever because you need to stay alive. And you know, sometimes that doesn't even work . . . but you have to try to do that.

Preparing and Supporting Children in Teacher Encounters

The preparation for encountering police was similar to the possibility of engaging with a racist teacher, with caregivers recognizing the onus for de-escalation and proving their humanity was on their Black child. One caregiver recounted the following story after her son and a teacher had a disagreement:

The teacher followed him from the library, down the stairs, down the hall, all the way to his locker door behind him, bantering constantly about getting off the computer. And at one point they were in the hall by themselves—and that was my concern. In that hall by yourself, there's no checks and balances. It's my word against yours. And at one point, the man was up in my son's face, so close that they were only inches—the noses were only inches away, and he's yelling at him. This has been going on now for about five minutes. And I told my son I was very proud of him because he did not allow that man to escalate the situation and to get him out of his character, which was what the goal was so he could then have a real reason to be in trouble or to be expelled or to whatever degree that would have gone to. So, in that particular situation, I had to go up to the school, address the teacher who was equally disrespectful, and then meet him in front of the dean of students, which only solidified what I was saying in the first place, and my son was able to see how having a sense of discipline . . . self-discipline—in that particular moment allowed him to prevail in the end instead of following suit to what the expectation was for him as a Black male student.

All the above pointed to the onus on Black youth having to prove their humanity, having to be in control, and having to suppress their emotions. Youth offered a complex analysis of these expectations, demonstrating awareness of their caregivers' perception and noting that it required them to control or modify their behavior despite awareness of the ways the adults are the ones in the wrong.

Child: They'll [parents] usually tell me stories about what's going on in the news. And of course, with social media nowadays, you can see people recording with their iPhone or something like that. Just a few days ago, there was a story about a ten-year-old boy running away from the police. They usually tell me I have to be home by a certain hour. And they tell me to choose who I'm hanging out with, choose what I'm doing, and don't get caught under self-pressure.

Then, specifically around police, the same boy notes:

> **Child:** My dad tells me, and my mom tells me, if a cop sees me and they start asking questions, keep my hands away from my pockets so they don't think I'm reaching for a weapon; don't talk back; do everything they say.

Black Caregiving, Schools, and Police

Evidenced in the narratives above and further supported by research is the centrality of race in Black families' socialization of their children. Racial socialization involves the messages children are given about the values, attitudes, behaviors, and beliefs around race, racism, racial identity, and interactions.[4] Specific to schools and schooling, this includes shaping children's understanding of the formal education system and their teachers' perceptions of them. For Black parents, this may connect to their own experiences of schools and furthermore may come with warnings about teachers and other agents of schools, such as school resources officers who will underestimate, ignore, or even act violently toward Black youth.[5]

Both research and colloquial understanding further point to the prevalence of "the talk"—typically framed as discussions about racism, racial profiling, and harm at the hands of law enforcement[6]—between Black caregivers and their children as one component of racial socialization that Black families engage in for the safety of their children. Policing is not limited to the police and is shown across literature and from youth and parent comments to be present in both the apparatus and the practices of schools. Disciplinary practices against Black children by teachers and administrators are more likely to be administered for subjective behaviors (e.g., disrespect, loudness), result in more punitive outcomes (e.g., suspensions or expulsions), and connect to carceral outcomes (e.g., alternative schools, juvenile detention, or prison). Thus, Black caregivers think about the safety of their children as a regular part

Figure 1: Racialized compensatory cultivation

Aims	Behaviors	Motivators/Drivers
Because Black parents want their children to have	they actively engage in	both to forward positive drivers
• Race-affirming knowledge • Race-affirming experiences • **Physical safety** • Positive academic experiences and outcomes • Positive social experiences and outcomes	• *Enrollment in programming (athletic, academic, race-focused)* • Forwarding counternarratives of race • *Directives of avoidance of certain peers/activities* • Participation/visibility in child's school • Connections with child's teachers	• Race pride (as protection, motivator, etc.) • Children's interests and abilities
		and to counteract negative drivers
		• School environment (micro-aggressions, racist practices) • *Localized safety concerns (recent occurrences)* • *Societal safety concerns (violence toward Black people)* • Caregivers' firsthand experiences

Originally published in L. Delale-O'Connor, J. P. Huguley, A. Parr, and M.-T. Wang, "Racialized Compensatory Cultivation: Centering Race in Parental Educational Engagement and Enrichment," *American Educational Research Journal* 57, no. 5: 1912–53.

of both school and out-of-school time and activity. They must further engage in complex knowledge and navigation of carceral systems to support their children.

In a previous article,[7] we described racialized compensatory cultivation as the processes by which Black caregivers support their children with in- and out-of-school learning to both cultivate their interests and strengths and account for deleterious (underresourced, racist, violent, etc.) environments. In figure 1, we illustrate the process of racialized compensatory cultivation with particular emphasis as it connects to potential police-perpetrated harm. In short, Black parents have goals for their children and engage in specific behaviors to both forward positive forces and counteract negative drivers. The negative drivers—which may include the school environment, localized safety concerns, and societal safety concerns—in part encompass the carceral environment caregivers note they experienced in their own youth and that they and their children currently face.

Violence and carcerality are a clear part of the context in which Black caregivers care for, educate, and socialize their children. Pittsburgh specifically offers a challenging and contradictory space for Black families to navigate, with hyper-segregated schools, racial disparities in access to educational and other resources necessary for thriving, and deep-seated histories of police violence against Black people existing alongside innovative programs and policies focused on Black communities and historically and contemporarily thriving Black arts scenes and community work.[8] Black caregivers must navigate this context and support their children in ways that prepare them for and protect them from police and teacher encounters; they also use out-of-school time to mitigate these risks. As caregivers noted, keeping their children safe from carceral systems and associated violence by focusing on activities that would keep the children busy and prepare them to act in ways that might be viewed as "appropriate" during police encounters and in school. Youth, in turn, noted their fears of violence and the ways that they modified their behavior to align with their caregivers' expectations but constrained them.

Notes

1. Leslie A. Anderson, LaRen Morton, and Andrea N. Trejo, "To Be Young, Conscious and Black: The Cumulative Witnessing of Racial Violence for Black Youth and Families," *Journal of Family Theory and Review* 14, no. 3 (June 8, 2022): 412–20; Michael J. Dumas, "'Losing an Arm': Schooling as a Site of Black Suffering," *Race Ethnicity and Education* 17, no. 1 (December 9, 2013): 1–29; Monique W. Morris, *Pushout: The Criminalization of Black Girls in Schools* (New York: The New Press, 2016).
2. Jennifer M. Threlfall, "Parenting in the Shadow of Ferguson: Racial Socialization Practices in Context," *Youth and Society* 50, no. 2 (September 25, 2016): 255–73.
3. Lori Delale-O'Connor et al., "Racialized Compensatory Cultivation: Centering Race in Parental Educational Engagement and Enrichment," *American Educational Research Journal* 57, no. 5 (December 6, 2019): 1912–53.
4. Chase L. Lesane-Brown, "A Review of Race Socialization within Black Families," *Developmental Review* 26, no. 4 (December 2006): 400–26.
5. Gloria Boutte and Nathaniel Bryan, "When Will Black Children Be Well? Interrupting Anti-Black Violence in Early Childhood Classrooms and Schools," *Contemporary Issues in Early Childhood* 22, no. 3 (December 22, 2019): 232–43.
6. Leslie A. Anderson, Tracy R. Whitaker, and Cudore L. Snell, "Parenting while Powerless: Consequences of 'the Talk,'" *Journal of Human Behavior in the Social Environment* 26, nos. 3–4 (January 20, 2016): 303–9.
7. Delale-O'Connor et al., "Racialized Compensatory Cultivation."
8. City of Pittsburgh, "Black Pittsburgh Matters," (n.d.), https://pittsburghpa.gov/bpm/black-pittsburgh-matters; Jodi DiPerna and Elaine Frantz, "Historical Context: Violence Occurring against Black Pittsburghers Today Has Been Happening for More than a Century-and-a-Half," June 19, 2020, https://pinjnews.org/historical-context-violence-occurring-against-black-pittsburghers-today-has-been-happening-for-more-than-a-century-and-a-half/; Pittsburgh Foundation, (n.d.), "Advancing Black Arts in Pittsburgh," https://pittsburghfoundation.org/advancing-black-arts-pittsburgh; Liz Reid, "An Unsuccessful 30-Year Effort to Desegregate Pittsburgh Public Schools," WESA, October 19, 2018, https://www.wesa.fm/education/2018-10-19/an-unsuccessful-30-year-effort-to-desegregate-pittsburgh-public-schools.

Notes from Upstream

Salmon Girl

Sheila Carter-Jones

Why do salmon swim upstream? This is not a trick question requiring some erudite response. Not a riddle or test to find out one's knowledge of ichthyology . . . that salmon are a bony fish. The answer to this question explains well how I became a teacher in a public school system and survived to retirement years later. In retrospect, I have come to realize that becoming a teacher is a lifelong endeavor, which requires compassion, courage, perseverance, and good common sense or what I like to call *intelligent wisdom*. It is not something that just happens because we say so or will it so or bring into existence through positive thinking.

In the beginning, I didn't have a deep desire to become a teacher. It was an idea my college adviser had, and I went along with it. I was really too young to know exactly what I wanted to do in my life. So when I first entered the teaching *profession*, it was just that. The word for what I was to profess, not what I was to become. And yes, with all my youthful passion, I did think that I had it by the tail. I had graduated from a prestigious university. I was energetic, creative, forward-thinking, and young. I loved the way students, who were slightly younger than me those first couple of years, discussed and put their ideas out there. They were open, and I was listening. At the age of twenty-two, I was a child myself, and I could relate. It's no wonder that the principal at my first school decided that I was an unsatisfactory teacher. I don't think I was a bad teacher but rather a novice with no mentor and no possibility of getting one. And I was not the normal *just do what you're told* person, even if it is harmful for a child's future. I was, for sure, not a *just go along with* type of person.

It has been determined that cool, clean, and well-oxygenated water is critical to a salmon egg's survival. I am Salmon Girl. I definitely did not have that kind of environment as a first-year teacher placed in what was not nurturing waters but rather an environment that was detrimental to healthy growth as a twenty-two-year-old teacher-professional. I had to create my own environment in which I could breathe, flip my fins, and swim.

So I became my own mentor, although I didn't plan it at the time. This meant that many times I had to return to my point of origin and rely on the upbringing I received at home and from the people in my small coal-mining town in Western Pennsylvania. It is where I learned the honest work ethic, the never-be-broken spirit, and the perseverance to live and stand for what's in your heart. Nourishment from home was a good thing because, from the start, I was targeted as a teacher, and home is where I went to be replenished again and again. Almost and mostly every Sunday, I would find myself reflecting on my week at school. I'd nearly be in tears sitting in the kitchen with my mother, or Miss Margaret's living room, or Mrs. Gladys's front porch, or Ms. Gaines's *Lord!Lord!Lord!* These were all domestic working women in my small coal-mining hometown who taught me how to live with dignity and respect. They are the ones who pulled me through to my own potential and capacity for compassion. They taught me to persevere, to see the bright side of possibility, which was teaching African American children toward the future. These were the most important and valuable things they could pass on to me.

The professional adults I encountered at school my first teaching year, on the other hand, functioned like fishermen to net or scoop me up or lead me by false praise to fall prey to hawks or kites and get eaten alive in a system spinning like an eddy within the institution called *public education*, sullied by a colonial consciousness. At first, I considered these people in charge of schools and content areas as obstacles. Later, however, each situation I found myself in with people who held transgressive ideas and ideologies proved to be a training ground that in the end catapulted me forward in strength of resolve and academic and credentialed achievements.

My first teaching assignment was in an urban high school teaching English to tenth and what was then called a *slow* class of eleventh graders. It was not the students, though, who challenged my growth. It was the negative and harsh treatment of the administrators and the English supervisors that forced me to rely on instinct, on what was good and worth it, and on what was detrimental to growth and not worth standing up to based on my own beliefs and what I had been taught by the women and men in my hometown. And it wasn't that they taught by words alone. Their actions and behaviors were far greater lessons than anything they ever said.

This was 1972, and having been bred in the '60s of seemingly contradictory ideologies of *make love, not war* and *the revolution*, I maintain that it was my flimsy blowing-in-the-wind afro hairstyle coupled with an understanding and empathy for students' ideas and concerns, which were not too different from my own, that the swirl of developing as a teacher was set in motion. There were other things various heads of English departments and administrators did throughout my teaching life that were intentionally done with intent to harm my spirit, my intellect, and yes, my physical body.

I remember clearly and still feel the punch, though not physical, of my first experience being observed by the English supervisor. In my first-period class of tenth graders, we were reading the curriculum-based novel *Silas Marner*, which, for urban kids, was dead weight. It was an anchor that helped keep them tied to dock, keep them from sailing out to fulfill dreams. They were completely uninterested. On this particular day, at the sound of the bell, the English supervisor hightailed it into the classroom and sat in the back with not so much as an introduction or a greeting of hello or good morning. She was completely unannounced. I would come to learn that this coming into the classroom to observe teachers for evaluation was more a tactic to intimidate and disparage and to document some already decided ranking of a teacher's ability to teach. They had to find some small thing like *Miss Carter didn't pass out paper until well into the class period* to justify an already determined unsatisfactory rating. The supervisor didn't ask the whys of anything. She didn't know that the reason for passing out paper when I did was because I had learned that paper too soon in the hands of students in that particular class would soon become flying paper airplanes or spitballs whizzing across the room.

When Anthony, in my first-period class at seven thirty-five that morning, raised a lolling right arm to say that he didn't like "this story," I was nervous, of course, but tried not to act like it. It was my first year—first few months, in fact—of teaching and my first time being observed. But what I said after that, I thought, was genius: "Well, Anthony, I don't like it either, but there are still some things we can learn from it." I thought to myself, *Oh my heavens! Brilliant! Simply brilliant!* I was euphoric the rest of the class period. I kept thinking, *Where did that come from!* like it was clear sight after a fog hanging over the river near my hometown. I just knew the English supervisor observing me from the back of the room was beyond pleased with my erudite response. However, what followed after that class was an attempt to put me in my teacher-place.

Since I had no classroom of my own, the follow-up conference took place in the hall. I was what was at the time called a *traveling teacher* equipped with a cart full of books and pencils and a stack of composition paper, which I rolled to empty classrooms when the teacher was having a preparation period. "Don't erase my board," "Don't use the pencils in my drawer," and "Make sure the desks are straightened before you leave" were some of the demands from teachers whose rooms I was assigned to use.

What the supervisor said at that time still baffles me. She said with vehement authority, "You never tell a student that you don't like a story." Huh? I was too young and inexperienced to not say something. So I did.

"Why not?"

"You just don't do that."

"But why?"

"You just don't."

She offered no educationally sound reason. In fact, she offered no reason at all. Instead, she walked away as if frustrated that I pressed for an explanation. I was genuinely perplexed by her lack of ability to give an educationally sound reason, but I was more disturbed by her rude behavior. And I never did get a sound educational explanation for that bit of direction and on-the-fly professional development. Instead, I got the adjective *belligerent* written into the anecdotal records that would begin to shape how I would come to be perceived by administrators, supervisors, and even colleagues, who were either intimidated or kowtowing to get favors or get out of the classroom altogether.

When a female salmon deposits her eggs, she covers them with loose gravel on the river's bed to form a nest. Once the ova develop into alevins, they become active and begin to journey up through the gravel. This process is called *the swim-up*, and this is the first time the alevins are exposed to danger. Predators. This first observation and follow-up conference with the English supervisor was my swim-up. It was the beginning danger of if I weren't careful—or, more like, resolved to live and become what I was beginning to embrace—I would be chewed and swallowed up by the system or chewed and spit out. Luckily for me, I chose another route. That route was the one given by my upbringing. Do what is true and right and stand by your beliefs. Like the women in my hometown always said, "Knees to floor don't have to knot up and hurt if you take care yourself."

All Writing Is Political

An Interview

Sheila Carter-Jones and Robin-Renee Allbritton

Sheila Carter-Jones is the author of three poetry collections: Three Birds Deep, Crooked Star, *and* Blackberry Cobbler. *Her poetry speaks to Black experiences of resistance, both personal and collective.*

Robin-Renee Allbritton: In what ways have you experienced connections between schooling and carcerality, and did this connection have any impact on you as a young poet?

Sheila Carter-Jones: Connections between schooling and carcerality. You know what? I don't know if I connected to the connection having an impact on me as a young poet. I would have to say at the time, as a young person, I don't think I even understood that there might be a connection between schooling and carcerality, that I just was not that aware. I come from such a small coal-mining town that the city was far off, and all the things that might have been happening around that were not, in a sense, I thought were not touching me, but in the long run, that they were. So the connection as an impact on a young poet would have to be in retrospect. That I would have to look back and think, "Well, yeah."

One of the things that I in fact have written about is that in June 1965, I was fifteen when two detectives and two of our small-town police set a road trap for my father. He was taking my mother to do domestic work in the wealthy neighborhood where all of the African American men and women worked after the coal mines shut down. Our small coal-mining town was located at the fringe margin of wealth and opportunity. My dad was beaten by cops and taken to a state hospital for the criminally insane. And this was just because he was a Black man with a voice, and he was not going to be disrespected, and he was going to stand up for himself as a human being. So that particular incident impacted not only my poetic spirit but my whole life up until this point. I still talk about and write about how that incident impacted me as a young person and just not knowing why and how all this was happening because my dad was such a nice guy and he was working.

And the whole little Black community was a very intimate kind of community where people traded vegetables from their gardens. There were two churches, and kids—I was one of them—recited speeches at Christmas and Easter. And that in itself was a training for being able to speak out within a community of people and to, at the same time, begin to hear the rhythms of a poetic voice. There was a certain amount of poetry that was flowing through the speeches that we were given to memorize.

The schooling then, to me (and I just actually wrote about this), happened more in my community than in the institutional school. And all of us got bused into a rich section to go to school. And in this section, all of our parents, men and women, did domestic work, yard work, chauffeurs. And so that had an impact that I needed to be able to even matriculate in a school of rich, white kids. And I was the only African American girl in a class of 400, 400 basically, actually 398. But I was the only African American girl.

RRA: Wow. How did the home education and your institutional education factor into your poetry? Would you like to expound on that a little bit more?

SCJ: The home education was the root of things where I could feel very comfortable with writing what I had to say. Then the institutional education part came in where I was reading and experiencing mostly, in fact, all white authors. And yet there was something that I gained from that, that I could apply to my own work and extend the stories and the happenings within my own cultural community. And, in fact, the Book Mobile came to our little town: a green, little bus type of thing with all the books in it. And there were no Black authors. So in a sense, by the time I graduated high school, I had read almost all the books in the Book Mobile because I could check out five at a time.

RRA: So you're saying that by the time you finished twelfth grade, you still had not read African American authors through school and the Book Mobile, but was that done at home?

SCJ: True, true, true, all of that. I think the first Black authors that we started reading was maybe I was in my second or third year at Carnegie Mellon University, and they got somebody from the community, Nick Flournoy, to come in and teach Black literature. And I don't know if you've ever seen that book called *Black Voices*. That was the first time I think that many of us had ever even read anything by a Black author. And the interesting thing was, even though it was a class that anybody could take, only Black students were in there. It was only maybe five of us or six of us at the time that he could come and have a class. And I had never had an African American teacher at all. I had a graduate student at Carnegie Mellon but not a full professor or anything like that or even a teacher in high school or any elementary school.

RRA: So other than home, community, and church, where you had Black teachers, Black educators?

SCJ: Right. And they weren't like, what would you call them? They were educators in the sense of informal, being informal educators.

RRA: And community educators, yeah?

SCJ: Yeah. One would think that when I entered the teaching profession, school administrators would think I would be an asset to any school. However, because of what happened with my father, I was more determined than ever, even as a novice teacher, that I would teach children, and particularly African American children, first to believe in their potential and then to use it to think critically. This was not a good idea to administrators. I remember vividly throughout my thirty-five-year teaching career how administrators treated me for being highly educated and for questioning the practices and policies that did not support the intellectual development of any children, let alone African American children. Because of my parents and all of the grownups in my small community who had migrated from the South, a moral responsibility had been instilled in me by word and deed.

How I was treated as a teacher in the city public school system [where I taught] was closely aligned with how my father was treated for six and a half years while being held at the state hospital for criminally insane for being a Black man with a voice in 1965, when he was beaten by the two detectives and two hometown policemen—all were white men. The first attack on me in the educational setting was by a white principal during my first year of teaching. I was only twenty-two years old. Sure, I had an afro, but I wasn't the militant he claimed. I just asked questions about sound educational philosophy and had supplemented the curriculum with enriching and culturally relevant literature given that most of my students were African American. I could see the educational differences and lack of opportunities for African American students as well as who really cared or not. I was seen as challenging the institution. A troublemaker, like my father. The principal targeted me as one to be marked *unsatisfactory*. He had called me to his office to scream at me, ranting repeatedly, "You want to set the world on fire, don't you? Don't you? Don't you?"

He pressured me with that sentence over and over until he was red-faced and frothing at the mouth. Finally, I relented just to stop his madness. "Yeah, okay," I said. Letters to the board of education were sent to be placed in my personnel file (and the letters did pile up over the years). I was insubordinate and a rebel. He didn't write *militant*. That would have been too telling on his part.

Although there were many other aggressions, both micro and macro, including being slapped by a principal, having one of my car tires slashed, etc., etc., I'm going to relay one other attack that was the most physical. This attack was similar to, but far less severe than, the attacks by white guards at the state hospital for the criminally insane, who actually murdered mostly Black and brown men by stomping them to death.

After being marked *unsatisfactory* for two consecutive semesters in a row, if a third occurred, that would be grounds for termination. So I was transferred to another school, where it seemed the principal was waiting for me. At the time of evaluation, he marked me *unsatisfactory*. However, he had forgotten to sign the form. I had taken it from my mailbox and read it over. There were anecdotes that had me doing things when school was not in session. In addition, not one single administrator or supervisor had observed me teach. And there were other small things inconsequential for white teachers, but for me it was different. There were consequences—such as being marked *unsatisfactory*. When I went to find the principal to get him to sign off on the evaluation, he assaulted me. I had asked him, "If all of this is true, why haven't you signed it?" He quickly said that he didn't have a pencil. I had one and extended my hand for him to use it to sign the evaluation. Instead of taking the pencil, he grabbed me up in my collar and started shaking me back and forth, then let go, pushing me backwards into a large metal cabinet five or six feet away. Only a hummingbird can fly backwards. I was flying backwards, but I was not a hummingbird. I was scared. He was a big, hefty, white man capable of hurting me badly if it came to that.

The next year, I was transferred again. I was twenty-four and trying to learn how to teach. In relation to most principals, I wasn't just a kid. I was a Black one. Like my father, in relation to the carceral system, he wasn't just a man. He was a Black man. And, yes, he came out alive. I did too.

RRA: Does political education factor into your poetic practice? And if so, could you describe that to me?

SCJ: I don't know that I would separate it out as a political thing. I think all writing that you do, not even exposing, but embracing and sharing your own narrative, is political. Just the act of writing, itself, is political because it causes people to have questions about things, to even question their own beliefs or their own ways of seeing things. So *political*—I would say that I would describe it as that, so that when I write about my dad and our experiences because of what happened, I would call that political in a sense. I think that it would cause people to have questions and begin to maybe open and see something in a different way.

RRA: Did this connection have any impact on the evolution of your poetry? The political education, the infusing of political education into your poetry, could you tell me how it impacted your poetry?

SCJ: I think it made me think more clearly and deeply about what I was saying and how I was saying it. Whether I was going to use a metaphor or simile, for the poem itself to carry the emotion, and how those literary elements and devices that I could use to be the movement or the underneath pushing forward of the emotion without basically cursing somebody out in the poem or something like that. To have it be shaped and sculpted in such a way that people could understand it and not be afraid of it, but question. Anytime I think that something I write causes people to question or to think about what's happening in the world and those happenings, how they are involved in that happening, that is how I try to carry forward the elements of poetry.

RRA: What would you consider some of your most valued work toward freedom in this context, and how would you define freedom?

SCJ: I think freedom is . . . Let me do that and then go back in. I think freedom is an ability to internalize one's own self-worth and to not be influenced by the outer shell of things.

RRA: So how does your poetry practice contribute to struggles for liberation?

SCJ: I think just being able to put it into words and to get it out into the public domain, that is a liberatory act. So one of the things that I have been doing in the community actually is that I have what's called the Sub Verses Social Collective. I cofounded it with another woman for African American women's voices from the community to be heard. They're not in academics or have book awards and all that kind of stuff. It's just the everyday woman who is from the community and working.

So we do have poetry writing prompts at a coffeeshop owned by African Americans in the Black community. So we're there, and they're very comfortable there. It's like home, and all the women, where we gather, share. And I think that's part of what I would say where freedom begins to move forward—that it's not just for me but that I'm adding to something that's in motion.

RRA: That's beautiful. Would you like to share a story to further illustrate your liberatory poetry practice?

SCJ: Poetry is not confined, I don't think, to just writing a poem. Poetry is the movement of life and how people take on and share their stories, their poetic spirit. When I was teaching school, I loved that the kids actually loved to write, once they realized that they could. That I did not give them, "Okay, write about this or write about that."

I would just give it open. And they were so afraid. I don't know, maybe because of the way schools are set up where the teachers just knows everything and nothing at all. So I love that these students that I had, and I'm still in touch with many of them. In fact, I'll talk to one tonight. She participated in the Sub Verses Social Collective activity that we did Saturday. She came with her little notebook and pencil. Well, she is thirty years old, but she's still like a child to me.

SCJ: But one of the things that we did do, and I think this was a great political act by the students. I don't know if you were born when Columbine happened in Colorado, where that first school shootings kind of—

RRA: Yes.

SCJ: We didn't learn about it until we got home from school. It was frightening, like what in the world, there's school shootings? People are coming into schools shooting up kids, and kids are getting killed and things. So when I went to school the next day, the class was completely quiet. And they're eighth graders, and they're never quiet, but they were really silent. They were so silent that I had to ask, "What's going on?"

And they said, "We're scared."

And I said, "You know what? I'm scared too."

And we decided that we would make a plan that if that ever happened, how we would get out of the room. Then after that I said, "Well, let's get started with the lesson."

And they said, "Well, we don't feel like doing that."

I said, "Okay, what do you want to do?"

So we ended up coming up with some ideas of what they wanted to write about instead. And they really came up with some beautiful work. I still have most of it from all those years. But it was such an impact on them and me. The writings that they did were beautiful. They made their own groups; they left notes on the board for the next class, "This is where we are." And then they put in some artwork that they had done in the art class. But they put it up in our little pod all along the wall, their stories and their flowers with the tissue flowers that they had made.

And the stories were so touching that teachers were coming through and reading them and crying because the kids were embracing their own hurt and fears of a brother being shot, somebody's mother had died, and just the whole grief; it helped them grieve a little bit more. And then we noticed that somebody had came and wanted to film it for TV and stuff like that, but it was all the kids. I had nothing to do with it other than to stand there and act like I had some sense. And they did some beautiful work, beautiful. And that, I think, was a political act.

RRA: Oh, it sounds like it. That's awesome. Thank you. So how do you engage your work and with whom, and what are the principles by which you work?

SCJ: How do I engage my work? I engage my work basically every morning. I have a set pattern of I get up and start. I read something first, and then I start working. And sometimes it's a bit of a dream that's hanging on that I can get started with. Or if I'm reading something and

I say, "Oh," and it's something that just takes my breath away, I'll put that down and begin writing. So I definitely write every single morning.

Just thinking of that part about the African American woman at the library, maybe I can name that little teeny section "The African American Woman" and then talk about her, how she supported me in the library. And then the whole idea of how Black women have been supporting the community, the family, the nation.

SCJ: Well, I don't know. I got so many books on this doggone table.

RRA: So are those the books that you read when you wake up, or are those just books that you read? Are those different than the books that you read when you wake up?

SCJ: Oh, no. When I wake up, these are the books I read. I read one every day. Every morning, I start with this one called *The New*, how do I get this over here, *The New Human Revolution*. And this talks about how to transform one's life to have an impact in changing the environment. I've been reading that.

RRA: What does a free world look like to you?

SCJ: A free world. They call this over here, the United States, *the free world*. I don't know what's so free about it, but that's what they call it. So a free world would be a more humane existence for everyone, much more humane. In fact, I was going around, just driving and thinking, "Look at all these boarded-up houses. This is crazy. And then look at these people, they're living in tents," T-E-N-T, tents, "right off the bridge there. And why are people standing on the corner for food?"

There should be no one in the world who suffers from poverty actually or having no food or housing. So that is part of it. But the other part is a spiritual freedom, I think, where people are free to be human, who they are, without any oppressive influences from the outside. And I think that would definitely call for an empathy for the suffering of others and education about how to live as a human being, which one of my students actually on his paper wrote down *human bean*, H-U-M-A-N, human, B-E-A-N, a human bean. I think that many bridges can be and need to be built from heart to heart, I would say.

RRA: Wow. Is there anything that you would like to expound upon? Anything that I missed or you would like to bring up that you feel might be really important for this chapter?

SCJ: I'm going to go back to the first question about schooling and carcerality. The schools, when I was teaching, there were so many students that were being put out of class for "you don't have a pencil." Just give the kid a pencil, for God's sake. What big deal is that? But this idea of authority or having ownership over someone or something because you think that you have a better position or station in life, which allows you to be able to treat others in a particular way.

There's one student that . . . I guess my room became the catchall for students that were thrown out of class for ridiculous reasons. And one teacher constantly called this one African American boy who was dark-skinned, had a dark complexion, and she kept . . . His last name was . . . oh, what was his name? It wasn't what she called him. What was Richard's last name? Blake? Branch. Branch. And she always called him Richard Black. And he kept saying, "That's not my name." And he would keep saying, "That's not my name" until she got angry and would throw him out of class because he kept saying, "That's not my name."

But her eyes were seeing Black and calling him that, like his complexion. And so those things were happening. The idea that some students did not belong in a gifted program—that, in a sense, carcerality is not just a physical thing, that it can really hurt your intelligence, your emotional state, and your whole being able to develop fully. So one of the things that . . . they honestly started calling me a *troublemaker*. I got to say that. And it wasn't that I was causing trouble; I was causing progress, I thought. That's what I called it.

So there was one African American student in the whole sixth, seventh, and eighth grade that went to the gifted program. And I wondered why. And so finally I said, "Well, we can't just go on test scores. There are other ways to show intellect."

And so they developed a portfolio system in the middle school, and maybe it went on to other schools or whatever. But the portfolio system for the gifted program in middle schools, I started it. I was fighting all the way. People were saying, "They don't belong there."

"They don't belong there?" How?

But that carcerality and schooling is almost as if in the institutional education that your schooling is geared toward, not necessarily a pipeline to a physical prison but a pipeline to a mental prison, where you think, "Oh, I can't make it there. So maybe I'll go out here, and some people are making a lot of money on the corner, or some people are doing certain things that I can make it that way, and I'll go that way."

And it's just that whole idea of schooling is more broad than the institutional way that we have it. And carcerality is more broad than the way that we think it is simply just going to prison, while prison is happening in the free world.

Resisting School Violence

Hip-Hop as Pedagogy for Black Freedom Struggle

Jasiri X, Christopher M. Wright, and Tiana Sharpe

Jasiri X offers insight into his personal experiences with racism in and out of schools. Through his experiences as a teacher, rapper, and activist, he details various ways in which art, specifically hip-hop, can serve as a pedagogical tool for Black consciousness raising and freedom struggle. He is cofounder of 1Hood Media, a Pittsburgh-based organization whose mission is to build liberated communities through art, education, and social justice.[1]

Christopher M. Wright: In your 2016 TED Talk at the University of Pittsburgh, you spoke about how you are originally from the South Side of Chicago and how your community and schooling experiences were almost exclusively Black. When you and your mother moved to Monroeville, PA, you experienced racism in school that led to a fight, then a suspension. So maybe you could talk about your experience with the suspension when you moved to PA and the carceral setup of schools and how racist they can be.

Jasiri X: Absolutely. My first day in Monroeville, I lived in a place called Cedar Ridge; it was an apartment complex. Monroeville had a large population of folks from India. They brown like me, you know what I'm saying? They dark, and it was two brothers darker than me who I kicked it with. My first day, I go outside, and a white dude came up and started harassing them. So I was like, "Pick on somebody your own size." But dude was like, "Okay, what's up?" So I knuckled this dude down. Day one I had to fight this dude. Then there was my first time in Monroeville Mall, where I was called a "nigger." When I got to school, and somebody had something disrespectful to say about my mom in a racialized way, I knuckled him down too. Then I got a school suspension.

My mom was all about education. She was valedictorian of her class at Roosevelt University and went on to become a nuclear engineer. For her, education was the way out for us as Black people. Her main concern was me getting suspended and it going on my permanent record and how that would affect the college I got into. She's not even looking at how it could possibly lead to me being in jail. She was more so like, "This could ruin your future." This is how I got into activism because I felt like I had to do something. I had to respond to the racism I faced, and there was a lot of it in school. I remember when I graduated, the principal was happy to see me leave. He was like, "Man, good riddance" because I was somebody that was always advocating for folks in my class.

Afterward I ended up going to college and dropping out, thinking I was going to be a rapper, and ended up participating in some other things too—things I shouldn't have been doing. Soon after, I came into the Nation of Islam. That really brought my consciousness back. At the time, I was a mortgage broker. The money was good, but I didn't like what I was doing. I was like, "Man, I want to do something. I really like working with young people."

I started working for Pittsburgh Public Schools. When I went into Pittsburgh Public Schools, for whatever reason, they sent me to Carrick [High School]. At that time, and I don't know the current statistics, but Carrick was the only predominantly white Pittsburgh public school, and they sent me there. I was mad. I didn't want to be there. I really didn't have experience with the south side of Pittsburgh.

When I went over there, it was so racist. Carrick was so clearly racist in how it treated the Black students. I would see vice principals basically antagonize Black students into being suspended. I started to have conversations with the Black students and began running afterschool programs. That's what I got hired to do. What I didn't know was that there was an unwritten rule at Carrick. They expected the Black students to leave after school and not be in that neighborhood. They didn't want the Black students to be in the neighborhood after school because it was predominantly white. So when I started a hip-hop club, they tried to shut it down. I was getting all of this pushback with the administration to the point where they actually fired me. Basically, the way the school worked was because we have a union, they couldn't fire me because I had one-year seniority. So they had to bring me back to Carrick. There was an intensity to the situation because they didn't want me there, and I didn't want to be there. They switched my position and had me in the classroom, and they had my lunch at ten in the morning. It was the first time I really became conscious of how racist schools can be toward Black students and teachers.

I ended up getting another job within Pittsburgh Public Schools where I became the first teen-parent advocate to work with teen fathers. That job enabled me to go to all the schools and offered a little bit more to see. I saw a similar pattern at all the schools, even with Black principals and Black VPs, about how specifically Black students were being treated. The buds and seeds of 1Hood[2] came out of that.

When I worked in the schools, particularly when I took the job where I would go to all the schools, I would have to wear a suit. I had to wear a suit every day, and because I wore a suit and I was a Black man, teachers would be like, "Yo, you need to speak to these bad kids," who were all Black male students. When we would talk, I would talk to them about hip-hop. When I talked to them about hip-hop, they would be engaged. I remember teachers would come into the classroom like, "Why is it so quiet in here? What are you talking to them about?" I was like, "We just talking about hip-hop." I would teach lessons through hip-hop. These were the seeds of what ended up becoming the 1Hood Media Academy. Then I started rapping to them.

So, to make a long story short, I had actually stopped rapping at this point because I was told so many times people didn't want to hear socially conscious music. When I heard about the Jena Six, again I saw what happened to those students in Jena happens every day in Pittsburgh Public Schools. I didn't have the ability to give money or resources to the movements in Louisiana, so I said, "You know what? I'm going to write a song about this." It showed me something. I remember thinking, "Oh, I was lied to. I was told people didn't want to hear this type of music, but I put this song out, and it's being played all over the country." It showed me that I had a place as an artist making conscious music. That was how I got into the lane where I became this artist that told these stories around what was happening to young Black people and police brutality and all that. Really Jena was that introduction. When the officers were found not guilty for killing Sean Bell, people started to message me saying, "We need a song from you." At that time, mainstream rap artists weren't addressing these issues. So I became that person that did.

CMW: Your music sounds like a rallying cry for Black people, like diss tracks to our oppressors. Is your approach to music similar, or complementary, to how you do work as an activist? I'm also wondering about your approach to songwriting. Do you approach it artistically like, "I got bars I'm trying to get off"? Or is it inspired by scenes of Black suffering?

JX: It's definitely changed over time. On "What If the Tea Party Was Black?" I talk about white supremacy so much because of the role it played in my life. Coming into Pittsburgh and seeing it in my face, it was like, "Okay, well, what am I going to rap about?" I'm going to rap about the pain that I experienced as a Black person coming into a predominantly white environment and what I faced. And so the first rap I wrote was inspired by Eldridge Cleaver's *Soul on Ice*. Because, again, I started rapping when I got to Monroeville. That's what I began to rap about.

I'm a political rapper. I rap about white supremacy. I felt like I do have a responsibility, almost like a lane. Even when I talked about Pittsburgh, I always felt like I want to show people the real Pittsburgh, that we are America's most livable city according to the world, but we have the poorest Black community in the country. I felt like it was my responsibility as an artist to show what's really going on on the ground. Everybody ain't popping champagne. Everybody ain't shooting and killing. A lot of people are struggling to get by. I felt like part of my responsibility was to represent those folks. And to go at the white supremacist power structure that I see is another role of mine.

CMW: Absolutely. You got a line in "The Whitest House," I hope I'm not butchering it, "Kill Blacks, kill Mexicans, kill Natives because the only real American can be Caucasian." That analysis extends to the only real student can be Caucasian, the only real teacher can be Caucasian, etc. All of these designations that we have for people in the United States are actually white designations. So when we enter these spaces and seek humanity, it's met with violence, right?

JX: Right. I mean, you'd know. I'm sure as an academic on these college campuses, they asking for your ID and, "Are you supposed to be here?" In their minds, an academic is this older white man that looks a certain way. We always have to play that second-class citizen's role in a sense. This is why we began to focus on media as an organization because around 2010, we participated in a study that the Heinz Endowment and Pew Center did around how Black men are portrayed, specifically Black men in the media in Pittsburgh. Ninety percent of the time it's crime; quality-of-life stories, on the other hand, are less than 3 percent. For us, it was like what I was doing with my music online was I was providing a different narrative. I was creating a different type of news from my perspective and from Black people's perspective. When we started our media academy for young Black men, it was about telling our own stories in our own authentic ways and not allowing a mass media or mainstream media to tell one story of us. The hood goes so far beyond what you see of it in these movies or even in music, right?

A Black child coming into a school, what support do they have? Automatically you're coming into a school, you got to face all of these stereotypes and ideas that you didn't create. Part of what we began to try to do is, again, change that narrative and tell our own stories. It was like, if Trump lost, it's not going to end white supremacy. Although he was a huge white supremacist, so is Joe Biden, you know what I'm saying? So are many Democrats. I was trying to reach beyond that.

CMW: I'm thinking about how you said you wanted 1Hood to be a space where you can come and be yourself. Sometimes what we see is alternative schools that are Black schools, with Black staff and Black curriculum, but don't necessarily engage the issues of Black people who are disabled, queer, gender-nonconforming, etc. So thinking about how we take this up in our striving for freedom, in our collective political education, how important is it to create Black educational spaces and organizational spaces that speak to the diversity of Black people, the diversity of Black life and all its multiplicity?

JX: Yeah, I think it's super important now. How we started to envision 1Hood really came out of the disappointment with the school system. I remember when I had a hip-hop club at Allderdice [High School], I would put flyers up in the school. For our first class, the flyer was Tupac, and the school took all the flyers off the wall. Literally tore them down. In their minds, Tupac meant violence. "This battling, are you all going to be fighting in there?" I'm like, "No, this is hip-hop." They had came to me one time and said, "You can't curse." I was like, "Do y'all walk around the hallways and listen to the students? How can I do an authentic class if I can't curse?" So this is why we did not do 1Hood in the schools. We did it outside of the schools. And we let our parents know, "Hey, we're going to be playing music that has curse words; is that okay with you? We're going to be watching stuff that has imagery that might be violent; is that okay with you?" We wanted to create a different space.

What we've seen as 1Hood is that when folks are in the space, those conversations come up organically about when disabled folks are in the space. About what our responsibility is to these different communities because we created a space where a person didn't feel like, "Oh, to come into 1Hood means you had to dim that part of you." Or, "Oh, I can't be queer or trans or whoever I am in this space." And a lot of times, unfortunately, we talk about our education spaces. A lot of times they come out of religious institutions. If they're coming out of a church, it is already going to have some different views, where you already know, "Oh, it's a church." You might feel like you can't be your full self because of how individuals feel. And so we just tried to create an environment where we didn't have that. That's why I didn't want to be attached to a school, where we could be able to do what we wanted to do, and as long as the parents were okay with what we're doing and signed off on it, it was cool, and we were able to create this different type of space. I personally believe that education is supposed to be about finding that thing you are passionate about, your purpose. It's so different for everybody. If you can't be your authentic self, how do you find your passion or your purpose? That's why I think it's important to create a space where you feel comfortable and just where you feel loved, where you feel accepted. To me, that's the beginning of actually getting into a real participating in class and feeling like your voice matters and your words count. Most schools don't do that; most schools don't really care if the students like the curriculum or not. "This what's being taught, and that's that." If the point of educating is serving that student, why shouldn't that student have a say in what they would like to do or how they feel like they might learn differently than what we think traditional learning is?

What became defined as the Black Lives Matter movement, for me it started really in 2008 with the killing of Oscar Grant and the movement of folks in Oakland around police violence. Folks started to push back on what people call *respectability politics*.

CMW: You most definitely are engaged in pushback against white supremacy and politically educating through your art but also through 1Hood. So I'm thinking about what does freedom mean to you within these contexts? Is freedom in the school, or must it be outside of the school, must it be outside of the institution?

JX: Yeah, man. Definitely not in the schools. I mean, it was a story that came out today that I was reading. I don't know if y'all saw it. It was a student that was killed last year in Oliver. Come to find out, his mother actually was trying to get him in remote learning because of his safety. She felt like remote learning would be a benefit to him but also that he'd be safer. The former superintendent rejected her request for remote learning. The school was down with it, the parents was down with it, but he rejected it, and the student ends up getting killed right outside of the school.

I don't think there can be freedom in schools if you got police there, but that's that white supremacist mindset. Shout-out to a group called Black Women for Better Education that had began to organize. They got that superintendent out of there who, although he was Black, to me, didn't have our children's best interests at heart. They also ran two school board members that we believe are more in line with what we need in our schools. So that's the type of organizing I'm supporting now. To me, our mission at 1Hood is to build liberated communities. It's these spaces where you have the freedom. It has to start with you have the freedom to be yourself. You have the freedom to be your full, complete self. To me, freedom is like, man, you can live out your dream unencumbered. We say life, liberty, and the pursuit of happiness, and that's what we're fighting for. Unfortunately, the way it is right now, bro, just saying a school is predominantly Black is political because the schools that have the most Black students get the least amount of resources, in whatever city you're in. That's political. That's political, you know what I'm saying?

Normally the schools that have the most Black students are the most policed. The communities that have the most Black people are the most policed, the most incarcerated, the most oppressed, you know what I'm saying? To me, what we're trying to do is like, "Okay, if we can create this space in this room, then now we have the idea, and we can create it on a larger scale." If we had the proper resources, we could create it on a larger scale. That's what we're trying to do, man. That's what liberation is to us.

Notes

1. https://www.jasirix.com/bio.
2. https://www.1hood.org/.

In the Space That Is Not Yet

A Dialogue
Marc Lamont Hill and T. Elon Dancy II

Dr. Marc Lamont Hill is a longtime scholar, commentator, and activist on global questions of Black life, carcerality, and Palestinian liberation. The following is excerpted from a wide-ranging conversation between Hill and Dr. Elon Dancy in which they discussed abolition, political education, histories, educational policy and reform, punishment, and more.

Elon Dancy: The question, Marc, asks you to think about perhaps study and struggle within the local. We have been very interested in the pedagogy of local struggle and interested in the intervention that local struggle can make on how we may be thinking. For us who are doing this work locally in Pittsburgh, I'm inviting you in to think with us about how might we do this work in relation to a school-prison nexus here but, specifically, the thought that we need to be having around place, around geography, and our coordinates of struggle. Even if you're just raising questions that might give us something to think about, to think more about: How do we do this work that is against a school-prison carceral relationship in Pittsburgh and within urban Appalachia?

Marc Lamont Hill: Pittsburgh is such an interesting place. Pittsburgh, for me, is special because, as I mentioned, so much of my activism is rooted in my work to free Mumia Abu-Jamal.

He was on death row at SCI Greene, which is in Waynesburg, PA. So I was coming up to see Mumia, and then I wrote a book with Mumia called *The Classroom and the Cell*. We did letter writing and phone calls, but I'd also go to death row to see him. So I would fly to Pittsburgh. So much of how I think about Mumia and the liberation of Mumia is bound up in Pittsburgh and SCI Greene. So I would fly to Pittsburgh and then drive to Greene.

So for me, that entire geography has personal significance and political significance. Waynesburg and Pittsburgh felt very much like Philadelphia and the urban parts of it, the Black parts of it. But what was fascinating to me was that in between those two extremes—in between Philadelphia and Pittsburgh—is this entire state that is politically conservative. And most of the people I know who are caged in SCIs—state correctional institutions—are caged in between Philadelphia and Pittsburgh.

Waynesburg is filled with people from Pittsburgh and Philly. When I would go see my own brother—he wasn't in Greene, but he was in another one—I still had to drive basically to Pittsburgh to see my brother. So at all times, these parts of the state, the more rural they were, the more white they were, the more likely they were to have as residents young Black men from Philadelphia and Pittsburgh.

When I would go to see Mumia, one of the things that was so noteworthy to me was you always wanted to get in before the guard change because if not, you could be waiting twenty minutes to an hour. And as I would sit there at the guard change, watching, listening, you'd see nothing but white men from rural Pennsylvania. Some were from Pittsburgh, some were from smaller towns like Waynesburg, but they were all rural white men, most of whom were high school educated. In my conversations with them, I realized that a lot of them were friends. They knew each other.

And they comprised a large percentage of the men in that town who had jobs. And the ones who didn't work there were, you know, electricians or carpenters. They did services to the prison. Some were bail bondsmen. So many people had their economic futures, personally, at the personal level, tied up in the existence of this prison. And then as a town, their congressional representation and their funding, all of it was built on the fact that they had more residents, and they had more residents because they were counting the prisoners as residents.

So for me, part of it, as I think about Appalachian cities, is that in many ways, those spaces, while not always marked as urban, they still, at worst, function as repositories for the contradictions, the economic and social contradictions and failures of urban cities toward the most vulnerable. So Waynesburg, PA, might not be a Black city, but it's a Black city. It may not be urban in that way, but it's urban.

Now, Pittsburgh is fascinating because it has multiple things happening simultaneously. Its Black men and women increasingly are being shipped out to those type cities, but Pittsburgh itself has an increasingly carceral space, with juvenile detentions, with jails, county jails, et cetera. And I think that when we think about, at a spatial and geographic level, what the prison is, we imagine it as an urban space, when in fact it's far more likely the prison physically is located and situated within these other places.

And it's not a minor point because it is the distance from home, it is the spatial distance between a Pittsburgh and a Waynesburg that marks a few things. The likelihood of going back to prison is dramatically increased when you're far from home, and it is no coincidence that most of these spaces are far from home.

So it breeds a certain kind of class warfare and racial warfare because as a Black person who's locked up near Pittsburgh or in Pittsburgh, I'm more likely to go back to prison. So we should be saying no prisons there, no people there. As a resident of that town, a white poor person with no resources who's been underserved by capitalism, I have every incentive to keep that there because we don't have the kind of class solidarity that would say, "We all losing at this," right?

As I think about what you all are embarking on, I think we have to start to ask different questions. I think so much of our understanding of the prison and its relationships are about urban space and nonrural space. We have to think about the relationship to the urban. I think, on the one hand, we have to think about how, even in the context of urban cities, we have to think about the relationships, the political, economic relationships between the urban and the rural because oftentimes the rural spaces, again, are where people actually get caged. They're where our people physically are located. And they don't just mark a geographic distance, which is often considerable—three, four, five, six, eight hours—but they also mark a certain kind of denial of the possibility of decarceration because the thing that makes you more likely to not recidivate is access to family. And then the phone calls are made so expensive that you can't just call home. So part of it just becomes a crisis of distance.

But we also have to think about it from the point of view of those residents of that town. We also have to think about it from the point of view of the people in Appalachia or in any rural space. How do they understand the role of the prison? They have a material investment in the maintenance of the prison because of centuries and certainly decades of divestment, isolation, whether it's stripping away farming subsidies, whether it's capital flight of corporations that have gone East, whether it's environmental abuses. All of these things have made it increasingly difficult for them to have a living wage, and the prison has been offered to them. Take wage out of it for a minute. And the prison has been introduced to them as a viable form of redress to the economic issue.

And it's too reductive to say, "These people are willing to lock up Black people, or poor, you know, lock people up to live themselves." It's that they have been incentivized to not critically assess the prison. How are we incentivized away from critically assessing the prison and toward ignoring the harm done by mass incarcerating the vulnerable? How is this incentivizing economic? How might we forge futures beyond the prison when so much of people's lives and futures are bound up in it? So part of what we have to begin to do as abolitionists is not just to examine the political economy of prisons within rural spaces but also, at the phenomenological level, begin to engage those people in those spaces, to understand their mindset and their thinking about this. And also to engage in political education.

In some ways this goes back to Du Bois's issue with the white worker back in *Black Reconstruction*.[1] They have to see the material investment in the big picture of divesting from prisons. They need to be able to form a class solidarity project rather than closing ranks around their whiteness. No one has been targeted more to close ranks around whiteness than rural white Americans, poor rural white Americans. They, more than anybody, have been told, "They're coming for you. You need to fight. And fighting means supporting right-wing neoliberal policies." There's a way that their material condition has been exploited by economic elites, and we got to unpack that. It's too easy to reject them or dismiss them with false consciousness. It's not enough to just say, "Well, they have false consciousness. They got the world wrong. They're racist." We have to figure out how to engage them in a way that speaks back to their economic exploitation. Otherwise, we don't get anywhere.

When I think about those white men during the guard change, that's exactly what I think about. There are white workers who are fighting to uphold the institution of slavery and closing ranks on whiteness, when in fact they, more than anyone, should be fighting to dismantle.

Assata said, "Because I've never been free, so I can only offer my vision to you of what freedom might be." I think in a world shot through so thoroughly with unfreedom, any claim I make about what freedom, again, is a provisional kind of truth. It's a speculative one. It's an imaginative, speculative one. Which is, I think, where Black freedom, in many ways, rests, has always rested. Our freedom dreams have always been imaginative and speculative. They live in the space that is not yet. What I know is whatever freedom is, and I don't feel confident saying what freedom is, but what I do feel confident saying is that whatever it is, it's a communal one. It's bound up in the full expression and articulation of humanity for all people. For all beings rather, not even people, for all beings, for all life.

Note

1. W. E. B. Du Bois, *Black Reconstruction: An Essay toward a History of the Part Which Black Folk Played in the Attempt to Reconstruct Democracy in America, 1860–1880* (New York: Harcourt, Brace and Company, 1935).

Part 4

"fierce grief shadows me"

Grief can map the entanglements of the heart and sociality. It makes maps that explode scale. What is the landscape that shares a mother's love, a boy's lyricism, and a murderous police state? How can one map reveal the infinite, intimate anguish and the structural impunity? Grief defies singularities. In the pages that follow, fierce grief is neither a state nor a condition. We invite you to reflect on its capacity, its shape, and its action. How does it help us untangle the forces of urban Appalachia? Can grief give us possibility even in its most irrevocable form?

Sabina Vaught

They Always Come (A Note to My Son)

For Ahmaud Arbery and Breonna Taylor and Those Suffering in COVID-19 and the Past, Present, and Future

Medina Jackson

Son

How do I prepare you for apocalypse?
How do I prepare you for the inconspicuous, loud, cyclical doom of White supremacy's tentacles
How do I prepare my nervous system for what seems like the inevitable, inescapable trauma
Of
Will I lose him someday?
Somewhere, somehow?

See

They always come
The wonder-less to the wanderers
To the free people
To those who are spacious

To those who hold themselves
To those shaped by expansive sky and ocean and dirt

It always comes
In a liberated moment
Parasitic travelers leaving bones and dust in the wake of dawn, and move on

I just want to keep you safe in a place that is trying to kill you a little bit every day
Or by bullets exploding from guns
Or by the relief of a needle from these troubles

It always comes
To steal the light from your eyes
But see
It suffocates them
They can't hold it

I just want to shield you with my open heart
The sinking of your muscles
Relaxed breath in my arms forever

It always comes
Ushering the terrifying unknown
Baiting us with bribes, trades, and fear of something worse
Ready to reclaim
An Earth they do not own

They always come
To dry up all the water
Set fire to the soil
Pollute the air with poisoned breath

They come in the night
They come in the day
They always come

Can I hold you one more time?
One more kiss on your forehead?
Soothing hands through lion locs
Can I keep you in my sight?
Can you stay with me while you spread your wings and sing
your sweet shower songs?

They always fucking come
Driving sticks into sacred ground
Walking woundedness and death
Teeth stained with someone else's blood
When we are simply
Living

They do not know
What true life, love and liberation is
So they consume it with impunity
And are never full

A Requiem for Antwon Rose II

Defending the Dead in the Afterlife of Slavery

T. Elon Dancy II, Christopher M. Wright, and Chetachukwu U. Agwoeme

I am confused and afraid
I wonder what path I will take
I hear that there's only two ways out
I see mothers bury their sons
I want my mom to never feel that pain
I am confused and afraid

I pretend all is fine
I feel like I'm suffocating
I touch nothing so I believe all is fine
I worry that it isn't, though
I cry no more
I am confused and afraid

I understand people believe I'm just a statistic
I say to them I'm different
I dream of life getting easier
I try my best to make my dream true
I hope that it does
I am confused and afraid
    ~Antwon Rose II, "I AM NOT WHAT YOU THINK"

Introduction

"When Antwon was five, and we moved into homes, Antwon would paint all over the house, all over his bedroom walls, all the way down the stairs, everywhere," remembers Antwon Rose II's mother, Michelle Kenney. She was sharing her story on a panel of mothers grieving children lost to the antiblack violence of the state.[1] "And I remember yelling at him," she continued, "'Boy, if you don't make something out of this artistry you claim you are doing, I am going to lose my mind!' And in hindsight, when I read the poem he wrote, I see he really was artistic... I knew then, I knew he had a talent."

In an essay about memories with her son and her premonition about the significance of his life, she remembered, "I would tell him 'kid, you're going to change the world. I don't know what you're going to do or how you're going to do it, but there's something special about you, and you're going to change the world.' I just had no idea that he would have to die in order for that to happen."[2]

When he was taken from her, she was convinced. "And the night Antwon died," she said, "I made up my mind I was never going to let anyone forget what happened to him."[3] On June 19, 2018, Kenney entered, in her words, "a club that doesn't need any new members": a familiar sorority of grief and mourning in which Black mothers do not have the choice to declare interest but are already selected. All of the beauty and wonder that fall short in describing Antwon's life were squeezed into the noose of a lynching. Antwon was murdered by Michael Rosfeld while running for his life, sparking a series of protests across the Pittsburgh area in the name of Black lives.[4]

Antwon was a brilliant thinker and talented writer. In 2016, he published his vulnerable and prescient poem "I AM NOT WHAT YOU THINK" in *Younger Black Pittsburgh*, a volume of Black Pittsburgh youth writing about their lives. As we embark on this chapter, which is shaped in a dialogue with Antwon's poetry, we heed the words of Michelle Kenney and the other mothers on the panel: "They have no problem using our children, putting our children's names on t-shirts and banners and advancing careers, but when they leave, we are all that is left."[5] We aim to center this understanding in our memories as we engage Antwon as a life, a scholar, a writer, and a poet. And we acknowledge that his mother's knowledge and experience with her son precede and exceed our own. Before this chapter, before his image was plastered across banners against police killings, and before his name was repeated night after night on the Pittsburgh and national evening news, he was his mother's child.

As Black men with Black boy experience in this world, we write *with* Antwon. We feel a kinship tie to Antwon; he is our brother, although we never got to know him personally. As a collective of scholars, we—Elon, Cheta, and Chris—come to this chapter through a history of interests and scholarship in racial political economies, gender and masculinity, education, and carcerality. Across these interests, we engage antiblackness theory for deeper thought, to guide a refusal of bourgeois remedies and to build revolutionary capacity.[6] We were deeply affected in collectively reading and discussing Antwon's poem. We were reminded of Du Bois's reflection on seeing the lynched body of Sam Hose, a Black man tortured and murdered by a white lynch mob in Coweta County, Georgia: "One could not be a cool, calm, and detached scientist while Negroes were being lynched, murdered, and starved."[7] Indeed, we could not be cool, calm, and collected scholars as we revisited the details of Antwon Rose's precious life and antiblack death. We shuddered. We were enraged. We cried. We mourned.

Following dialogue, we decided that this chapter had a threefold purpose: (1) to bear witness to Antwon's life and endeavor memorializing and watching over Antwon in his death; (2) to dialogue with Antwon as a poet, as we would any poet within Black intellectual tradition, in advancing a theory about antiblackness as a violent world order and to place these words within a constellation of thinkers across conversant knowledges; and (3) to advance a theory of Black will-building to refuse antiblackness and end the world through which it is built, with a focus on Pittsburgh.

We organize our discussion underneath the guiding frameworks of Antwon's poem in value of close reading, collective dialogue, and reflection. Our engagement surfaced three areas of thinking that shape the chapter's sections. The first section, "I am confused and afraid," engages antiblackness and the afterlife of slavery[8] as a condition for Antwon's poem's emphasis on fear and confusion. The second, "I touch nothing so I believe all is fine," analyzes the question of Black childhood within antiblackness, arguing that court discourse about Antwon cast him as the antichild and, by extension, antihuman. And, finally, the third section, "I understand people believe I'm just a statistic / I say to them I'm different," discusses the relationship of antiblackness to Pittsburgh statistics and Antwon's refusal and dreams of freedom.

"I Am Confused and Afraid"

What Blackened[9] people must have felt in the hold of the slave ship exceeds words. In the vast yet crammed black abyss, bodies are stacked on top of one another with lacerations and bodily fluid cocktailing with cold, salty seawater. Life as it once was becomes "literally suspended in the 'oceanic,'" and pain and suffering become quotidian.[10] We wonder what their thoughts were, what emotions were elicited, how the fear of death and uncertainty engages all of their bodies' senses. The very habitat of the ship, the open sea, and the strange land upon which we would arrive conditioned Africans with confusion and fear when they would enter the new-world terrain as "Blacks." Antwon's words recompose the realities of the passage: *I am confused and afraid.*

Antwon Rose's poetry about his own feelings espouses a collective Black knowing and lived experience shaped within histories of slavery. The transformation of people from what we now call *African* to *Black*—and, by extension, *slaves*—is an ongoing project that orients our world. While chattel slavery and the traditional plantation has "ended," Black people's vulnerability to violence has remained constant. We remain confused and afraid. This is logical. Saidiya Hartman argues that slavery formulated a political arithmetic and social stratification that still exists today in what she calls the "afterlife of slavery."[11]

Why is Antwon Rose "confused and afraid"? Why is it a Black reality to languish[12] in induced fear and uncertainty? For engagement with these questions, we turn to Black critical theorists who think deeply about how chattel slavery is constitutive to the modern world. Such a turn leads us to antiblackness. Rinaldo Walcott is helpful in our understanding of what it means to be human and the ways this category functions against the Black body. He argues that the terms of human social engagement are always already shaped by logics of antiblackness that sanction unintelligible and commonsensical quotidian violence. Walcott continues, "This global antiblack condition . . . still and again manifests itself in numerous ways that have significantly limited how Black people might lay claim to human-ness and therefore how Black people might impact on what it means to be human in the world."[13]

The barring of Blackness from humanity through the violence of accumulation and fungibility is inherent to our worldwide sociality. The result is also a world consciousness that excludes the Black from the human family and thus sanctions the regularity in which Black people suffer.[14] Antwon testifies to the recomposition and impact of these processes in his daily life, and in so doing, he becomes a part of thought tradition including many Black intellectuals. His writing about his fear and confusion bears witness to a world order shaped through enduring slavery technologies that prevent any social recognition of Black humanness. He reveals the experience of this in how he feels, what he sees, and what he desires: *I am confused and afraid / I see mothers bury their sons / I want my mom to never feel that pain.*

Antwon remembers a maxim that speaks to the trap and hold of antiblackness: "I hear there are only two ways out." Dumas[15] reminds us that antiblackness is not easily resolvable—it is not just a matter of racial conflict to be resolved through political struggle—but that it represents an ontological relation to the world that is irreconcilable and requires its structural ending. It is a trap and a hold. We might refer to this irreconcilability as an *antagonistic* relationship between "the Black"—a constellation of Black people and imaginings of Blackness—and the world. In conversation, Antwon luminates the ontological suffering of Black people and wonders if the stakes of escape are only made possible through short and long forms of death, which Wilderson might locate within Blackness's "grammar of suffering."[16]

Antwon's repeated line, "I am confused and afraid," echoes Black voices from the past, present, and future. No matter how hard we try, we are not in control of how the world sees us. As Fanon notes, "The Black has no ontological resistance in the eyes of the white man";[17] the argument critiques a world of Black slavery in which we are the slave not by our actions or wrongdoings but as a matter of flesh. Blackness produces an anxiety that makes shooting Black flesh always a reasonable response. We are *confused and afraid*.

"I Touch Nothing So I Believe All Is Fine"

Antwon's line *I touch nothing so I believe all is fine* echoes the loving Black mother wit guiding Black children in a world in which Black childhood is dangerous and endangered. During our reflective dialogue on Antwon's poem, Elon remembered a childhood story his mother once recalled to him about his grandmother's direction during a trip to the town's white-owned grocery store in the Jim Crow Alabama South: "When we go into this market, you say 'yes ma'am' and 'no ma'am' and *don't touch nothing*." This is part and parcel of Black "home training." Our caregivers' rearing praxis prepares us for a world that teaches, as Toni Morrison writes in *Beloved*, no matter "the manners" of Black people, "under every dark skin [is] a jungle. Swift, unnavigable waters, swinging screaming baboons, sleeping snakes, red gums ready for . . . blood."[18] The reality reminds us of how knowing Black people as existentially in need of discipline shapes the home and family. We—Antwon, Elon, Chris, and Cheta—learned this ancestral wisdom in our lives as our foremothers learned in theirs. It is therefore axiomatic that Black children's learned response to "touch nothing" reflects an always already antagonistic relationship of the public, its laws, and its institutions to Black people as terror incarnate. For instance, the public discourse around the deaths of Emmett Till, George Stinney, Tamir Rice, and Trayvon Martin, among others, associates Black boys with what is pathologized about *adult* Black men as one way the terror relation shows up: always up to no good, suspect, meaning ill will, and a physical threat. Antwon's mother, Michelle, remembers her knowledge about the state's automatic blame of Black people as common sense: "I'm biracial and Antwon was raised to hang out with white kids. Antwon knew he was Black as far as common sense, but based on the people he hung out with, he didn't understand what that meant. I felt that if anything was to ever happen or the police were called, even if he was at a party, they would automatically blame Antwon. The blame would be put upon him before they would be put upon the kids he hung out with. That's the harsh reality, but it's our truth."[19]

Michelle understands that, no matter his manners, her Black child is marked for blame and guilt; *Black child* is an oxymoron within a world in which Blackness negates childhood or childhood possibility. The result is the ontological un- or the antichild. A conversant idea has shown up more popularly in literature and media in examinations of adultification or as the phenomena of engaging Black children like adults.[20]

Public engagement of Black youth "as adults" applies to all Black youth. When nine-year-old Bobbi Wilson gleefully walked her neighborhood to find lanternflies for her science project, her neighbor, Gordon Lawshe, called the police on her, stating, "There's a little Black *woman*, spraying stuff on the sidewalks and trees . . . she is a real tiny *woman* wearing a hood."[21] Although Bobbi is doing the work of study and imagination for a school project, her neighbor and police respond to venom. And while the little girl must endure the unnerving context of police inquisition for being outside, we also know she could have been killed in an instant. She is neither a "neighbor" nor a "child." Antwon's poem suggests the rocks and hard places (the impossibilities) established where Black family insistence on Antwon's life and the global state insisting on his death meet: "don't go outside," "don't go inside," "don't whistle," "don't play," "don't wear a hood," and for God sakes, whatever you do, "don't touch anything."

While scholars have offered the framework of *adultification* to name the public and social engagement of Black children and their bodies as adults,[22] we contend that this term is one way of naming what Dumas and Nelson[23] argue is a condition of the "unimagined and unimaginability" of Black boyhood and Black childhood deriving from humanity's antagonistic relationship with the Black. In his childhood, Antwon already knows he is forced not to touch anything but also knows the failure of this counsel to erase the antiblack condition. And this is the reality of Black childhood: it is one in which the possibility of some future adulthood cannot be assumed—not because of a general "life unpredictability or unknown" but because Blackness represents life's ultimate unpredictability and unknown.[24] We contend, too, it is the unimagined and unimaginable childhood of Antwon that advances the reasonableness of his killing as articulated around the acquittal of his murderer, Michael Rosfeld.

The killing of Antwon Rose II and the acquittal rationale of his murderer are a rejection of the idea that Antwon is innocent, a child, and a human being, more broadly. State platitudes when *children* are killed (e.g., school shootings) are usually a discourse of innocence, hope, and potential forever lost in the deadly aftermath. It is also common public advice, from elected officials, educators, families, and police themselves, that *children* should run when assailed by strangers.[25] However, the shooting of Antwon Rose II (while running away) is rendered justified and justifiable, underscoring how what happens to Black children happens within the recomposed horrors of enslavement, which works to excommunicate Black children from the childhood project and closer to death. In her open letter to colleagues following the 1992 Los Angeles police beating of Rodney King, Wynter[26] argues that through the logics of racialized classificatory systems, "humanity" recognizes itself by ranking Black people as "non-evolved lack of human"—a logic revealed in the LAPD's use of *NHI*, or *no humans involved*. In these logics, white people are the prototypical human, and Black people, including Black children, are the prototypical slave. These organizing principles, a white-human alignment and a Black-human antagonism, more specifically, were apparent in the Michael Rosfeld trial and discourse around Antwon.

Within the geography of antiblackness, Black people are disallowed space, *human* space, including the space to flee and the space to be children. Antwon's decision to flee harm from police reflects Black knowledges that have long understood interactions with police (formal or informal) as death-dealing, no matter the circumstances. However, because this reality is a nonissue in the Michael Rosfeld trial and American jurisprudence altogether,[27] Antwon's decision to run for his life is illegible; it cannot be understood as reasonable to do with a state police force nor as even children's behavior (as his history is outside of what is considered a *child's* history or experience). Antwon's decision to run from police is met with disciplinary tactics revealing reenacted police force slave-catcher strategies and the coterminosity of these strategies with what it means to "protect and serve" the "public." His decision to run for his life requires his death to keep "the public" (which unimagines Black people) safe. When the jury acquitted Rosfeld, their determination that he was actually the one who had a "reasonable fear" renders necessarily *unvisible*[28] the realities of Black pain and suffering necessary for Rosfeld's personhood and his status as the only possible claimant to safety and life.[29]

The discourse around Antwon and his murderer reasserted Antwon's antihumanity, antichildhood, and antivictimization to enforce the core antiblack knowledge that Black people's attempts to assert claims over their lives is *the* illegal and unconscionable show of capacity; the fleeing Black body compounds the already chaotic Black presence and therefore requires discipline, and the tactics are deadly. Any possibility associated with dialogue or "cultural norms" about innocence, benefit of the doubt, or childhood is impossible for Antwon in his shooting death and in the "reasonable fear" rationale, supporting an analysis that his presence alone constituted reasonable fear and no childhood question was applicable. And no childhood question applies because no human question applies within a world in which Black people are inherent slaves, whether or not we can identify an "owner"; the rationale in this case resurges the opinions and decision in *Dred Scott v. Sanford*,[30] in which the idea of Black people's ontological slave status was upheld.

While Michael Rosfeld murdered Antwon Rose, the state's court and prison systems do not and will not end Black death as the antiblack state requires the violence context we experience. Hence, our aim in an analysis of court discourse and verdict is not to advocate for a "guilty" verdict, which would suggest legitimacy in state institutional processes to deliver "justice." Rather, we are reading the unimaginability of Antwon's personhood and childhood as it played out in the court (even if the verdict was "guilty"). When George Floyd's murderer, Derek Chauvin, was found "guilty", a similar discourse around George Floyd still emerged, with the conviction actually suggesting Chauvin was guilty of sloppy police work rather than violating George Floyd's life or "rights."

Before Antwon was taken from us, his poem gave voice to his knowledge of the impact of this relation and his anxiety about it. Antwon knew. He *knew* the world he was surviving was against Black people, and he dreamed of freedom from this bondage: *I dream of life getting easier / I try my best to make my dream true / I hope that it does.*

"I Understand People Believe I'm Just a Statistic / I Say to Them I'm Different"

Spillers[31] explains that the ways enslaved Africans are "unmade" in the Middle Passage require Black bodies as quantifiable cargo to be bought, sold, and accumulated—an unidentifiable mass to the world with infinite utility. Antwon's reflection "I understand people believe I'm just a statistic" underscores the Black as statistic as a global norm.[32] His attention to statistical context evinces awareness of how Black people are positioned in the world, more specifically in Pittsburgh. The "statistic" in Antwon's prose reveals one manifestation of slavery's condition—a focus on what Spillers defines as "quantities." These statistics in slavery's afterlife recall the skewed life chances Hartman refers to: "limited access to healthcare and education, premature death, incarceration, and impoverishment."[33] As Black flesh is converted into quantifiable masses for various preoccupations, that very conversion illuminates and maps the Black pain and suffering required for multicultural-neoliberal measures of "livability" and "progress."

In contrast to books of statistics that do not measure but suggest Black shared experiences of pain and suffering,[33] Pittsburgh has also been deemed the ninth most livable city in the United States by various market metrics.[34] However, we argue that what is often discussed as an irony obscures an analysis of social death—namely, that habitability (social life) is contingent on the uninhabitability (social death) of Black people.[35] Applying to Black people everywhere, social death refers to the complete and ongoing negation of humanity through gratuitous violence, natal alienation, and general dishonor, which maintain the Master (the world) / Slave (Black) relation.[36] The tethered Black-death-to-non-Black-livability characterizes Pittsburgh as a progressive dystopia, a place where social "victories" require Black social death.[37] Through this lens, the statistic's function comes clear—Antwon Rose's murder, which adds to the city's statistics of Black death, enhances habitability for Pittsburgh's populace. It is proof positive that the police innocently keep its "citizens" safe.

Antwon's rejection of this world's practices is his wake work: what Christina Sharpe conceptualizes as "a mode of inhabiting and rupturing this episteme with our known lived and un/imaginable lives."[38] In the second half of the couplet, he is emphatic: "I say I am different." At first read, one might misinterpret his assertion of difference as a claim to an exceptional Blackness that should elevate him among Black masses. This would be a misreading. We argue his rhetorical use of "difference" is his critique of an antiblack world's imagination of him and Black people. He is refusing to accept the role of the recomposed slave and asserts his life. Antwon's assertion of difference is a critique of parasitic relation and a declared refusal to be the world's parasite host; it abhors the abject that the world requires and decodes the statistical preoccupation as one area in which antiblackness plays out. Despite a world powered on Black impossibility, Antwon still dreams of "life getting easier." His dreams invite us down a pathway of imagining what freedom might require. His poetry and his decision to run for his life that fateful day are wake work and freedom work; they dare claim ontological space in a world hellbent on denying it.[39] His words and attempted escape are fugitive praxis and bound for freedom. Both his dream for an easier life when he was with us and his lifeless body that followed indict the state for its hubris about livability and progressivism. Antwon's work to make his "dream come true," with his poetry as but one example, was his own way station within freedom dreaming[40]—imagining the possibilities of life when Blackness is centered and embraced. But what might it mean to do this?

Conclusion

In the last couplet of his poem, Antwon hopes that his "dream comes true" but ultimately ends on a note of fear and confusion. It is within this tension that we think and write *with* him. What does it mean to end on a note of fear and confusion? Why is this sentiment the final word? And what of us who are still living in the afterlife of slavery? We interpret his dream as a call upon those of us who are still here to work to build a Black will—a will to end the world of the Black/slave relation that generates Black pain and suffering—that builds upon his will and undertakes the charge of study and struggle in honor and mourning of Antwon. His call for us to engage in wake work is a call that honors and defends our dead (both physical and social). What would it mean for us to think about study and coalition-building as requiring a deep inhabitation of the wake? What resources lie within it? What would it mean for us who are still here to rupture the world and envision new ways of living in what are known as Pittsburgh and Appalachia, which require Black people to be placeless? Such a process must begin locally; as Audre Lorde contends, we must do battle right where we are standing.[41] Organizing, studying, and struggling against the Pittsburgh project is where we reissue Antwon's call to make his dream come true.

The war to end antiblackness must be fought on fronts that work to dislodge "the Black" from "the slave." This requires fierce resistance to the project of modernity (including its invention of humanity) and will undoubtedly produce global and local anxiety. It will mean that what is "reasonable" must contend with the antiblack power dynamics that produce reason as well as what structures our imaginations of the world and its programs: the public, childhood, citizenry, human, life, and safety. Such a process is one that requires deeply radical and collective study that uncovers the complexities of slavery's afterlife so that we may begin its undoing and imagine worlds anew. It is essential to center study of the pain and suffering produced in the afterlife of slavery within organized struggle as pain and suffering maps the terrain in which struggle *must* take place. We continue this work and have learned a great deal about this terrain from the writing of Antwon Rose II. And we are grateful for his life and brave poetry.

Notes

1. Center for Urban Education, "CUESEF 2023: Embodied Pedagogies: Memory, Mothering, and Making through Grief," July 11, 2023, video, 40:18, https://www.youtube.com/watch?v=A4BvFf3zLtY&list=PLsZ39MWpeY4V3iihKtFSIPL0U4XNH79ci&index=1&ab_channel=CenterforUrbanEducation.

2. Michelle Kenney, "I'm Antwon Rose's mother. My Son Had to Be Killed by Police in Order for Him to Change the World," Good Morning America, July 10, 2020,

https://www.goodmorningamerica.com/news/story/im-antwon-roses-mother-son-killed-police-order-71677745.

3. Center for Urban Education, "CUESEF 2023," 42:00.

4. John Bacon, "Antwon Rose Jr., Unarmed Teen Shot by Police Officer, Laid to Rest in Pennsylvania," *USA Today*, June 25, 2018, https://www.usatoday.com/story/news/nation/2018/06/25/antwon-rose-unarmed-teen-shot-police-laid-rest-pennsylvania/731392002/.

5. Center for Urban Education, "CUESEF 2023," 1:23:24.

6. We capitalize *Black* when referencing Black people, organizations, cultural products, and kinships associated with the self-determination of this racialized social group. Like Dumas (2016), we do not capitalize *antiblackness* as the term does not refer to the definition of Black people noted in this footnote per se "but a social construction of racial meaning" (Michael J. Dumas, "Against the Dark: Antiblackness in Education Policy and Discourse," *Theory into Practice* 55, no. 1 (January 15, 2016): 11–19, p. 13), or what is imagined *about* Black people rather than what Black people and organizations self-determine.

7. Derrick P. Aldridge, "W. E. B. DuBois in Georgia," *New Georgia Encyclopedia*, July 21, 2020, https://www.georgiaencyclopedia.org/articles/history-archaeology/w-e-b-du-bois-in-georgia.

8. Saidiya Hartman, *Lose Your Mother: A Journey along the Atlantic Slave Route* (New York: Farrar, Straus and Giroux, 2008).

9. *Blackened* is used here to underscore how *Black* as a racial identifier is mapped onto stolen African peoples to demarcate property. Before Blackness, African people understood themselves through Indigenous cosmologies and epistemologies that varied across the continent. Practices of commodification effectively muted the agency of the African subject and produced the Black body as a desired object for exploitation in the American marketplace (S. E. Smallwood, *Saltwater Slavery: A Middle Passage from Africa to American Diaspora* [Cambridge, MA: Harvard University Press, 2007]).

10. Hortense J. Spillers, "Mama's Baby, Papa's Maybe: An American Grammar Book," in *The Transgender Studies Reader Remix*, ed. Susan Striker and Dylan McCarthy Blackston (New York: Routledge, 1987), 93–104.

11. Hartman, *Lose Your Mother*.

12. To be sure, the assertion that it is a Black reality to languish within civil society advances an analysis of global antiblackness. It is not an essentialist argument (one that argues that all Black people live the same lives and experience identical suffering), a characterization of "individuals," or an assumption that Black people are inherently weak. Further, the purpose of the *languish* phraseology is to assert that the condition of Black slavery organizes Black suffering, and this language describes the experience in the hold in which any one Black person's emotion or disposition was forced to reckon.

13. Rinaldo Walcott, "The Problem of the Human: Black Ontologies and 'the Coloniality of Our Being,'" in *Postcoloniality—Decoloniality—Black Critique: Joints and Fissures*, ed. Sabine Broeck and Carsten Junker (Frankfurt: Campus Verlag, 2014), 6.

14. Sylvia Wynter, "1492: A New World View," in *Race, Discourse, and the Origins of the Americas*, ed. Vera Lawrence Hyatt and Rex M. Nettleford (Washington, DC: Smithsonian Institution Press, 1995), 5–57.

15. Dumas, "Against the Dark."
16. Frank B. Wilderson III, *Red, White and Black: Cinema and the Structure of U.S. Antagonisms* (Durham, NC: Duke University Press, 2010).
17. Frantz Fanon, *Black Skin, White Masks*, 1st Evergreen ed. (New York: Grove Press, 1982), 96.
18. Toni Morrison, *Beloved* (London: Vintage, 1987), 41.
19. Kenney, "I'm Antwon Rose's Mother."
20. Ann Arnett Ferguson, "Making a Name for Yourself: Transgressive Acts and Gender Performance," in *Men's Lives* (7th ed.), ed. M. Kimmel and M. Messner (Boston: Allyn and Beacon, 2007); Gloria Ladson Billings, "Boyz to Men? Teaching to Restore Black Boys' Childhood," *Race Ethnicity and Education* 14, no. 1 (January 2011): 7–15; Kiara Alfonseca, "Ralph Yarl's Case Spotlights Racial 'Adultification' of Black Children," *ABC7 Eyewitness News*, retrieved June 15, 2023, https://abc7.com/ralph-yarls-case-spotlights-racial-adultification-of-black-children/13158342/; T. Elon Dancy II, "The Adultification of Black Boys: What Educational Settings Can Learn from Trayvon Martin," in *Trayvon Martin, Race, and American Justice*, ed. Kenneth J. Fasching-Varner et al. (Rotterdam: Sense Publishing, 2014), 49–55.
21. Tod Perry, "Young Girl Who Had the Cops Called on Her for Studying Lanternflies Wins a Major Award," Upworthy, December 13, 2022, https://www.upworthy.com/bobbi-wilson-wins-science-award-rp2 (emphasis added).
22. Ann Arnett Ferguson Dancy, *Bad Boys: Public Schools in the Making of Black Masculinity* (Ann Arbor: University of Michigan Press, 2000).
23. Michael J. Dumas and Joseph Derrick Nelson, "(Re)Imagining Black Boyhood: Toward a Critical Framework for Educational Research," *Harvard Educational Review* 86, no. 1 (March 1, 2016): 27–47.
24. Calvin L. Warren, *Ontological Terror: Blackness, Nihilism and Emancipation* (Durham, NC: Duke University Press, 2018).
25. https://www.wikihow.com/Protect-Yourself-from-a-Stranger-(for-Kids).
26. Sylvia Wynter, "'No Humans Involved': An Open Letter to My Colleagues," Libcom.org., 1994, https://libcom.org/article/no-humans-involved-open-letter-my-colleagues.
27. K-Sue Park, "Conquest and Slavery as Foundational to the Property Law Course," SSRN Electronic Journal, 2020, https://doi.org/10.2139/ssrn.3659947.
28. Katherine McKittrick, *Demonic Grounds: Black Women and the Cartographies of Struggle* (Minneapolis: University of Minnesota Press, 2006).
29. According to McKittrick (2006), to be unvisible is to "not really [be] invisible; rather an 'imperceptible' social, political, and geographic subject who is rendered invisible due to [one's] highly visible bodily context" (emphasis in original), 18–9.
30. *Dred Scott v. Sandford*, 60 US 393 (1857).
31. Spillers, "Mama's Baby, Papa's Maybe."
32. Warren (2018) argues as African existence is murdered through chattel slavery, it produces the Black as "available equipment" for the purpose of supporting the existential journey of the human being (p. 27). As available equipment to the world, Black bodies are reduced to things such as statistics to "serve the needs of the human ontological project" (Warren, *Ontological Terror*, p. 47).
33. E.g., Junia Howell et al., "Pittsburgh's Inequality across Gender and Race," 2019, https://pittsburghpa.gov/gec/reports-policy.

34. "Pittsburgh, PA Is the #9 Best City to Live in the USA," Livability, 2022, https://livability.com/best-places/2022-top-100-best-places-to-live-in-the-us/top-100-2022-pittsburgh-pa/.

35. Orlando Patterson, *Slavery and Social Death* (London: Harvard University Press, 1985); Frank B. Wilderson III, *Afropessimism* (New York: Liveright Publishing, 2020).

36. Frank B. Wilderson III, "Blacks and the Master/Slave Relation," in *Afropessimism: An Introduction*, ed. Frank B. Wilderson III (Minneapolis: Racked and Dispatched, 2017), 15– 30.

37. Savannah Shange, *Progressive Dystopia: Abolition, Antiblackness, and Schooling in San Francisco* (Durham, NC: Duke University Press, 2019).

38. Christina Sharpe, *In the Wake: On Blackness and Being* (Durham, NC: Duke University Press, 2016).

39. Thomas Low Sternberg, "What Else, What Else, What Else?: Character Tension, Textual Multiplicity, and the Development of the Post-Slavery Imaginary in Toni Morrison's Song of Solomon" (Master's thesis, Haverford College, 2017), http://hdl.handle.net/10066/19313.

40. Kelley, *Freedom Dreams*.

41. Audre Lorde, *Sister Outsider: Essays and Speeches* (Berkeley: Crossing Press, 1984).

What They Say What They Said 2
D. S. Kinsel

What They Say What They Said 2 is a continued place for open dialogue, building on the original *WTSWTS*[1] series from the #kinselcollection. *What They Say What They Said* 2 intends to represent a dialogue that centers community experience and uplifts community voice. Understanding that to create policy and/or procedural change the focus must be placed on the voice of community members' needs in relation to community-police interactions, *What They Say What They Said* 2 serves as a space to present the ever-evolving conversations that are actively happening around community-police relations.

The original work included two text sources. The first source originated from responses reflecting interviews with Black men between the ages of sixteen and twenty-four who reside in Pittsburgh's East End; each interviewee was presented with the prompt: What do the police say when they see you?

The second source reflected the executive summary of *The Final Report of the President's Task Force on 21st Century Policing*, which was created by President Obama's Task Force on 21st Century Policing.[2] Placing these two texts in conversation with each other displayed how the experiences shared resulted in the high-level policy and procedural changes suggested in *President Obama's Report on 21st Century Policing*. *What They Say What They Said* 2 includes the Drop 12 Demands[3] submitted for consideration by the Allegheny County Black Activist/Organizer Collective in 2020 as a text source included in the final design. A singular police officer outline is placed in the center of that field, and the Drop 12 Demands serve as the final overlay for the entire piece.

D. S. Kinsel, *What They Say What They Said 2*, 2020

The responses to the prompt "what do the police say when they see you?" paired with the executive summary from *The Final Report of the President's Task Force on 21st Century Policing* brings unique movement and pattern behind the police officer's silhouette. This text collage of the two sources represents the increased public consciousness regarding interactions between Black men and law enforcement officers. It also displays how this issue has become a larger part of critical dialogue in the United States concerning social justice–focused reform. Placing the Drop 12 Demands submitted for consideration by the Allegheny County Black Activist/Organizer Collective presents viewers with an update on the conversation—adding the latest local contribution that is directly based on the shared experiences of community members.

Notes

1. "Past Project: Activist Print: D. S. Kinsel: What They Say, What They Said, May 1–August 31, 2016," *The Warhol*, 2023, https://www.warhol.org/exhibition/d-s-kinsel-what-they-say-what-they-said/.

2. "President's Task Force on 21st Century Policing," *Wikipedia*, last edited December 23, 2022, https://en.wikipedia.org/wiki/President%27s_Task_Force_on_21st_Century_Policing.

3. "'Black Activist and Organizer Collective' Delivers List of Police Reform Demands to City, County Officials," *CBS News Pittsburgh*, June 15, 2020, https://www.cbsnews.com/pittsburgh/news/black-activist-pittsburgh-bill-peduto/.

Prison Took My Daddy

Nekiya Washington-Butler

Nekiya Washington-Butler graduated in April 2024 with a bachelor's degree in Applied Developmental Psychology from the University of Pittsburgh and is completing a specialized master's degree program in K-12 Special Education and K-4 Early Education.

My time in high school I attended City Charter High School in downtown Pittsburgh. While there, I was allowed to figure out what I wanted to do post–high school. And I was encouraged to act in such a way that I felt I was able to get a taste of what my life would and could look like. This led me to the University of Pittsburgh and gave me some before-knowledge of what I actually wanted to study. In ninth and tenth grades, I was in a class called Informational Literacy that was to teach us how to write a research paper and also to get us ready for our senior projects on a topic that could be researched in length.

I had a hard time picking a topic, but I was so moved about learning about the prison system because my father was in prison. Although I knew I wanted it to be based on prison, I was not sure what about prison exactly. So one day my Informational Literacy teacher and I were talking, and I was telling her about my father's school experience and then ending up in prison. She brought this topic to my attention: the school-to-prison pipeline. After that conversation I did some slight research on it and knew that was my topic.

Now, my father's education experience is a little complex. My father went to school in the southern area of Pittsburgh from pre-K to about fifth grade. Then his family moved to the Hill District of Pittsburgh, and he did middle school in that area. However, things went for a turn when drugs were brought into his home, allowing CYF (Office of Children, Youth, and Families) to get involved. So my father and his three other siblings got split into different foster homes, and that is where my father finished the rest of his education career. He graduated from Penn Hills High School, where he was a star track athlete and earned honors in history. Post–high school, my father went to the army for about two years but came home early because his first wife was pregnant, and he did not want to miss out. My father later on went to culinary school and got his certification.

When I look at his life in this aspect, it's kind of interesting because my father has done a lot but still ended up in prison. This makes me question much about the world, the systems we live in, and the correlation between schools and prisons. Did my father actually do something horrible to the world, or did the world do something horrible to him? I think about not having that father figure around and what it felt like to not have my dad at high school graduation. After doing my research on the school-to-prison pipeline, I was no longer mad at him, but I was sad for him. Knowing and now understanding the impact that school and his life had on him has helped me understand him and the systems.

My study also helped me understand my own schooling in Pittsburgh and the way my mother had to navigate the systems here.

Both of my parents graduated from high school and had a little bit of education afterward. However, their educational backgrounds built how they wanted my education experience to be. My mother lived in a Black community in Pittsburgh called Homewood. Rich in many ways, Homewood was made economically poor by the racist systems of the city. My mother attended elementary and middle school there. Then when it came to high school, she went to a magnet school named South Vo-Tech on the south side of Pittsburgh. The school's message was to promote trades, meaning that they actually allowed students to opt out of some classes and attend a trade program that would either give them a certification with graduation or put them on track to get it after graduation. During this time, my mom was facing many personal obstacles. After high school, my mother graduated with honors and a certification in cosmetology. She then went to a community college located in downtown Pittsburgh called Bradford Community College, where she got her associates degree in computer science.

My mother's experience made her have certain expectations for herself, so when I attended school (pre-K through twelfth grade), she wanted to do whatever was in her power to make sure I had a good education by the schools she chose for me. That meant, to her, not going to schools in poverty but sending me where she believed to be where the best education was.

School was not something that came easy for me: educational, social, and love life. As a child, you have certain expectations of school that were pushed in your head by parents and/or other social factors. However, if someone else was looking at my transcript from pre-K to twelfth grade and only looking at the schools, they would probably think I was pretty fortunate. Because I went to so many schools that had high rankings in the great education that was given to the children. Now if someone looked at my grades, maybe the standpoint would be different. I only know this because from pre-K to sixth my grades were terrible, if I was the one to describe them.

Now when I look back, I remember this time of my life being extremely hard because I transitioned from so many schools, in different states, and it felt like I could not keep up. I can remember when I was in pre-K through kindergarten my mom got me tested for different disabilities. By the time I finished second grade, my mom was ready to move again, and we did, and that was back to Pittsburgh, Pennsylvania. When I came back, educationally, I struggled significantly in the third grade, and my teacher suggested to my parents that I go back to the second grade. I did, and that was embarrassing, but what I will say is that I appreciate it now because look at who I am today.

When looking back and reflecting on my own school experience and my family's experiences, I can say that it was tough. I thank my parents for their commitment to build me up and for myself to have my own experience—even in the unfair society we live in.

Boy

Sheila Carter-Jones

Other teachers think he is strange. It isn't
his almond colored skin. It is his eyes.
They are blue as if the ocean is in him and
water has risen up past his lids into his pupils.
His eyes are placid. The calmness makes
teachers question. They want to know how
this ocean happened. It is odd. Doesn't make
sense. Makes them uncomfortable. He isn't
what they expect. Not mean. Not loud. Or a
smart aleck. It would be easier to label him a
troublemaker if he had regular eyes. Remove
him from their discomfort. They would feel
less threatened by the way his body in motion
appears to be still. He is just a boy with a soft
voice. When he makes comments or answers
questions in class his eyes are words and his
voice is held back by a blush. When his mouth
swells into a smile his cheeks puff up as if to
make his eyes two distant, blue suns rising
together and scattering light. Other teachers
ask over and over if I can believe such a thing
as a brown boy with blue eyes. I say, *Yes, I see
him*. I see how he dreams in his Air Jordans.
How his voice carries him up before his body
Is a bubble bursting. Before other teachers

insist, *he will never be anything.* I wish they
could have seen him beyond their horizon.
How he wouldn't become a negative statistic
but graduate with a scholarship. How he would
become an engineer, outstanding employee
and a fine example. See his wife, a scientist,
and their baby born with a smile. How he works
full time, has his own side business clearing weeds,
landscaping, and making way for planting seeds.
The young boys he hires are quiet. They blush too.

Part 5

"listen little sister / angels make their hope here"

Dreaming. Possibility. Freedom. We begin the final section of this text with an image that invokes freedom, transcendence, and the "primordial blackness as a source of divine power" and conclude with an image that asks us to "inhale and exhale and smile . . . breaking free from archaic thinking." The works in this section urge us to look both forward and backward for visions of freedom: young people's understandings of what freedom feels like, along with conversations between elders and youth that invoke the principle of sankofa—reaching into the past to draw and build from knowledge to make a positive future—with each piece illustrating that there are different ways of imagining and depicting what freedom is or could be. When invoking the logics of freedom, some focus on resistance, while others focus on imaginaries they haven't yet seen and can't yet describe.

As you read, we encourage you to consider what freedom looks like to you. Does freedom / how does freedom draw from the past and what has come before? How is freedom related to collective healing and collective action? How do we work to move toward freedom across difference and toward common purpose?

Lori Delale-O'Connor

The Flying African

Mikael Owunna

The Flying African, part of my *Infinite Essence* series, is an exploration of resistance, transcendence, and the primordial Blackness as a source of divine power. The piece depicts a celestial Black body floating in the vast expanse of space, drawing inspiration from the African American myth of the Flying Africans, which tells the story of enslaved individuals taking flight and returning to their African homelands. This tale of defiance and liberation embodies the theme of *Black Freedom Struggle in Urban Appalachia* as it highlights the resilience and strength of the Black community in the face of oppressive systems. As a Black artist from Pittsburgh, I feel a strong personal connection to the subject

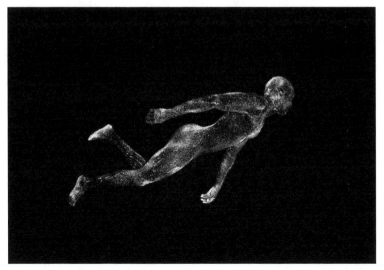

Mikael Owunna, *The Flying African*, 2018

matter and the book's examination of these systems within the context of urban Appalachia.

The *Infinite Essence* series is deeply rooted in Indigenous African knowledge systems, drawing on Nigerian (Igbo) and Malian (Dogon) cosmologies to create a unique visual style that captures cosmic grandeur and Blackness as the divine origin of all things. In *The Flying African*, the fusion of art, science, myth, and technology serves as a vehicle for Black transfiguration, reflecting the multidimensional voices and experiences featured in *Black Freedom Struggle in Urban Appalachia*. The piece not only aligns with the book's aim to give voice to underrepresented identities but also embodies the spirit of resistance, resilience, and reclamation central to the ongoing struggle for liberation in the Appalachian region and beyond.

What a Free Future Looks like to Me

A Prose Poem

Cadence Spruill

Cadence is a senior at Margaret Milliones University Preparatory School in Pittsburgh. She is a reader, a writer, and a seeker of knowledge.

A free future looks like being able to breathe the air deeply on the sidewalk with yourself and others, without having to wear a mask and worrying that you may catch something or the polluted air may get in your lungs, killing you or harming you. Being able to feel the warmth on your skin as the sun blazes on you with its welcoming hug and its blinding light.

It's when you go to your school and don't have to worry about "the big test!" Failing on it, getting anxious. Worried about how the system will deal with you. Will they help you? Will they encourage you? Or will they ignore you or punish you? It looks like when you don't have to worry about your children coming home from the park, on the sidewalk, or on the porch because it's getting late. Having to tell them, "Look out for strangers! Don't speak to anyone you don't know!" Or programs telling you to go to the nearest adult for help but don't know for sure if an adult will help you.

A free future looks like when people of color are not being killed just because of who they are or the color of their skin. It looks like when women's bodies aren't being controlled just for the sake of "'My body,

My choice' is ridiculous nonsense." It's when you can freely express yourself without having to worry about your body, how you are shaped, from head to toe, to face to hair or the name of your race.

A free future is when you can feel the prickling grass under your feet or the fine lines and bumps on wood, lightly grazing it, amazed by it. It's when everybody is not at each other's throat shouting, screaming, proclaiming, raging "INJUSTICE!" In reality, we all should be able to be equal—to *feel* equal. To know that we are all the same. Just different heritage, race, eyes, hair, culture, land, and people.

A free future is when the people who are in need get their needs instead of staying in need or having to reach out to people, hearing the words "I'm sorry I can't help you" or "Get away from me!"

A free future is when we do not blame others for the atrocities happening to our land. If we can call it that. It's when we fought so hard to push our "home" forward. Instead, we continue to go backward. HISTORY! is going into the past; the struggles are thriving and hurting more than ever before. It's when we help our earth instead of killing it.

A free future is when we can feel the cooling breeze of the fall, smell the humidity, and step and hear that satisfying crinkle of a leaf crunch.

Now for sure, we are finding ways for all of these problems to become a solution. But it can't become a solution when it's continuously being ignored by the majority. It's like when you take off your socks and shoes and place your feet in the sand. Feeling grains of minerals go through your toes sticking to you, feeling soft, until you dip them and feel that swish, swirl, and tiny waves between your toes in the saltwater of the ocean.

A free future is when you, as a person, make your future free. It is when you, as a person, are the happiest you can be. No matter what or who you want to be. No repercussions. No violence. Just serenity and peace. It's when those who wish to be married regardless of sex can be married. Who cares? Why blame it on someone else? A higher-up.

A free future is when a person is allowed their own choice. Not from pressure or wishes or looks of disappointment. Why discriminate when on their document it states "_____" because those who were taught that something or someone is not the same as you, to hate it. That it's not right and to be afraid that the problem will spread as our world falls deeper into a depression; the division widens in our world as the people get angrier! Then it is noticed. Then it is too late to handle or too deep to solve and resolve peacefully. Back to stage one.

A free future is when you can look forward instead of looking over your shoulder in the night, *afraid* that someone may grab you and that you will be fighting for your own life. Scared that you'll never see family or friends, terrified if you don't know if you'll make it out alive out of that situation. Search parties, crying families and friends, weeping and scared, you holding on to your will so you won't lose hope. But by the grace of your family or by the evil of those hearts, you will find a way. But it's either crying, healing, loving, getting your justice, or in a coffin. No one deserves a coffin.

A free future is like a paradise. Enjoying yourself with the people you love as you all dance near the heat of the fire, full bellies, not a worry in the world, not having to worry about the next bill. Bill? A bill. A free future is when you aren't having to worry about the next bill, having to be paid because you aren't able to afford it; "It's coming too close," saying the repeated phrases, "The bills are too high," "I might have to get a second job," "What am I going to do?": now you find alternatives, more jobs, worried you might get a notice in the mail, in that line. That dreaded line, the bill: $_____ your power will be cut off in the next week. Running water is no longer a luxury, electricity is no longer a fun activity, and keeping the gas on so you can be warm and not freeze to death, keeps your meals hot! A free future is when poverty isn't holding you back from feeding you and your family, not stopping you from getting a shelter or even a safe place to sleep at night, a home. Thousands and hundreds of thousands of people have to deal with poverty, *every day*, and the next day struggling just as much. Getting by is no longer a choice, an option. It's survival, a must to keep living. Working hard and getting time off is no longer a balanced scale.

It's when you can put your hands together, like a bowl, dipping your fingers first, then the entirety of your hand, lifting your hands out from that body of water as drips and drops fall from it and you sip it. Feeling the dryness of your throat and mouth slip away with the cooling, clean water quenches it. And as you go for more, you don't worry about what it's in. Because you know that this water is safe; it's what's keeping you alive right now. It's when you are near running clean water, hearing the rushed sounds flowing down the river as you inhaled deeply, tuning your senses in, body relaxing into the soft grass, as you look up through the peering leaves and feel beaming sunlight on parts of your body as the brisk wind and shade keep you chill. The birds flap their wings, and their chirps send out to one another as the wind.

A free future is when everyone is able to have and provide for themselves and to feed the children and animals. But how can they when conflict is stopping them from keeping food on the table? Why must they fight to survive when there's plenty of food? Because of access and availability, extreme weather conditions, conflict, food waste, one's gender—back to it again, the main problem is conflict! So many people are affected by this.

A free future is when our crops are living, breathing, and greener than ever before. It's when crops are meeting society's present needs without sacrificing and experiencing the food we need to preserve and save us. Instead of our people ending in the ground, why not feed the earth? It's soil making it healthier to stop killing our trees, to not spoil the water, to give to the people, to stop carbonating our oxygen—*that's* what it means to have a free future. A free future is a laughing yell that echoes through a tunnel, you feel as though you're flying. That your mind, body, and soul have all synced. That instead of going backward and forward, you're balanced. You feel like you could do anything you set your mind to. And you can. Take a stand and do what you feel is right.

A free future is when you're outside your home, on your porch, or on a balcony staring at the life around you. It reminds you of those peaceful morning walks through your town or through a small hike. You take in the fragrances relaxing your mind. That all the worries in your mind are simply swiped from the ocean floors of the beach. Nothing but words in the sand. Nature gives as you give back, making you both in complete harmony. An everlasting melody.

Our People That Came before Did an Awful Lot to Be Free

An Interview

Tamanika Howze, Cameron Shannon, and DaVonna Shannon

This interview was conducted by Cameron Shannon, a ten-year-old boy who attends Penn Hills Charter School for Entrepreneurship. Cameron loves football, building intricate Lego sets, and being an awesome big brother to his brother, August, and sister, Kaliya. In this interview, Cameron sits alongside his bonus mom, DaVonna, as they learn from community matriarch, leader, and advocate for children, Ms. Tamanika Howze. Cameron hoped to learn from Ms. Howze her motivations, goals, and experiences with freedom and justice for children and for the education system. From this time they shared, Cameron said, "I learned why it's so important to fight for other people" and that "I have a voice and I can help people, too, and make schools a safe and fun place."

Cameron Shannon: What are some interests that you like to do?

Tamanika Howze: Well, I'm interested in learning more about your school and what interests you have about your school. It sounds exciting to me. I might have to ask you to repeat questions sometimes. I think my greatest interests, and it might be corny, but I am so passionate about children, and I'm passionate about justice. I'm passionate about real education, and I'm passionate about liberation. If you want me to break any of that down to you, please let me know.

CS: Well, some of those things you just said that I have questions for.

TH: That's great. I love questions. I think children should question all the time. Question, question, question as a part of real education.

CS: My first question is, how did you come to understand the relationship between school and prison?

TH: How did I come to understand the relationship between school and prison? It was a long process. It was a journey—me being an activist around education for a very long time. I read. I love to read, and I would read a lot. I would go to as many education forums and conferences as I possibly could to learn more. I think that was basically it, because I read a lot, listened to people. I like to listen. I like to learn. I think it's necessary to do that. So that's how I came into my knowledge of that.

CS: Okay. My next question is: How do you define freedom?

TH: How do I define freedom? That's a very broad and very, very important question. I don't think I can answer it as an individual, but through my history of my people, freedom has meant many things. To say that we still are not free, first we need to have a free mind to think clearly, to think collectively. Not what is just good for one person but what is good for the collective to break the shackles of oppression. Shackles are like chains. Like you can break a chain. And break the chain of exploitation so that people have the freedom to live free. Free from those things that oppress them, that kind of hold them down. There are many things that hold us down as a people, as Black people, and as a class of people. So those things, those shackles, have to come apart, and it takes a collective body to break those shackles.

Our people that came before us did an awful lot to be free. They needed their physical freedom. They needed to break away from being enslaved. There were many things that they did to gain their freedom. They also knew they needed to have the freedom of mind. So we have to think of our own, think clearly. And my position is not to think the way some of the school systems have taught us to think but to think independently and to think "what is best for us?" Then we know: what is best for us eventually will be best for other people who have been held down.

CS: What has been some of your most valued work toward freedom in this context?

TH: I have to mention, there's a program that is near and dear to me. It was the Children's Defense Fund Freedom Schools, and they have some of the best national training I have seen. They took that model—was an organization that happened a long time ago called SNCC, Student Non-Violent Coordinating Committee, and it kind of laid the blueprint. They said, okay, here's the example of what can happen and should happen for Black children to learn. They knew then that because the education system, the school system for Black people, was not fair at all. It was not fair. So Black children didn't learn. It wasn't equal of what Black children learned and what white children learned. And so they started in a place, in a state called Mississippi. They had Freedom Schools there.

Later, after some years, a woman by the name of Marion Wright Edelman said, "Okay, I think we need to—let's rebuild Freedom Schools." So it was built in a different way. And so they had an insight, too, of when you are not educated in the right way, you are imprisoned in your mind. Imprisoned in your mind. The school system, the public school system, is not built for Black children to have a free mind. It's not built that way. It's built a certain way so they will have workers for this big society, what I call a capitalist society.

I learned from there how when education's not taught properly and when people don't have the things that they need—which is called *resources*—when they don't have that, it takes them off track. And then it's a rebellion. And I love the rebellion of young people. I love it. They rebel in the school system and say, this is not for me. Some would say, "Oh, they're acting out," but actually they are rebelling, and so we need to give them a voice. I think young people should always have a voice.

Cameron, even if you disagree with me, I ask you to disagree with me respectfully. Speak up and say, "Ms. Howze, I don't think that's correct" and tell me why. And I should listen to you. I should listen deeply to you so you have a voice. Young people should have a voice in how the education system should work. And so when things aren't working in the school system, unfortunately and sadly, they drop out. First, they drop out mentally, and then they drop out of school altogether. That leads some of them to go into things that are not correct, and they end up in what some people call the *prison industrial system. Industrial* meaning they're making big money off it. It's prisons all over this country, and having prisons is big money. United States has more imprisoned Black people than anywhere else, and we need to ask why. How do we stop that? This is not justice.

The other part is about thirty years ago, a little over thirty years ago, I got involved with an organization called the Advocates for African American Students in the Pittsburgh Public Schools. It was organized by this brilliant, brilliant woman by the name of Dr. Barbara Sizemore. I said *Dr.* Sizemore—she was a scholar, she was a warrior. I say *warrior* because she fought, and she was an activist. She fought. She fought for justice for Black children in the school system. So Dr. Barbara A. Sizemore, scholar, warrior, activist.

She formed this organization called the Advocates for African American Students in Pittsburgh Public Schools. She said, "Wait a minute. Things aren't right. Black children are not learning the way they should learn. What is the matter?" So I became involved in that. What evolved after that, would follow that, Dr. Sizemore had left Pittsburgh, and we kept it going. Then we formed a group called the Equity Advisory Panel,[1] and that is still operating now. As a matter of fact, I was on a meeting yesterday in regards to that. We still, our organization, because we kept going. These were parents who had children in the school system and said, okay, we need to stand up. Not just for our children.

What's important is we didn't just stand up for our children; we stood up for all of the children. We didn't have money for an attorney, so we filed what's called a complaint with this big organization in

Pennsylvania called the Pennsylvania Human Relations Commission. After a while they said, "You know what? Pittsburgh Public Schools is not doing all right. Okay, we agree with you." After a while, they found things, and I'll break it down real simple. They found ninety-four things. Ninety-four. They said, "Okay, Pittsburgh Public Schools, this is what you need to do to make things better for Black children." And so we know that's to the school-to-prison pipeline. We still have that organization of thirty years, and we're still fighting on behalf of Black children. We know when we fight on behalf of Black children and improve things for them, guess what? It's going to improve the whole system. But it's been a long, long fight.

I think I've been involved in a lot of community organizations prior to Freedom School. And the advocates just always, we just never get what we need. Ultimately, I think we need to have our own schools.

Davonna Shannon: So, Cameron, do you have thoughts about Ms. Howze just told you a really thorough story about a time that she was inspired to become an advocate for Black children? Or in other words, to stand up for Black children in Pittsburgh Public Schools, which is the other larger school system. You don't go to the Pittsburgh Public Schools, but some of your friends do. She talked about her experience, knowing from research, knowing from her own experience, learning from other parents that Black children were not getting a fair shot in school and were actually being, in some ways, mistreated and oppressed. Do you have thoughts about that?

CS: I'm just curious on why you would help all those people for that one reason. Why would you help everybody but only for one reason, not for other reasons?

TH: Thank you, Cameron, for answering that because it's something I forgot to mention. I think it's very important. I thank you, thank you, thank you for asking that. My mother was my example, and I'm sure that is why I'm involved, I've been involved as an activist being active in trying to find justice for Black children. I remember my mother, and you might not know anything about this, but way back in the day, there wasn't a lot of opportunity for Black women or Black men in terms of jobs or whatever. And so my mother worked in white homes as what they called a domestic. She cleaned their houses. She took care of their children. I don't know if you ever had to mop your kitchen floor or whatever, but my mother used to have to get down on her hands and knees and scrub these white people's floors. That's how she made her living to support us.

It was in this place, this wealthy place called Mt. Lebanon,[2] mainly where she worked at. She would come home and talk about the school system there. I realized in elementary school, she said I'm not getting that. They were learning a language in elementary school, and I'm like, what? I didn't take a language until I was in high school, and she just used to talk about the different things, and I knew something was indifferent.

I had my first encounter of racism when I was in elementary school. The teacher who opened the world of reading to me was a white librarian. Once a week we went to our reading time at the library, and I was always anxious to go and hear and listen. This one particular day she read a book called *Little Black Sambo*, and she showed the pictures. It made Black people look really, really, really bad. We always sat in a circle, and she made one of my classmates run around in a circle until he was just exhausted. You know sometimes you just play so hard, you get so tired? That's what; he just collapsed. I was very fond of this teacher, and that's when that went away. I said, "This is not right."

I never told my mother because my mother was an advocate for me, but I was afraid if she went up to the school what would happen. She didn't have vacation days or sick days, but whenever there was a school fundraiser, my mother was there. She was there, and I was so proud of that. I was very, very proud of that. I remember one day was a thing called a school bazaar, and they were selling different things. My mother was behind the line, and I think her part was the hot dogs. There was a child behind me who didn't have a ticket to buy a hot dog. My mother raised me: you don't lie, you don't cheat, you don't steal, that sort of thing. And I saw my mother give this child a hot dog. I'm saying to myself, I think it might be stealing. But that was my example of: this is how you care for children. She was a type that, people in the neighborhood, in *our* neighborhood, would come to her and seek knowledge and wisdom. If they had a problem, they would go to her.

My mother didn't graduate from high school. She quit high school to take care of her mother, who was sick. And so my mother was the example of how you care for others and how you look out for children. People in the neighborhood knew my mother would look out for children, and so that was my example. Then in high school, I came across a book—it just happened the book was misplaced—by Mary McLeod Bethune. That did it. That got me into education. I loved it. For then on, I just had that interest.

So my mother was definitely my example. From there were other people. I lived in a community that was raised in a very poor community in the Hill District, but people cared for other people. My next-door neighbor ended up being my mother's best friend. When I had contracted pneumonia and my mother knew she had to work in order to make money, my next-door neighbor, Madea, came and sat with me in the hospital all day long until my mother got off work. Even there were other people in the neighborhood who would encourage us to do good in school and even to do the right things. So it was a community that cared, and it wasn't a community where you would say there was a lot of high academic people, whatever. But it was a community where people worked. Many worked; some didn't, but they worked in their homes. So that was important to me.

DS: Can you think of maybe a role model that has taught you a valuable lesson about life?

TH: My mother. There are many others.

CS: Probably my parents.

TH: That's great. That's great.

CS: With whom do you do this work? Who should be involved?

TH: Oh. Everybody needs to do it. Anybody who believes in justice, anybody who believes and understands the value of liberation. Anyone who has children. And it doesn't have to be their child by birth. It could be their niece, their nephew, their grandchild, their cousin. Anyone who has a business or an agency, an organization. Just people, period. There are some people who are actually fighting to make things better, but it's not as many as we need, and sometimes those people get tired. I think it's unfair that you just have a little bit of people doing great, a whole lot of work, and we need to have more people involved. But in order to do that, it's like anything else that's worthwhile.

I do believe in what SNCC (Student Non-Violence Coordinating Committee) used to do, and always said in Ella Baker and Fannie Lou Hammer, it's you go to the people. Go to the people. So if we are sincere about education, we need to go to children and ask them, "What is it that you want? What is that you need?" And ask the families, ask the community. I always reference this one organization that's no longer together, but it is a different organization by Dr. Jerome Taylor, who has been, talk about a real warrior. He has been fighting for true justice in education for over fifty years. They used to have a program called Right Start. The example of going to the people, they went and asked some of the grandparents and others, "What is it that you want for your children?" As a result of that, they develop a program called Values for Life.

DS: Cam, have you ever been asked by maybe one of your teachers or one of your mentors even in an afterschool program about the things that are important to you or what you want to learn about? You know how we talk about learning the truth in school and that sometimes some of the curriculum or what the teachers are teaching you is sometimes not the whole truth, but some of it's not the truth at all, so we learned the truth at home? Has anyone at school ever asked you some of those questions like what is important to you when it comes to education? [He indicates no.] No one's ever asked you those types of questions? None of your teachers? If one of your teachers or someone you respected did ask you for your input, how do you think that would change the way that you think about school?

CS: I really don't know if I would change what I think about school. But I think it would help me more understand school.

CS: Is there anything that you would like to share that we haven't covered?

TH: I'm trying to think on that and trying to think of it in the context or in the way that this is supposed to be put together. The one thing that even when I was asked to be a part of this and some questions put before me, and even the whole title, it made me think, okay, this is just for people in this high academic community. Just college. For those who have doctorate degrees and for school systems. It concerns me. Well, no, this is how they put it together, so I can't knock that. But I'm always thinking, do we use the language, how people talk, if we need more parents? People talk about parent involvement, and I think about family. When I think about being involved and it's a part of being engaged, but my main thing is being empowered. And so those parents, those families, and the children would speak up and say, "This is not right. This is what I need for my children. This is what we need for our community."

So if the academic community and those who are actually living it, have been through it, unite and hear the voices of parents and families, those who are caregivers, hear their voices and act on it, respect what they have to say. I loved how when SNCC went down South, they stayed with families. They knew. They couldn't come down there thinking that they're better than anybody else. These people will give up their couch, give up their bed, their food. They have very little food, but they accepted them in. And so these big universities and colleges, they need to accept the people. Accept the people, how they are. Go to the people. Don't always think people should come to the university. Those kind of things have to happen. And I'm sorry I've gotten off track with your question. I apologize.

CS: How long have you been an activist for schools?

TH: Oh goodness. I started when I was eighteen, after I graduated from high school. I am seventy-three years old, and a couple months I'll be seventy-four, and I've never looked back. Never looked back. I've always felt that. A part of my life, too, I have to say, is that when I was eighteen, well, I was always interested as a child in civil rights. Because back then we had—and I know you wouldn't know, and DaVonna wouldn't know—it was a black-and-white TV, and you would have to get up and change the channels. But I would see how things, the injustice, the things that were wrong against Black people happened down South, and that laid in my mind.

Then in my home, there were, like, *Jet* magazines, the *Ebony* magazine. These were Black magazines, and it would say what was going on with our people. As I had to walk up a place called Center Avenue, we didn't have a place like Giant Eagle [supermarket] or places like that. There were small stores, and that's where we'd go to get our dinner. There was a place called CORE, Congress of Racial Equality. I would stop past, and they would tell me, they would talk to me about different things. There were a lot of times the freedom marches would start in the Hill District.

I can't remember what it was, but I remember this day. My mother sent me to the store to get dinner. I got pork chops and cream-style corn. I'm coming down Center Avenue. I see my sister standing on the corner, and I just had to join this march. I had to. And I asked her to take dinner home. She said, "No, Mommy's going to get you." So I just held in there, and I went on the demonstration, walked back home, back up to the Hill, and I thought I was going to be in big trouble. My mother never said a word. Never said a word. So my interest started at a very young age about justice.

CS: Thank you for giving us some of your time. Thank you for the questions.

TH: I thank you for your time. I wish you the best, and I would hope that you would learn what justice is. There are children your age that made a difference. I was telling DaVonna how there was a walkout in the South, and they said this education is not right. And so children your age and teenagers, they turned things around. That's what we teach in Freedom Schools. Freedom Schools say, "I can and must make a difference in self, family, community, country, and world through hope, education, and action."

Notes

1. For more information on the Equity Advisory Panel, see the chapter by the EAP in section 2 of this book.

2. Mt. Lebanon is an affluent suburb of Pittsburgh in Allegheny County, Pennsylvania.

Let's Go Find Out

Win Nunley

Win is a cofounder of and creative for Black Dream Escape, a therapeutic arts practice focusing on Black and Indigenous rest.

By age three, I was the Squirrel King of London. My throne was not easily won. It took a couple of weeks and many bags of cashews for my subjects to recognize me as their rightful sovereign.

My kingdom spanned from St Augustine's Tower, to the secret walled garden, to St. John at Hackney. Though the land wasn't expansive, its character and beauty were immeasurable. The worn stone walks, the wise and friendly trees, crumbling walls lined with moss-covered tombstones. My kingdom was populated by the squirrels and our nemeses the pigeons.

No one is born a ruler, for me to become a proper king, I had to learn the rules and customs of the squirrels. No random flapping of the arms, no stomping of the feets, no ululations. Patience, stillness, and personal space are a must. I abided and sat in quiet communion with them. After a month of daily etiquette training, they gave me my first task, defense against the pillaging pigeons. As I distributed the daily rations to my people, our enemies would attack us and pilfer our provisions. For generations the squirrels let them, for they valued their safety and were pacifists by nature. But enough was enough; they saw value in my stomping feet and flapping arms. They allowed me to wail at the enemy, and sure enough they were able to feast in peace. After that one defining moment, they would greet me, gather round, take nuts from my hand, and chitter happily with me.

After a few months, I explored other territories. If I was gone too long, I would be loudly chided about my absence. But no matter how long I'd been away, they'd always remember me. After my family returned to the States, I visited my kingdom one last time and was greeted warmly.

I was home educated my entire life; because of this, I often get questions about whether I missed out on crucial learning moments. I always tell them that I honestly feel as though I learned more than an average American school student. In addition to learning fundamental concepts, I also was allowed to explore and work at my own pace. Had I been put in school, I would have missed many magical moments and not have known the lessons one can find in them.

It is impossible to be young and without questions. Sometimes those questions do not have to be answered by adults but are instead revealed through experience, so as with the squirrels. The lesson that my mother valued with the squirrels was the practice of patience and stillness. Every moment was a teachable moment in my household. Though the underlying message of the squirrels was that of being in harmony, my mother also took the opportunity to discuss the animal kingdom in more depth with me. A bird was not simply a bird; it was a moorhen, coot, or pigeon. Asking why it rains was met with a discussion of the water cycle. If the answer was unknown, the response was "let's go find out."

For purposes of clarification, a big misconception people have is that they believe "homeschooling" is synonymous with "home educating." One of the key differences is that homeschooling follows an established curriculum, which is aligned with the state's objectives and methods of learning. Many homeschoolers choose to take their child out of school because the school is failing their child. They go on to use the exact same methods and deadlines that schools use. Rigid structures, curricula, punishments and rewards, binary thinking.

There are core concepts that are fundamental for a child to learn to become a functioning adult. The way in which they're taught can differ. I know πr^2 is the formula to find the area of a circle, but I learned it from sewing before I learned it in a textbook. There are lessons in everything, and everything is connected. That is the central philosophy of home education. Home education is proactive as opposed to reactive. Home education assumes that learning is always happening.

The phrase "let's go find out" was crucial to my education. It showed me that it's okay to not know something and nurtured the ability and discipline to research. Being aware of where one lacks information and being excited to learn is empowering. It often frustrates me that many people have been taught to be ashamed of the gaps in their knowledge or that there's only one right answer. The most important tool of a home-educated child is their drive and enjoyment in the search of knowledge. As John Holt has said, "We destroy the love of learning in children, which is so strong when they are small, by encouraging and compelling them to work for petty contemptible rewards, gold stars, or papers marked 100 and tacked to the wall, or A's on report cards, or honor rolls, or dean's lists, or Phi Beta Kappa keys, in short, for the ignoble satisfaction of feeling that they are better than someone else."[1]

Because lack of information is stigmatized, people feel like they have to be right all the time or that they need the answer to everything. This attitude doesn't allow people to grow, makes them remain in ignorance, and/or doesn't give them openness to being corrected. Being open to new ideas and new information leads to a more cohesive and unified community.

The premise of our home education began with the fact that everybody involved was a human being who deserved to be heard and recognized. These are the basic building blocks of forming a community. Home education is a way of being and a lifestyle. Community was part of that lifestyle for my family. My mother always said, "Every parent is a home educator regardless of whether they do it full time or not."

As they say, it takes a village to raise a child. In Western society, it can be a bit harder to have a village. But you can still build one around you nonetheless. When I was younger, there was a librarian named Ms. Leann, who spent a long time talking to me. I originally was not the biggest fan of reading, much to the dismay of my parents. They couldn't figure out what it was I didn't like about reading. They provided for me all the Afrocentric or culturally relevant fantasy, fairytale, and folklore books that a kid could want. I was reflected in every book on my bookshelf. What Ms. Leann found was not a lack of representation but that my interest was in nonfiction. She directed my mother and I to the nonfiction section, where I was most delighted to discover books about bats, bugs, trees, and marine life. She helped instill a love of reading in me. She would ask me how my book was when I finished it. She had recommended a book that I loved so much that I wrote a sequel, which she shelved so I could check it out whenever. She took me and my interests seriously.

Sometimes the littlest things further a child's education. Being seen, being heard, being taken seriously are some of the most critical components to engaging a child's desire to learn.

Oftentimes I find that people who have gone through orthodox education view learning as something which is passive, or something that is done to you, as opposed to something inherent to the human experience. They often lean on hierarchical structures which are meant to condition children to fulfill their state-sanctioned role. These roles have manifested for Black people as laborers, entertainers, or athletes.

Orthodox education gives the illusion of training people to become functional members of society while purposefully denigrating some of its most critical components. A one-size-fits-all approach is not beneficial and ignores perfectly valid jobs such as mechanics, plumbers, sanitation workers, electricians, etc. In addition, it doesn't leave room for people with different learning styles.

In schools, children wake up early every day, get told the "right information," what to memorize, when to eat, when to go to the bathroom, what not to wear, etc. Schools believe they have a right to a child's time, taking the remainder of their waking hours with assignments. This is not a healthy model of learning or a healthy lifestyle in general. In fact, many times it hinders the learning of children. School consumes the time people need to (as my great-grandmother would say) contemplate their navels. It does not allow people to study in depth what they find important to themselves. Furthermore, schools do not offer the time for adequate nutrition, exercise, and rest.

This ties in to the illusion of America. We pretend to be a country where anyone can make it if they work hard enough. The truth of the matter is that this country wants those who are not upper middle class to generate profits for the owning class. Schools are a model of how to be subservient and an indoctrination to be indentured to the corporations or a model prisoner. If corporations are considered entities, then workers are as disposable as cells. This is made evident by the disciplinary systems in place in schools, where children are disposed of on a regular basis through suspension or expulsion. There is no inquiry into the unmet need causing a child to be disruptive. There is no conflict resolution practiced. There is no humanity.

This is not to say that there are no good concepts within the schooling system. However, they cannot be used in a beneficial way in our current society. A more free society would have a balance of the two modalities. Schools would allow children to learn in the ways best suited to themselves and allow for change in what a child believes they need. Some people like and need a rigid structure. Some people thrive with a more open-ended education. And others, such as myself, like something in between. To be a human is to change constantly; you are not the same person you were when you were seven; you're not even the person you were a minute ago. Stagnation is unnatural and can be problematic. That's not to say that specializing in something that makes you happy is wrong.

Though I was always a patient kid, the squirrels taught me a different level of patience. Because of what they taught me, I was prepared for a different adventure. I have always loved nature, and my upbringing grounded and stabilized that within me. For instance, when I was younger, there was a redbud tree in our front yard—we called her Mrs. Redbud. When we first moved in, she was on the brink of death and was growing away from our house. My father pruned and tended to her; my mother pulled grass and weeds away from her roots and installed a natural playground for me under her leaves. My friends and I would play underneath her heart-shaped leaves and hug her and sing songs to her.

After the first year, she had totally bounced back; she was flowering profusely in the spring and had started growing toward our house. Every fall when she started losing her leaves and producing her seed pods, my mother would create a leaf crown for me and my friends. Adorning ourselves, my friends and I would gather the rest of the fallen leaves, seed pods, and the prettiest of rocks and would make what we called redbud soup. We would put the ingredients in a wheelbarrow and stir it together and bring it to her to drink as a token of our gratitude for her shade. Mrs. Redbud was one of the people I missed most when we moved from Pittsburgh for the second time. Through her I learned more about botany, the seasons, and creative thinking.

At this moment in time, I am currently learning about horticulture in a more formal manner. It has been a culture shock for me. Learning about plants as something we manipulate and control is very different from how I learned to coexist and partner with nature. I am being taught the importance of conservation but not through a lens of altruism and helping our neighbors but through the lens of human gain. While self-preservation and the continuation of the species is something found in many people, there is a different energy found at the core of the material I am being taught. I believe these textbooks would look very different had the authors been part of a kingdom of squirrels.

Being in a classroom setting has made me even more grateful for the education I had prior. Being able to learn on my terms was one of the greatest gifts my parents gave me. Not having the pressure of failing, being penalized for tardiness, or getting good grades allowed me to take control and enjoy my education. Being told what to learn, how much to learn, what timeframe one needs to metabolize the knowledge, and even how to learn is limiting and stressful. I do not understand how people have full, rich, and complete lives while immersed in formal education. My intention is not to appear ungrateful for what I am learning at this moment but to compare two different systems of education.

Ultimately, a free society allows people (including children) to have, make, and learn from choices. My mother and grandfather always talked about how people who remain close to the earth are very similar. A common theme that one finds is reciprocity and allowing children to experience and learn from the world around them (even if their teachers are squirrels). Learning from your choices is essential and inescapable in life; facing those consequences head on from the time you are born allows for a child to practice freedom and truly understand the responsibilities that come with it. Learning how to make intentional choices comes with the aforementioned practice and being in a loving and safe environment. Sadly, not every family is capable of providing a loving and safe environment because of the wounds they bear from the unsafe, unloving systems that are in place in our society. How I grew up was in a way revolutionary but also returning to precolonial ways of being. My mother was very deliberate in how she chose to raise and educate me, deciding to continue and honor how her father raised her and how his mother raised him.

Note

1. John Holt, *How Children Fail* (New York: Da Capo Press, 1995).

Discipline, Punishment, and Black Childhood

How Carceral Education Shapes Time for Black Youth

Ariana Brazier

Educator and organizer Qui Dorian Alexander writes that the "conflation of discipline/punishment, power/abuse and structure/fear become normalized" through ideologies of fear that teach us the only way to "create discipline is through punishment."[1] Motivated to address the harmful outcomes of the conflation of these terms, I facilitated the development of an interactive Youth Undoing Institutional Racism (YUIR) Pittsburgh workshop to disentangle discipline from punishment. YUIR was an intergenerational, multiracial, youth-focused, antiracist organization focused on undoing institutional racism within the education and criminal legal systems and disrupting the phenomenon often referred to as the school-to-prison pipeline. A microcosm of the prison industrial complex, the school-to-prison pipeline can be understood as the phenomenon by which the school serves as a site of engagement for a nexus of punitive systems—by criminalizing students with marginalized identities, schools have become a state-sanctioned carceral apparatus. More specifically, situating select students within this nexus ensures "the ongoing function of public education as a form of incapacitation or enclosure."[2]

Through narrative reflection on the YUIR workshop at Woodland Hills High School in fall 2019, this chapter considers how the intentional conflation of discipline and punishment stems from and reinforces institutional racism. Woodland Hills School District is located in a suburban area just within the limits of Pittsburgh, Pennsylvania. The median household income in the district is $46,733, with 16 percent of the population living below the poverty line.[3] Woodland Hills Senior High School consists of approximately 60 percent Black students, and 88 percent of the total student body participates in the free lunch program. The school maintains a college readiness index of 11.5/100.[4]

Citing language around suspension policies in Pittsburgh Public Schools Code of Conduct and Woodland Hills High Student Handbook, I argue that Black students in the Greater Pittsburgh area are subject to violent, state-sanctioned restrictions on their access to and width of temporal and spatial movements in their school communities. These restrictions are further exacerbated by the disjunctures between Black students and the conventional white-centered developmental narratives that are mapped onto Black children. Such narratives are consistently disrupted due to social constructions of age and a racialized temporal order that are neither inclusive of nor applicable to the lived experiences of Black children. As a result, Black students in the school-to-prison pipeline experience "managed delays"[5] throughout childhood that continue into adulthood. These delays are enforced under the guise of "disciplinary policies" and "codes of conduct." Finally, I conclude with a commentary on play as a method of restoring students across racial, ethnic, and gender identities and socioeconomic status to community via a shared temporal-spatial dynamic.

YUIR Pittsburgh Workshop

Standing at the center of the room, with about thirty Woodland Hills High School students seated in a circle around me, I asked them to shout out any and every word that comes to mind when they think about the word *punishment*. I recorded every word in a column on the left side of a sticky note hanging on the wall next to me. We repeated the exercise with the word *discipline*.

I then asked someone to read the dictionary definition of *discipline* and someone else to read the dictionary definition of *punishment* from our *YUIR Pgh Zine*.

Discipline, Punishment, and Black Childhood · 211

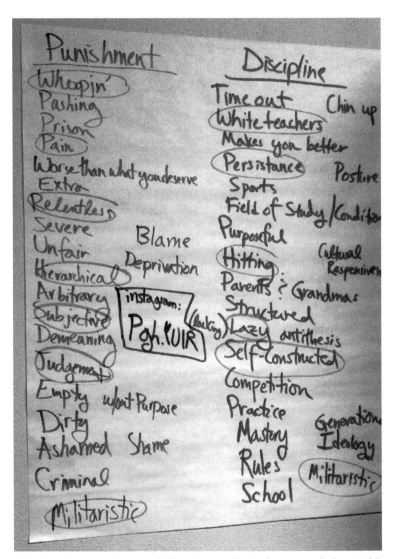

From the YUIR Pgh Workshop facilitated in Seattle, Washington, with the People's Institute for Survival and Beyond

Acknowledging some overlap, I asked the students to identify major differences between the two words.

From there, I prompted the students to name some of the most salient policies and procedures in the Woodland Hills High School's Code of Conduct. When a student made a comment about the dress code,

Discipline	Punish[ment]
noun 1. the practice of training people to obey rules or a code of behavior, using punishment to correct disobedience. • the controlled behavior resulting from discipline. • activity or experience that provides mental or physical training. • a system of rules of conduct. 2. a branch of knowledge, typically one studied in higher education.	noun 1. the infliction or imposition of a penalty as retribution for an offense. • the penalty inflicted. • rough treatment or handling inflicted on or suffered by a person or thing.
verb 1. train (someone) to obey rules or a code of behavior, using punishment to correct disobedience. • punish or rebuke (someone) formally for an offense. • train oneself to do something in a controlled and habitual way.	verb 1. inflict a penalty or sanction on (someone) as retribution for an offense, especially a transgression of a legal or moral code. • inflict a penalty or sanction on someone for (such an offense). • treat (someone) in an unfairly harsh way.
Synonyms: Development; education; method; practice; preparation; self-control; will; self-mastery; regulation; punishment	Synonyms: Abuse; chastise; execute; expel; harm; incarcerate; castigate; injure; oppress; scourge
A methodology or system that can cultivate positive socialization and increased productivity in a person/child/student	Punishment + policing have been used to contain and neutralize Black student protests and mobilization efforts in public schools
Culturally relevant and sensitive school-based discipline policies can promote accountability, communication skills, and self-confidence	"School policies are often designed by individuals raised with White middle-class values and the assumption is made that all students are raised with a similar perspective" (Nelson)
Can create opportunities to analyze and discuss consequences of an individual's actions in order to learn from the experience	Institutionalizes fear, silence and disorder, and can enable the internalization of self-loathing and condemnation
The key to positive discipline is teaching a child what behavior is okay and what behavior is not okay	"[can] produce ideas about what constitutes deviance at the same time they legitimize the attending consequences" (Wun 182).

Discipline can be a positive method that teaches children appropriate behavior and develops their character, while punishment inflicts pain and creates resentment; as a result, the child rarely learns the intended lesson.

"Discipline" and "Punishment" are frequently conflated in classrooms; as a result, Black children are punished at disproportionate rates.

Amy C. Nelson, "The Impact of Zero Tolerance School Discipline Policies: Issues of Exclusionary Discipline."
Connie Wun, [illegible] Black Girls in School Discipline Policies [illegible]

YUIR Pittsburgh, "YUIR Pittsburgh's School-to-Prison Pipeline + Our Vision for Our Future," Issuu, June 4, 2018, https://issuu.com/yuirpgh/docs/digital_zine_june4.

I asked them what they were learning, or what was gained, from the enforcement of the dress policies. There was no immediate response. Together, we reviewed the handbook. The dress code was broken into two categories: "Students Rights and Responsibilities" and "Unacceptable Clothing." The final bullet under the latter category reads, "Anything

Differences:

Punishment
- Focused on Hurt
- Something to someone
- Unbalanced Power
- To Break · Dehumanized
- View as Less than/Deficit
- Fear-based
- Push Out
- Reactionary

Discipline
- Positive · Strengths based
- Relational
- Different Meanings
- To Build · Humanized
- Something with someone
- Mutual · View as someone w/ Potential
- Bringing In
- Why? Self-Reflection

— Difference in Intension —

- Locking the Doors vs. Asking Why
- Black children labeled disruptive for talking, overdiagnosed as did it
- "Insubordination" as a catchall
- Excuses given to white students — Leadership, Civically engaged, Devil's advocate
- Is the environment even nurturing?
- Teacher/Student dynamics
- Linguistic Racism is real — Python
- Discipline can look like Punishment to some.
- Intent ≠ Impact

From the YUIR Pgh Workshop facilitated in Seattle, Washington, with the People's Institute for Survival and Beyond

else that the administration deems as a detriment to the educational atmosphere at Woodland Hills Senior High School."[6] As they stared at me, eyes wide, silence filled the room. I noticed a few students directing suspicious glances at the two participating teachers. I had piqued the students' curiosity and could sense their indignation.

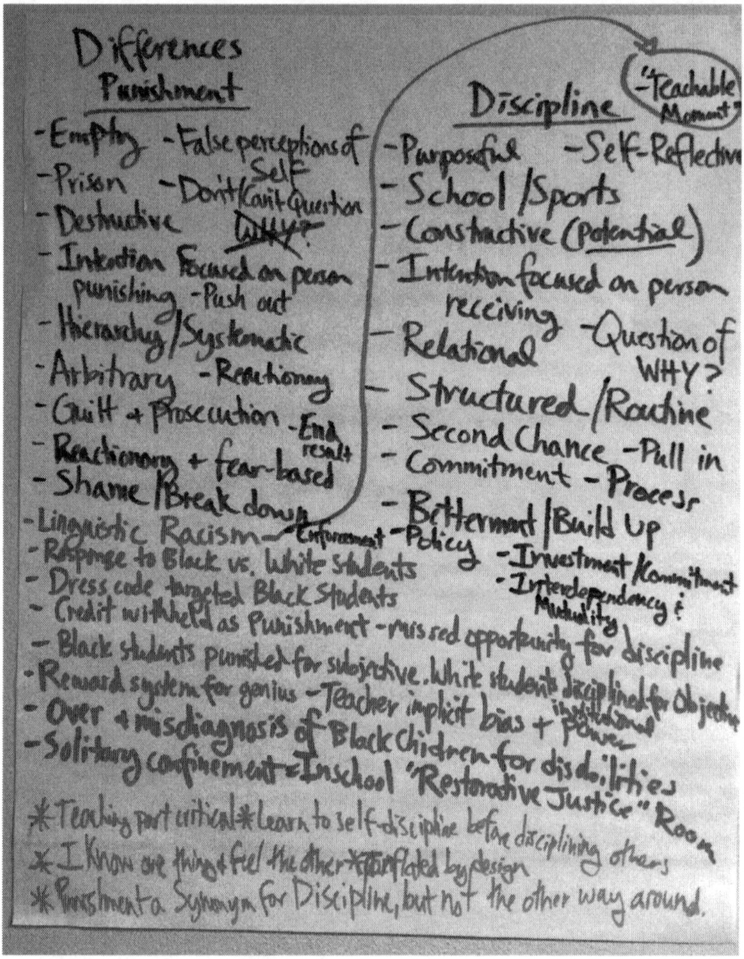

[Handwritten workshop notes:]

Differences

Punishment
- Empty
- False perceptions of Self
- Prison — Don't Want Question Why?
- Destructive
- Intention Focused on person punishing — Push out
- Hierarchy/Systematic
- Arbitrary — Reactionary
- Guilt + Prosecution — End result
- Reactionary + fear-based
- Shame/Break down
- Linguistic Racism — Empowerment — Policy
- Response to Black vs. White students
- Dress code targeted Black students
- Credit withheld as Punishment — missed opportunity for discipline
- Black students punished for subjective, White students disciplined for objective
- Reward system for genius — Teacher implicit bias + power
- Over + misdiagnosis of Black Children for disabilities
- Solitary confinement = In-school "Restorative Justice" Room

Discipline ("Teachable Moment")
- Purposeful — Self-Reflective
- School/Sports
- Constructive (Potential)
- Intention focused on person receiving
- Relational — Question of WHY?
- Structured/Routine
- Second Chance — Pull in
- Commitment — Process
- Betterment/Build Up
- Investment/Commitment
- Interdependency + Mutuality

★ Teaching part critical ★ Learn to self-discipline before disciplining others
★ I know are things I feel the other ★ Stimulated by design
★ Punishment a Synonym for Discipline, but not the other way around.

Another page from the YUIR Pgh Workshop.

I proceeded to explain that "discipline" is a methodology or system that can cultivate positive socialization via skills development and self-study. Discipline is a field of knowledge and/or a knowledge-building practice; it can generate mastery, preparation, regulation, and development. This generative component exists because discipline can create opportunities to analyze and discuss the consequences of an individual's actions in order to acquire critical insights from the experience. Culturally relevant and sensitive discipline can cultivate positive socialization, increased productivity, and self-confidence for students and enhance empathy and understanding for educators and authority figures.

During the session, I shared how, contradictorily, *punishment* in noun form can mean "the infliction or imposition of a penalty as retribution for an offense," and the verb form can mean "to treat someone in an unfairly harsh way."[7] Acknowledging that punishment denotes "infliction" highlighted how the act of punishing is inherently hierarchical as someone and/or some institution[al policy] determines both what is "offensive" and what the consequence of offending will be. Through the omnipresent threat of punishment, administrations maintain control and institutionalize fear, silence, and disorder, thus enabling the internalization of shame, loathing, and condemnation.

Throughout our conversation, we discussed the racial disparities that undergird the school-to-prison pipeline in their own and neighboring public schools. As students, both Black and white, exchanged and recounted narratives about their experiences, it became apparent how numerous white students had received the benefits of discipline, and Black students were managing the ongoing trauma of punishment. Authorized by school policies, students were internalizing and receiving starkly different messages about themselves and each other. These messages dictate how white students are able to influence collective educational and recreational time, capitalize on their own unstructured time, and navigate socioemotional and spatial movement on school property; these messages also dictate how Black students are subject to carceral time in which the prison state infiltrates school time and "uses time against"[8] them as a punishing mechanism.

Codifying Deviance and Temporal Disjuncture

Speaking to disciplinary codes within schools, Connie Wun asserts that disciplinary codes "produce ideas about what constitutes deviance at the same time they legitimize the attending consequences. Less about controlling violence, these policies regulate students' non-violent movements, labeling expressions and forms of communication as 'defiance' and 'disobedience.'"[9] Similarly, Christie, cited in Meiners, explains, "Crime does not exist. Crime is created. First there are acts.

Then follows a long process of giving meaning to these acts. Social distance is of particular importance. Distance increases the tendency to give certain acts the meaning of being crimes and the persons the simplified meaning of being criminals."[10]

Neither deviance nor criminality naturally exists; rather, a behavior or an act is determined to be deviant, and this necessitates punishment and policing. Although behavioral differences enacted/embodied by Black children are not inherently deviant, punitive school-based codes legislate normativity based on white middle-class values.[11] Black children, therefore, are suspended and/or expelled for historical perceptions and conditions that existed long before their personal entrance into the classroom.[12]

Actively punishing students while discursively asserting the intention of promoting discipline is another way of operationalizing the consequences of anti-Black racism. Anti-Blackness is embedded in the language of institutional policy and procedure, thereby "legitimiz[ing] the attending consequences" of what is assumed to be deviance.[13] Together, Wun and Christie illuminate how education systems propagate the belief that everyone reaps the positive benefits of discipline as administrators preserve a false notion of safety for the (assumed) victims of a student's actions, while the student aggressor gains experiential knowledge and personal growth in retrospect.

The consequences of Black children's physiological growth, bodily motions, and emotional expressions within the classroom result in disproportionately high rates of suspensions and expulsions. Studies have indicated that classroom teachers' and instructors' implicit biases toward Black children lead them to perceive the children as aggressive and threatening: "these correlations alone suggest that factors other than child behaviors contribute to the high rates of expulsion and suspension."[14] The primary factor is the operation of whiteness as early educational institutions sanction punishment and play deprivation via the operation of these violent readings of Black children, which then necessitate exclusionary policies to maintain classroom control.

For example, in 2018–19, the Pittsburgh Public Schools (PPS) Code of Conduct added the category of "Physical Aggression/Altercation," under which "over 45% of the 1062 K-5 student suspensions" were categorized in 2018–19.[15] Notably, "Physical Aggression/Altercation" was described in the PreK-5 Code of Student Conduct as "threatened or actual use of violence by a student on another person when there is no major injury as determined by the school administrator. *Administrators may use professional judgment in cases where the investigation yields a clear aggressor/initiator and may differentiate consequences accordingly.*"[16]

"Physical Aggression/Altercation" has since been removed from the most recent iteration of the Code of Conduct. Nevertheless, like Gilliam's broad gesture toward "factors other than child behaviors"[17] as reasons for racial disparities in preschool suspension data, "research suggests that the disproportionate representation of African-American students in [PPS] disciplinary referrals generally reflects subjective perception and interpretation of student behavior on the part of staff, as there is no evidence that students of color engage in more serious or disruptive behavior than white students."[18]

Criminalizing both students' physical movements and aesthetic expressions illuminates how certain bodies develop physically and are subsequently and arbitrarily considered to be indecent. Essentially, the desire to map developmental narratives, rooted in a white supremacist pseudoscience, neatly onto Black students is consistently disrupted due to social constructions of age and/or temporal order.[19] The ability to abide by the code of conduct, regulating dress and managing behaviors, then becomes a metric of development and a means of codifying innocence and policing deviance along racial and gendered lines. When a Black child is already being perceived as more aggressive and threatening, and the administration is the final arbiter of the consequences, "any movement—whether inoffensive, playful, and/or life-sustaining—is liable to be punished."[20]

As a result of racist fears and paternalism, Black students are forced into a liminal space due to age-defined compulsory education laws, which fixes them "in a child's role . . . [while denying them] a childhood, along with the privileges (of play, of an extended education, and of an eventual nostalgia) that 'having a childhood' [entails]."[21] Both infantilization and adultification[22] can be understood as states of "arrest" (or a series of "arrests") in which various institutions seek to deny/halt their development by subjecting Black students to violent, state-sanctioned restrictions on their access to and width of temporal and spatial movements. This, in an effort to deprive them of the holistic opportunities for individual and collective growth that are most meaningfully facilitated through the socioemotional learning produced through culturally responsive, developmentally appropriate discipline and cooperative play.

The restrictions on temporal and spatial movement are emblematic of the ways "white people dictate the pace of social inclusion."[23] Brittney Cooper articulates how "restricting African American inclusion is a primary way that we attempt to manage and control people by managing and controlling time."[24] When Black children are subject to inordinately punitive school-based policies, they are placed at a social distance from their peers and fixed within a sociopolitical category of deviance. Positioned here at this distance, Black students' experience of time is continuously arrested by their school systems and the state-sanctioned institutions in partnership with their respective schools. Circling back to the racial disproportionality in suspension rates, in-school suspension has been broadly described by students and activists as an isolating experience not unlike solitary confinement used as a form of punishment within prisons.[25]

Physically removed from the group learning space, and forced to navigate the "deferred effect" of that removal and subsequent isolation, Black students are made vulnerable to a series of managed delays. The *deferred effect*, a term encapsulating the way "the past gets grasped . . . namely as read through its future consequences,"[26] produces a rupture, or a sense of disjuncture from shared chronological time. These delays obstruct (though they cannot fully eradicate) Black students' access to the socially constructed metrics of success (e.g., graduation, marriage, career) as well as the pleasures of cultural exchange, collective worldmaking, and personal evolution.

Temporal disjunctures challenge us to reflect critically on the myriad ways that Black students are indefinitely suspended, and in some cases expelled completely, from the category of "child," particularly within institutions based on conceptualizations of vertical growth, biological categories of age, and chronological forms of temporal order.

Play as Coevalness

Standing at the center of another circle, my peer facilitators, Woodland Hills teachers, and students seated around me, I shouted, "Calling all my friends who have siblings!" Everyone with siblings sprinted across the circle in a race to grab an open seat. Everyone was making an effort not to be the next person left standing alone at the center. The chaos of disorderly movement, uninhibited laughter, colliding chairs, and winded bodies filled the entire room. This game, Calling All My Friends, is my favorite community-building exercise as much for the mapping of commonalities as it is for the empathic witnessing of differences. The game demands active participation from every person in the circle—all must be committed to sharing and responding vulnerably, taking and making space, spending that time locked in with the group.

Students must learn through experiential practice—through discipline—the struggle to stay present and in community with one another. Inherent to the application of discipline is a move to answer the question of "why?" Asking students "why" opens pathways to transformative justice that simultaneously center the individual and collective well-being of the people within a learning space. When educators inquire about the motive behind a student's decisions and actions, educators are provided narratives that reveal contextual landscapes shaped by systemic policies that ultimately enable and/or compel certain responses from students. By acting on their curiosity and posing critical questions, educators initiate an understanding of how disorder is created and managed by the daily, sociopolitical circumstances informed by a person's intersectional identities.

Asking "why" of students necessitates that educators commit to a lateral alignment with their students across time and space: "'Why?' often leads us to grief, abuse, trauma, mental illness, difference, socialization, childhood, scarcity, loneliness. Also, 'Why?' makes it impossible to ignore that we might be capable of a similar transgression in similar circumstances. We don't want to see that. Demonizing is more efficient than relinquishing our world views."[27] Yet undoing racism requires that we grapple with and navigate such tumultuous emotional terrain in real time.

Our YUIR Pgh workshops were introductions to this "Why" framework, the uncomfortable emotional terrain catalyzed by critical introspection, and community-organizing discipline as our workshops used multiple modalities, self-reflective practices, and art making to examine the structural history of the US education system as well as students' own school system and document their personal stories within these institutions. Arguably, the most prominent modality and practice were the cooperative play breaks interspersed throughout each session. Strategically incorporated, we understood how "infusing play with antiracist principles allows us to identify the operation of racism, as we move against traditional, hierarchical educational settings in which Black people are expected to consume as little space as possible."[28] Moreover, the activities engaged were grounding tools that situated all participants in a body-to-body struggle to achieve a collective end. Within the constraints of a particular game, students experienced the "concept of coevalness or co-temporality as the 'recognition of actively sharing the same time' with others as opposed to the fixed time of keeping others in their 'marginal place.'"[29] Play is restorative justice as it is a universally accessible, collectively joyful method of bringing one back into a shared spatial-temporal dynamic via their participation in the body politic.

Through cooperative present-mindedness, we were shifting time forward. The freedom we enjoy in our bodies enlivens and makes urgent our daily endeavors for abolition and liberation. In a moment of play, we experienced the abundance of time and space, without the discriminatory ideological constraints of identity politics, for which we are all organizing around and striving toward.

Notes

1. Qui Dorian Alexander, "Thoughts on Discipline, Justice, Love and Accountability: Redefining Words to Reimagine Our Realities," The Feminist Wire, October 26, 2016, https://thefeministwire.com/2016/10/reimagine-our-realities/.

2. Erica R. Meiners, *For the Children?: Protecting Innocence in a Carceral State* (Minneapolis: University of Minnesota Press, 2016), 9.

3. Census Reporter, (n.d.), Census Profile: Woodland Hills School District, PA, retrieved April 17, 2023, https://censusreporter.org/profiles/97000US4216500-woodland-hills-school-district-pa/.

4. Overview of Woodland Hills Senior High School, retrieved April 17, 2023, https://www.usnews.com/education/best-high-schools/pennsylvania/districts/woodland-hills-school-district/woodland-hills-senior-high-school-17123.

5. Kathryn Bond Stockton, *The Queer Child, or Growing Sideways in the Twentieth Century* (Durham, NC: Duke University Press, 2009), 40.

6. Woodland Hills School District Student Handbook, 2022, 22–3, retrieved April 17, 2023, https://resources.finalsite.net/images/v1660843409/whsdk12paus/wn8d3t9cggpbumwzeozk/StudentHandbook22-23docx.pdf, 21–22.

7. https://languages.oup.com/dictionaries/.

8. Meiners, *For the Children?*, 191.

9. Connie Wun, "Against Captivity: Black Girls and School Discipline Policies in the Afterlife of Slavery," *Educational Policy* 30, no. 1 (2016): 182.

10. Meiners, *For the Children?*, 122.

11. Amy C. Nelson, "The Impact of Zero Tolerance School Discipline Policies: Issues of Exclusionary Discipline," *National Association of School Psychologists* 37, no. 4 (2008): 33.

12. Ariana D. Brazier, "'Yea. I'm in My Hood. No Strap': Black Child Play as Praxis and Community Sustenance" (PhD diss., University of Pittsburgh, 2021), 34.

13. Wun, "Against Captivity," 182.

14. Walter S. Gilliam, "Early Childhood Expulsions and Suspensions Undermine Our Nation's Most Promising Agent of Opportunity and Social Justice," Moriah Group, 2016, 6, https://buildinitiative.org/wp-content/uploads/2021/06/428RWJExpulsion.pdf.

15. OnePA, "Suspended Education: Pittsburgh Public Schools 2016–17 to 2018–19," 2021, retrieved April 17, 2023, 16, https://412justice.org/wp-content/uploads/2022/12/ERNsuspensionreport2021B.pdf.

16. OnePA, "Suspended Education," 17, emphasis added.

17. Gilliam, "Early Childhood Expulsions," 6.

18. OnePA, "Suspended Education," 21.

19. Katharine Capshaw and Anna Mae Duane, *Who Writes for Black Children?: African American Children's Literature before 1900* (Minneapolis: University of Minnesota Press, 2017).

20. Brazier, "'Yea. I'm in My Hood,'" 34.

21. Capshaw and Duane, *Who Writes for Black Children?*, 5.

22. Ann Arnett Ferguson, *Bad Boys: Public Schools in the Making of Black Masculinity* (Ann Arbor: University of Michigan Press, 2000).

23. Brittney Cooper, "The Racial Politics of Time," February 21, 2017, https://www.ted.com/talks/brittney_cooper_the_racial_politics_of_time?language=en, 6:00.

24. Ibid., 7:02.

25. Eli Hageri, "When School Feels like Jail," The Marshall Project, November 11, 2015, http://www.themarshallproject.org/2015/11/11/when-school-feels-like-jail.

26. Stockton, *The Queer Child*, 14.

27. adrienne maree brown, "What Is/Isn't Transformative Justice?" July 9, 2015, http://adriennemareebrown.net/2015/07/09/what-isisnt-transformative-justice/.
28. Brazier, "'Yea. I'm in My Hood,'" 182.
29. D. Soyini Madison, "Co-performative Witnessing," *Cultural Studies* 21, no. 6 (November 2007): 827.

Budding Off a New Kind of Tree

An Interview

Tereneh Idía, Nekiya Washington-Butler, and Chelsea Jimenez

The following narrative is from excerpts of a conversation Nekiya Washington-Butler and Chelsea Jimenez had with designer and writer Tereneh Idía, whose work focuses on justice. Her works explore creating a just society especially in race, gender, environment, arts, and culture.

Tereneh Idía: Idia'Dega[1] is really about incorporating Indigenous adornment and innovation into contemporary, sustainable clothing. My writing, hopefully, is about that sense of seeking justice, the sense of interconnectedness all while centering ownership, agency, innovation, creativity with women and primarily Black women and primarily African diasporic women. So I work with the Maasai community in Olorgesailie, Kenya, and I also work with artisans in the Oneida Nation of New York. And we make clothing and jewelry. This past year has been focused on a renewable energy project, where we install solar village lights around the community and solar kits as well as designing wearable solar products, headlamps, bracelets, utility bags and tote bags, and a phone pouch that has solar panels incorporated into the design. So you're charging batteries, small electronics, and things as you're wearing them.

So one of the things that I talked about when we did one of our first collections together, which was the healing collection, I was thinking about because both the Oneida and Maasai communities were talking about natural healing and different healing elements. And I had gotten sick, actually, when I was in the Maasai village one year. So they were making me teas and different things to help make me feel better. And I started thinking about women being the first scientists in communities and being the first doctors because in a lot of traditional work, they are gathering herbs. They are finding the different things that help. If you cut yourself, what is it that's going to heal that scratch? So the collection was about women being the first scientists. But we expressed that through design. The Oneida women beaded maple leaves and strawberry blossoms and rose petals because those are symbols of different medicines they use. The Maasai women created beadwork that represented fire and water and air because they are connecting those key elements of existence as the basis of their healing.

And it was also a way to share but without giving away any secrets to what they use. So it's just the sense of remembering who we are. How do we remember who we are, even if it's generations back? I think about that sense of freedom and reimagining because it already existed. It exists in my body. It exists in my ancestry. I just have to remember it. I have to uncover it. Education is part of that uncovering, and finding out what it is my body forgot, because I'm not supposed to be here. I'm not meant to be in Pittsburgh. I'm not meant to be in America. My history, my trajectory, my Indigenousness has been kind of cut. And now it's budding off a new kind of tree.

The way that I deal with antiblackness and misogynoir specifically is collaborating with the Maasai women in such a way that, I hope, it's a partnership. It's not me dictating what happens. It's not me providing a Western standpoint, a way of thinking. It's us working in collaboration with the community and centering them. For example, when we're installing the lights in the village, the children are seeing their mothers and their aunties and their cousins installing solar lights or selling, designing, creating new things and buying food for the family.

It's been really, really challenging, actually more challenging than fighting antiblackness. It's fighting specific dislike and disdain for Black women. There's been times when we'll be designing. We'll be talking, and there's so much animosity and so much negativity that I have to stop and say, "Look, in this space we love women. I don't know what happens before. I don't know what's going to happen when you go home. I don't know, but in this space, right now, we love women. Let's try to work in that way."

Chelsea Jimenez: Could you define Blackness as you view it? It's been helpful to hear you talk about Blackness across different dynamics.

TI: I've never thought about a definition of Blackness. And I say *Black*, and I talk about Blackness all the time. But to define it is something that's very, very interesting. Blackness really is an invention and creation that comes from the Afro-Atlantic. It's multicultural. It's multinational. And although it came out of the misguided attempt to dehumanize us of the African diaspora, I think that what it's become is the source and the creation of all humanity, really is what I think Blackness is ultimately. It's the source. It's the beginning. It's dark energy, dark matter. It's the cosmos. What's the cosmos' main ingredient? Black and Blackness is, and to me it just feels like it's the greatest blessing of my life is that I'm Black and a woman. Those are the two best things that's happened to me in my life.

I was just thinking about one of the reasons why, when I'm in Africa, I struggle with the idea of Black and Blackness. I had a professor at Kenyatta University tell me that I can never call her *Black*. She just was so offended, and I understand why. She's Kikuyu, which is one of the forty-three ethnic groups in Kenya. She goes, "My people were here before Black was invented. So if you're going to call me anything, call me *Kikuyu*, which is K-I-K-U-Y-U. *Kikuyu* or call me *Kenyan*. But don't call me *Black*."

There is such an interesting mix of things. So on one hand, it's me collaborating with the Maasai women of Olorgesailie Valley and the work that they do. A lot of that is taking some of the traditional forms from that portion of the Maasai community. And there's approximately a million Maasai between Kenya and Tanzania. It's not a monolith of cultures or people. But the Maasai in Olorgesailie say, "We use all the colors." The Maasai traditionally use black and white seeds to create their work. So a lot of times you'll see black and white beadwork as a frame because they use seeds. And the seeds were white and black, and that's what they created the work with. These size 11 glass beads were actually the same beads that the Oneida used and are from Czechoslovakia. And they actually use the same size, which is kind of interesting because there's a wide variety of sizes.

And a lot of the design, a lot of the texture is very geometric and linear. When I ask them about color, *black* is *narok*. And narok is the color black, but Narok is also the name of one of their originating co-deities. And the co-deities, one is red, and one is black. The red one is more mischievous and maybe more the one that will try to teach you a harsh lesson. Narok, the black one, is benevolent and kind and healing. Interestingly enough, the gods did not necessarily have human form. And they were nongendered, so they were nonbinary, and they were maybe not human, which I find really, really interesting. But so the sense of color is very, very different. For example, if someone is healing, they'll wear black to heal.

One of the things that I realized is that, growing up, my parents would ask me what I was reading about. And then they would give me additional readings, which I hated as a kid, but now I'm so grateful for. Because it'd be like, "You're learning about this. Okay, here is what Black people, here's what African people, and here's what Indigenous people did." So that was always really helpful. But I also was under this false idea that I was not antiblack, that I did not have antiblackness and that I wasn't raised with antiblackness. So I had this false sense of security until I guess the past ten years, really, when I had to look and think about some of the things that I was taught, some of the things that I believe, even the way things were talked about in my home as a child surrounded by African art, surrounded by Black authors, being told about how much Black people contributed to the world and African history, et cetera, et cetera.

I still was surrounded by antiblackness, and I had internalized antiblackness. And I have to admit, I probably still do because it's so hard to not have any antiblackness in such an antiblack world. And also as a Black American working in Kenya, working in Africa, there's a whole other conversation about antiblackness as specifically anti-African, which also comes into play. So I've had to challenge even my notion of

Blackness, even my definition of African American when I'm living and working with Africans because they'll challenge me and say, "You're not African American. You're from Pittsburgh. That's not the same thing. You can't claim Africanness." So it all can be very, very challenging.

In the American school systems from pre-K up through graduate school, unfortunately, that education is white, patriarchal capitalism. That's the politics. That's the economics. That's the spirituality of the education system as it stands right now. I don't see that changing anytime soon. But I think that there are ways to incorporate pro-Blackness, pro-humanness. I'm going to say pro-life, but I don't mean *pro-life* in the bad way. I mean living, all living things. I mean the beyond-human family life because a lot of times we talk about life, we only talk about human life. And one of the things that—especially working with Indigenous communities of artisans—I'm learning is my connection to other living things and all living things and the sense of, really, the beyond-human family.

When I live in the Maasai village, there is connection with the livestock and connection with the other animals that live in that community, so I'm very much into the idea, the understanding, of when we talk about freedom and liberation and creating a community, a thriving community, that I really do think we need to include all living things that share this space with us. And if we can think that way, we're going to create a world that might actually exist with humans in it rather than us becoming extinct. So art plays a role, even though it keeps getting erased.

CJ: We want to understand the ways in which different community members and their work have connected to the school-to-prison pipeline. And if not exactly a school-to-prison pipeline, has any of your work discussed topics on the funneling of Black bodies or Black lives from being centered in culture, in mainstream society, in education?

Nekiya Washington-Butler: So with your childhood and how you've seen the school-to-prison pipeline, how did that affect you now as an adult? How do those teachings frame you as who you are now?

TI: When you talk about the school-to-prison pipeline, I guess there's two things that I thought about. One was just growing up and the way that I grew up. And then the second thing was as an adult trying to connect with the prison system in a way that I would hope would be creative and community-building. So first, I would think when you think of the school-to-prison pipeline, growing up as a Black kid in Pittsburgh, I feel like it was top of mind of my parents and particularly my dad to make sure that we didn't end up in prison. And although I don't know all Black parents, I feel like for Black parents, that's something that is a part of their thinking and their fears.

Because for us, for me and my brothers growing up, I felt like it was always a part of our lives. I had my own challenges. But with my brothers, they would get stopped by the police for no reason all the time. And I did not have that experience. So when I think about my experiences of being very vulnerable on the street, even times I've gotten beat up because I didn't like someone and their cousin, so and so, "Oh, she thinks she's all that, but she's not, and we'll show her." That kind of thing versus the police stopping my brothers because they fit a description.

And I was so afraid to do anything wrong because I felt like my dad would see it, no matter where I was. He would just get this sense, "Oh, wait, Tereneh is messing up. Let me do something about that." I was just always afraid of breaking rules, and I'm still like that. I'm still like I can't break rules. I'm going to get in trouble, blah, blah, blah. So that sense of if you do anything wrong, you're going to go to prison meant that when I was in stores, I remember I had to keep my hands behind my back. And we had to walk around and look at things and nod and say, "Don't touch anything. Don't touch. Don't touch, put your hands behind your back, stay quiet."

And it got to the point where it was somehow that kids could be seen but not heard. And it was really, really important, but I almost felt like we had to be invisible. It wasn't even seen and not heard. It was like we didn't even want to be seen because even being seen meant that there was a possibility for something to go wrong. So I remember growing up feeling very much like I had to shrink myself down to the smallest form possible so I didn't get into trouble.

And I remember when I was about seven or eight, maybe six, and there was a penny candy store when they had penny candy stores. And I took a piece of gum, but I took one of these expensive gums. It wasn't the penny gum. It was five cents. I remember that. And the reason why I remember it was five cents is because I was chewing gum later that day, and my mom knew I didn't have any money. So she was like, "Where did you get the gum?"

I said, "I just took a piece from the store." Well, in addition to getting a spanking all the way up to the store, all the way down to the store, I had to apologize to the store owner to say I stole this piece of candy. I had to pay him the five cents, and then I got a spanking all the way back.

And my mom, "Do not ever, ever steal anything from anybody ever, ever, ever again." And it was that kind of sense of you could end up in jail.

I was raised to be fearful. At the same time, I was told to study hard. "You can do whatever you want" and all these other things. At the same time it was, "But you're a Black woman, and so you are a threat. So you have to behave." My parents felt like they were teaching me the right thing and teaching me how to be safe and to survive. And I think my dad feels like he was justified in the way that he raised us because he'll even say, "I was really harsh on my kids. I was really hard on my kids. I was really disciplined, but none of them went to jail."

Once I came back to Pittsburgh, I guess this was 2015, and I was really interested in sharing the work with the Maasai community. I wanted to go to Shuman[2] and talk to the kids about working with the Maasai and even share video of the Maasai village and seeing the way a traditional African village functions and what are the kids doing at their age. I tried a couple times, but I was told no. They said they would have no interest in having me go speak to the students. And I'm still upset and confused by that because I think it would be really an interesting thing to have a Pittsburgher, like them, born from a family that didn't have a lot of money and found a way, created a way for themselves to travel around the world to teach overseas, to work with this African community. I just thought it would be an interesting thing to share but no, no, no. They didn't have interest in it, and I haven't tried again. I have just focused on the work.

No matter what you're doing, if you have the reason for what you're doing, that's what matters. And how you do that could be a multitude of ways. That was one lesson that I've been carrying through. So for me in my design work, I guess my "why" is to make sure that women, primarily Black and African and Indigenous women, are at the center of innovation and creativity and providing for themselves and others as a result.

Notes

1. The global eco-design cooperative founded by Idía and in collaboration with women from Maasai and Oneida Nations.

2. Former juvenile detention facility in Allegheny County.

The Journey to Freedom

A Conversation on Freedom Struggle

Sala Udin, Briayelle Gaines, and Christopher M. Wright

Sala Udin was raised in the historic Lower Hill District of Pittsburgh and went on to dedicate decades of leadership and activism to Black freedom in the city.

Briayelle Gaines: How did you come to understand the relationship between schooling and prisons, and why is it important to know about this in Pittsburgh?

Sala Udin: I come to the school board as a freedom fighter. I started my freedom-fighting work in 1965 in the Mississippi Delta under the tutelage of Fannie Lou Hamer. Then I returned to Pittsburgh as a community organizer and freedom fighter. One of the early organizations we formed was to attack the failure of the education system to educate Black children. It was clear to us from the beginning, the failure to properly educate Black children resulted in the repopulation of the prison systems. So, from a strategic standpoint, working toward improving the quality of education for Black children was directly connected to preventing them from incarceration. I've been doing that work since 1968, when I returned to Pittsburgh from the Mississippi Delta. That's how I got involved.

Christopher M. Wright: I'm going to ask another question that piggybacks off of what you just offered. I want to ask a question about the importance of political education for Black folk, especially Black children.

I read in another interview you did that you moved away from home as a teenager and went to New York City. It was there where you began to gain consciousness and began to come into your calling as a freedom fighter and organizer. I'm wanting to know if you could tell us a little bit more about that time—the shift—and why it was important for you to take what it was you learned and come back home and continue your work here in Pittsburgh. I know you went from New York, then to the Mississippi Delta, back to Pittsburgh, is that correct?

SU: Yes. I had failed at school and failed at education, and I was told by a counselor that God made us all, but he didn't make us all equal. He made some endowed with skills that they could implement with their hands, and he made some endowed with skills that could be implemented by their brains. Judging from my performance in school, it was easy to conclude that I was not endowed with a heavy payload of brains. So I thought perhaps I could find my calling by enrolling in a trade school. Maybe God had endowed me with talents in my hands that I hadn't realized. That was my exit interview, and I left Schenley High School mad at God for not giving me the brains that I needed and mad at Pittsburgh.

Some of my friends introduced the idea that we should abandon Pittsburgh and go to Harlem, the land of milk and honey. People come back from New York and flash big bundles of cash and drive in shiny cars. My plan was to figure out how to make a living hustling, shooting pool, shooting dice, and a couple other hustle games I had learned in the streets of Pittsburgh. That was my plan. Fortunately, my mother had two sisters who were nurses who lived in Staten Island. When I called one to let them know I was in New York, she said, "Your mother is worried sick. She has no idea where you are, how you're doing, what you're doing." I was dead broke and hungry as hell. She asked me, "Do you have any money?" I said, "Sure, I got money." She said, "Have you eaten?" I said, "I'm full, I'm fine." She said, "Well, come on over here to Staten Island and give your auntie a hug." I hung up the phone and jumped for joy. I found my way to Staten Island. They got me back in high school, where I learned that I was not dumb after all. I made the dean's list, graduated from high school, and I didn't have to be mad at

God anymore for making me dumb. In Harlem, on Saturday mornings, after we played basketball and had breakfast, we would go and try to find Malcolm X.

CMW: In the street?

SU: In the street. But you never knew where he was going to set up shop. Malcolm was a heavy influence early in my life. He used to travel around Harlem, speaking from a bed of a pickup truck or on a ladder with a megaphone, and you had to drive around. When you saw a large crowd cheering and saying, "Right on, brother," that's how you knew you found Malcolm. When the opportunity came to travel to Washington, DC, from New York, all the civil rights leaders were going to be there despite the fact that Malcolm had criticized the march and criticized the leaders. I knew it was a big event, and I wanted to be there. I attended the March on Washington and heard, firsthand, Dr. Martin Luther King deliver the speech "I Have a Dream." I knew, at that time, that that experience of the 1963 March on Washington answered questions that I had been asking myself like: Who are you? What are you going to do with your life? What's your plan? I decided, at that moment, I want to join that army. Before you knew it, I was on a bus on my way to the Freedom Office in Lexington, Mississippi.

BG: Do you think your life would've been different if you would've stayed in Pittsburgh? Do you think you would've ended up where you're at today?

SU: I'd be in jail or dead.

BG: So you think when you moved away, it was a better decision?

SU: There's no question. It's not a decision. I would not advise young people who may not have two lovely, generous aunts who were willing to take you into their home and get you back on the right track. I was just very, very fortunate that that was my experience, but I would never advise it for anybody else because if you think that you're going to make a life and a living hustling on the streets of either Pittsburgh or Harlem, you are destined for a short life.

CMW: Can you speak to how you sat within the tensions? You mentioned how Malcolm was extremely important and influential early in your coming to consciousness and you went to the March on Washington even though he had criticized the civil rights movement and its leaders. How did you and other folks who you were in community with sit within the tensions of the two ideologies?

SU: Well, I understood that there are different tensions in the larger Black dialogue. I wanted to be a witness, and therefore I had to get myself to Washington, DC, where I could see it for myself. I didn't need to take sides. I just needed to bear witness.

BG: Okay. How would you describe what freedom is for Black people, and where do children in school fit in?

SU: Freedom is the removal of obstacles and the opening of the pathway to success. Anything that is blocking that pathway, anything that is an obstacle has to be confronted and removed. The fight for freedom is a fight to remove those obstacles. If it's an obstacle to being able to earn a living and take care of your family and have a job, then you have to fight for that. The first time I went to Mississippi, the courts had decided that the schools had to desegregate. The white folks in Mississippi decided that rather than have their children sit next to Black children, they would pull their children out of schools and educate them either at home or in white Christian churches. They were not going to allow their children to be educated sitting next to Black children. So the fight for freedom in that instance was to open the possibility for children to attend school, to get a public education, and, obviously, to give children and their parents a voice in the fight for freedom. Whether it's an education, getting a job, or to be able to walk home without the fear of danger approaching in the form of racist police, all those are challenges that have to be confronted and defeated.

BG: Do you think the freedom in New York City was different between freedom in Pittsburgh?

SU: No, the difference is the level of consciousness that you have about your freedom journey. Everybody has a different journey. They have a different level of consciousness, they have different insights, they have different aspirations for who they are and who they want to be. So it is different in the sense that we are different, all of us are different, but it is not different in the sense that we have to confront obstacles in our freedom journey and defeat those obstacles. There's a wide variety of obstacles in Pittsburgh, and a wide variety of obstacles in New York, and a wide variety of obstacles in the Mississippi Delta. You got to decide who you are and what your relationship is going to be to the obstacles that are in your way while on your journey. If you are willing to confront them and fight them and defeat them, those are the differences. My first attempt at freedom started when I gave myself permission to run away from home in Pittsburgh and drive in this raggedy Buick convertible, where the rain would come through when it was raining, to get to New York and begin a whole new chapter in life. Being able to run away from home, to get away without me being caught by my father. If my father had caught me trying to run away from home, that would've been my first freedom struggle, trying to get out of his grip. Oh, but he was asleep, and I snuck past him and snuck out of the house. So my first freedom struggle, at the age of sixteen, having dropped out of high school, was to accept my friend's offer to drive to New York to start a new life. That was the first freedom decision that I ever made in my life.

CMW: I'm wondering if you could speak to a time in Pittsburgh, where you saw your work toward freedom have real impact on the folks who you struggle with. Maybe a story or significant moment where you can say, "We fought, we struggled, and we won" or, "We fought, we struggled, and the community felt what it is that we were trying to achieve."

SU: I think the first experience of that confrontation in Pittsburgh was when we learned about how the work we were doing for the Black liberation struggle in Pittsburgh could take a leap forward. That leap forward was for us to try to replicate what Amiri Baraka was doing in Newark, New Jersey. He had found an experience in Newark that took the work from the streets and put it on stage in a play. They learned how to communicate the freedom message on stage in a way that was much more interesting than the way we were trying to do it with a microphone standing on stage giving a speech. Amiri Baraka had created this group called the Spirit House Movers. When I came back to Pittsburgh, Rob Penny, August Wilson, myself, and many others decided to create a theater group here in Pittsburgh called the Black Horizons Theater. That's how we all got involved in theater. We discovered that it was a more effective way to tell our story and to get people mobilized rather than just preaching to them in a speech.

CMW: Could you speak a little bit more about the importance of art in freedom struggle? How important has art been in your work?

SU: It's like the difference between sliding down a sliding board that is not finished. It's rough, with splinters and pain, versus a smooth ride down the sliding board that's an aluminum sliding board and being able to get to the bottom without pain. You got to find the right sliding board. For us, theater was that sliding board, and it made our work much more successful and much more effective. We created a camaraderie of friends who became attached to each other for life. That's what I learned from that experience. Art, study, and work. That's the path, the successful path to freedom. I don't want to gloss over the importance of study. Freedom work requires hours and hours of study. There's a whole mountain of work and a parade of individuals who came before us, all of whom have different messages for us to learn from. We have to discipline ourselves to learn and hear those messages and learn how to apply them to our lives today. The messages in history are there. That's why history is so important. That's why Black history is essential. They contain the nuggets of success that we have to follow in order to be successful ourselves. It's not a matter of us just using our own brains and our own theories; we've got to study what the masters have said. What did Mandela have to say about this? What did Du Bois have to say about this? James Baldwin and Ida B. Wells, what did they have to say about this? What did the slaves have to say about their experience? Those are the things we have to study and be as disciplined in our study as we are in other aspects of the freedom work. Study.

CMW: So next, I want to ask a question about your time that you spent as a child in the Hill District. I know that you were there during a lot of development, during a lot of pushout, during some of the demolition of the Lower Hill, where you're from. I'm wanting to know if you could speak to that a bit. What were some of the changes that occurred within the community, and what were the reactions of your friends and your neighbors and folks who had to change schools or move into Bedford Housing? Can you speak to that a little bit and tell us about how those experiences have sort of stayed with you moving forward in your work?

SU: We stayed above a grocery store in a small apartment, and we played stickball in the cobblestone streets. That was our playground, and we got an attitude when a car approached and we had to stop playing to let the car go by and hope the car didn't run over first base and destroy it. The first experience that I recall of real fear was when the rumors started going around that they were going to tear the whole neighborhood down and everybody was going to have to move. I didn't know, who's "they"? And why are they deciding to tear our houses down, and where are we going to move? What's going to happen with our friends? Who are we going to school with? It was a frightening rumor that was going around that didn't have many answers, and my parents didn't have many answers.

Eventually, the day came when my father pulled up in a truck and loaded everything that we owned onto that truck and told us that we were moving to a new neighborhood around the corner and up the street. They had enrolled us in a new school, and everything was going to be all right. We moved at night. I don't know how many people will know about the experience of moving at night, but we moved at night, and we were taken upstairs to this new apartment building that was three stories high. We walked in, and the rooms were freshly painted; there were no holes in the walls. We went in through the kitchen—it had a brand-new refrigerator, a brand-new stove, a new sink, new cabinets—and I thought, "Damn, Daddy must have hit the numbers." I had never seen anything like that. It was new. We never had new kitchen equipment and appliances, new furniture. We had unlimited heat and unlimited light. It didn't matter if we left the lights on because the lights was included with the rent. So it softened the landing of having to move away from our old neighborhood and figure out how we were going to learn our way to school and learn to meet new friends and all of that. It was a frightening and terrifying experience.

My father used to take us for a ride in his car, and most frequently, he would go back down Bedford Avenue to Crawford Street, where the demolition of the Lower Hill District was taking place. He would look on at the demolition. He'd park the car, get out, and look. You could see him remembering the good times in that neighborhood. You could see him wondering, "What were the answers to our question? Who decided they were going to tear this neighborhood down? Why did they decide that? What are they going to build in its place? What is going on, and do we have any say so in this?" No. That was our Sunday afternoon entertainment: for my father to take us for a ride. Then we'd end up in Oakland at Isaly's and get a big, tall ice cream cone, and that would soften the blow and get us ready to start school Monday morning.

CMW: When we think about freedom work in the past, present, and future, where do you see resistance to that kind of demolition? How important is it for the community to resist and assert that their voices be heard and considered in those processes? Do you see that as an obstacle to be overcome in freedom struggle?

SU: Absolutely. People have a natural desire and need for self-determination and self-efficacy. People have to have a say in where their lives are going and how they're going to get there. So the reason why the demolition moved eastward from downtown and only got to Crawford Street was because an older Black woman who owned a gospel music shop near the corner of Center Avenue and Crawford got together with some other folks and put up a billboard at the corner of Crawford and Center that said, "Not another inch." They stopped the demolition that was planned to go all the way from Crawford Street, beyond Kirkpatrick Street. That act of self-determination, self-efficacy, was the lesson for me that answered my question, "Who decided, and do we get to say anything about this?" Yes, but only if you assert yourself. If you wait for them to give you permission, you will never get a say in these kinds of decisions. So yes, it is as important as breathing oxygen from the air. You have to decide where the boundary stops. Like Ms. Frankie May Pace—that's the lady's name who had the gospel music store—who said, "Not another inch." So now there are many organizations that work in the Hill District to refashion the future growth of the Hill District. What is it going to look like? Where's our commercial district going to be? Where's our housing going to be? Where are the playgrounds going to be? There are still people, even though a lot of people left the Hill District during that demolition, who stayed and took the lessons of the freedom fighters like Frankie May Pace and those who put their billboard up at Freedom Corner and said, "Not another inch." People are still working to rebuild a new community after the demolition.

Happiness & Freedom

Cue Perry

Freedom to me means growth in a positive direction. Leaving old ways and old thinking in the past. Breathing new life into the existing world. Those are the emotions expressed in this piece. To inhale and exhale and smile. And breaking free from archaic thinking, processes, and policies should be a goal of everyone in the region.

Cue Perry, *Happiness & Freedom*, 2022

Acknowledgments

J. Z. Bennett
I would like to thank my Lord and Savior, Jesus Christ, who reminds us in Luke 12:48 that to whom much is given, much will be required. This principle has guided me throughout my academic journey and this project. My heartfelt gratitude and appreciation go to my coeditors, Christy, Lori, Elon, and Sabina. Thank you for being outstanding thought partners and exceptional colleagues. I extend my thanks to the Center for Urban Education at the University of Pittsburgh, which played a critical role in refining my thinking and writing, pushing me academically to explore the intricate relationship between criminology and education. I am also thankful to Abby Freeland at the University Press of Kentucky for her assistance in launching this remarkable work. My gratitude extends to all the contributors of this project. To my beautiful and loving mother, Martha Bennett, thank you for being by my side at every step of my academic journey; I hope I have made you proud. Last, I owe a deep debt of gratitude to the Ronald E. McNair Scholars Program, Carl McNair, Jeffrey T. Ward, James Earl Davis, and M. Christopher Brown II, who have profoundly shaped me into the scholar I am today.

Christy L. McGuire
Immense gratitude for my supportive, thoughtful, inspiring coeditors. Juwan, thank you for being such a fabulous friend and colleague. Elon, thank you for your loving guidance, and for modeling ways of being and knowing that are rooted in grace, generosity, and authenticity. Thank you, Lori, for the genuine love and care you have always shown to me and countless others and for teaching me to trust the process. And Sabina, thank you for inspiring me on so many levels and for helping

me learn how to observe the unthinkable. Thank you to all of the contributors in this work: youth essayists and interviewers, artists, organizers, and academicians. To Abby Freeland at the press, thank you for your incredible support! And of course, thank you to the two most intensely fabulous people I have ever known, Zora and Ezra. You inspire, challenge, delight, and amaze me and give me hope; may you always be able and willing to imagine future's future.

Lori Delale-O'Connor
My deepest thanks to my incredible coeditors—Juwan, Christy, Elon, and Sabina. You have made the work of this volume both generative and fun, and I have learned so much from each of you. Thank you for bringing me into this project. Thanks also to Abby Freeland at University Press of Kentucky, as well as the anonymous reviewers who offered encouragement and feedback that significantly enhanced this book. I further offer my sincere appreciation to all the book's contributors for sharing their stories, their art, and, most importantly, their visions of the past, present, and future of urban Appalachia. Without your generosity and imagination this book would not have been possible. Finally, to my family— my parents, Rose and Joe; my children, Anna and Alex; and my partner in life and all things, Jason—you are my support and inspiration. Thank you for your belief and encouragement.

T. Elon Dancy II
I am grateful to my marvelous editor colleagues, Juwan, Christy, Lori, and Sabina, for their hard work and tenacity in crafting the sculpture that is this book. Special thanks to book chapter authors—the scholars, thinkers, writers, artists, and storytellers who lent their intellect, labor, and time to this project. I'm so proud of what we have all accomplished together. Thanks to Abby Freeland, the University Press of Kentucky staff, the Appalachian Futures series coeditors, and peer reviewers for engaging with this book's content seriously, thoughtfully, and generatively. To my wise and loving parents, Gwendolyn and Theodis Dancy; my brother, Theron; my partner, homeplace, and the sweet love of my life, Zawadi Colbert; my forever mentor, M. Christopher Brown II; and my brotherly student and colleague Christopher Wright—thank you so

much for uplifting me and my scholarship. Finally, my sincere gratitude to Black Pittsburgh, the inspiration for this book and without which this book would not be possible.

Sabina Vaught

My first thanks go to the extraordinary team that pulled the stories and ideas of this book together like so many stars and then shaped them into a magnificent constellation. Juwan, Christy, Lori, and Elon, my infinite gratitude for a wonderful coeditorial journey. Thank you to Abby Freeland at the University Press of Kentucky. Your generous, enthusiastic support gave this project life. I have immense gratitude for our thoughtful, brilliant reviewers, who made this book so much better. Thank you, contributors, for trusting us with your ideas and words and images. Together you made such a beautiful book, and you made more possibility for freedom in urban Appalachia. Finally, and as ever, to Cecilia, Carmen, Satya, and Ishkode Miigwanens, everything is for you, and nothing is without you.

Contributors

Chetachukwu Agwoeme (Graduate Student and Academic Scholar)
Chetachukwu Agwoeme is a doctoral student in the Urban Education PhD program at the University of Pittsburgh. His research focuses on Black students in K-12 schools, antiblackness, student safety, and carcerality.

S. L. Akines (Community Member)
S. L. Akines is a PhD candidate in the Department of History at Carnegie Mellon University, where her studies center the history of the Black radical tradition in education. Her areas of specialty are African American transnational history, the history of Black education, and US history since 1865 with a focus on Reconstruction, race, and resistance. She has been a home educator since 2008.

Robin-Renee Allbritton (Graduate Student)
As a West Philadelphian, first-generation college student, Robin-Renee Allbritton embodies Pitt Education's mission-vision to disrupt and transform inequitable educational structures. From her work in advising underrepresented first-generation college students to her research about success mechanisms for first-generation, African American, and Latinx college students, Allbritton brings years of skill and passion to Pitt Education's Center for Urban Education.

J. Z. Bennett (Coeditor)
J. Z. Bennett is an assistant professor and associate director of the Center for Justice and Communities in the School of Criminal Justice at the University of Cincinnati.

Ariana Brazier (Academic Author)
Ariana (Ari) Brazier, PhD, serves as the VP of Products and Storytelling at Daymaker. Daymaker is a compassion platform helping companies and their employees empower kids in their local communities by running giving campaigns like back-to-school and holiday giving. Her research centers Black children and families, housing insecurity and poverty, and cultural play practices.

Sheila Carter-Jones (Poet and Community Member)
Sheila L. Carter-Jones taught in the Pittsburgh Public Schools and in Chatham University's and the University of Pittsburgh's Education Departments. She earned her BA from Carnegie Mellon University and both an MEd and a PhD from the University of Pittsburgh.

T. Elon Dancy II (Coeditor)
T. Elon Dancy II is Helen S. Faison Endowed Chair, executive director of the Center for Urban Education, and former Associate Dean for Equity and Justice in the University of Pittsburgh School of Education.

Lori Delale-O'Connor (Coeditor)
Lori Delale-O'Connor, PhD, is an associate professor at the University of Pittsburgh Center for Urban Education and chair of the Department of Education Foundations, Organizations, and Policy.

Beatrice (Bea) Dias (Academic Author)
Beatrice Dias is an assistant professor of Digital Media, Learning, and Leadership in the Department of Teaching, Learning, and Leading at the University of Pittsburgh's School of Education. She formerly served as a project director and the codirector of outreach at Carnegie Mellon University's Community Robotics, Education and Technology Empowerment Lab (CREATE) Lab.

Breanna Ewell (Youth Author)
Breanna Ewell is a 2023 graduate of Urban Pathways Charter School in Pittsburgh and is now a first-year student at Indiana University of

Pennsylvania, studying sociology and communications/media. She loves writing, cooking, and listening to music.

Briayelle Gaines (Youth Author)
Briayelle is a senior at West Mifflin Area High School. She plans to go to college to study Criminal Justice/Criminology. She is driven, adventurous, and diligent. In 2021, she was featured in PublicSource's series "Unmasked: Candid Reflections on a Warped Year of COVID School in the Pittsburgh Area."

Tamanika Howze (Community Member)
Tamanika Howze has been a longtime activist for justice and liberation on multiple levels, primarily on behalf of the African American community. She has advocated for equitable education in the Pittsburgh Public Schools for over forty years.

Tereneh Idía (Community Member)
Tereneh Idía (MSc, Kenyatta University) is a designer and writer seeking justice through creativity and community. Her works explore creating just society especially in race, gender, environment, arts, and culture. Her award-winning designs via the company she founded, IdiaDega, are often done in collaboration with other women of global majority and Indigenous makers.

Medina Jackson (Poet)
Medina Jackson, MSW, is the Director of Engagement for the University of Pittsburgh's P.R.I.D.E. Program (Positive Racial Identity Development in Early Education), which focuses on helping young Black children understand race and embrace their heritage through several community-based projects.

Jasiri X (Community Member)
Jasiri X is the first independent Hip-Hop artist to be awarded an honorary doctorate, which he received from Chicago Theological Seminary in 2016. Still, he remains rooted in the Pittsburgh-based organization he

founded, 1Hood Media, whose mission is to build liberated communities through art, education, and social justice.

Jennifer Johnson (Academic Author)
Jennifer Johnson is a citizen of the Seminole Nation and a descendant of the Sac & Fox Nation. She was an elementary school teacher on Tribal reservations in Arizona and Florida. She is currently an assistant professor in the Department of Education Policy, Organization & Leadership at the University of Illinois Urbana-Champaign.

Chelsea Jimenez (Graduate Student)
Chelsea Jimenez is a doctoral student in Urban Education at the University of Pittsburgh. Jimenez recently graduated from the University of South Carolina with a BA in Early Childhood Education and a specialization in Urban Education.

D. S. Kinsel (Visual Artist)
D. S. Kinsel is an award-winning creative entrepreneur and cultural agitator. He expresses his creativity through the mediums of painting, window display, installation, curating, action-painting, nontraditional performance, and #HASHTAGS. Kinsel's work puts focus on themes of space keeping, urban tradition, hip-hop, informalism, and cultural re-appropriation.

Marc Lamont Hill (Academic Author)
Marc Lamont Hill is the Steve Charles Professor of Media, Cities, and Solutions at Temple University. Prior to that, he held positions at Columbia University and Morehouse College. He is currently the host of *BET News* and the *Coffee & Books* podcast.

Christy L. McGuire (Coeditor)
Christy L. McGuire, PhD, EdD, is the Community Engagement Program Manager with the Center for Urban Education as well as part-time instructor with the University of Pittsburgh School of Education.

Win Nunley (Youth Author)
Win is a cofounder and creative for Black Dream Escape, a therapeutic arts practice focusing on Black and Indigenous rest. Using music and meditations, they guide clients out of a state of unrest. They have also served on the Board of Directors for Dreams of Hope, a queer youth theater organization.

Esohe Osai (Academic Author)
Esohe R. Osai is an assistant professor in Applied Developmental Psychology in the School of Education at the University of Pittsburgh. Dr. Osai operates as a community-engaged scholar with an interest in how communities and schools can support social justice, development, and well-being for children, youth, and families.

Morgan Overton (Visual Artist)
Morgan Overton is a Pittsburgh native and visual artist who believes the arts are a powerful platform to challenge the status quo. Her work amplifies the voices and visibility of society's historically silenced.

Mikael Owunna (Visual Artist)
Mikael Owunna is a queer Nigerian American multimedia artist, filmmaker, and engineer. Exploring the intersections of visual media with engineering, optics, Blackness, and African cosmologies, his work seeks to elucidate an emancipatory vision of possibility that pushes people beyond all boundaries, restrictions, and frontiers.

Cue Perry (Visual Artist)
Cue Perry (also known as C. B. Perry) is an artist in the city of Pittsburgh. Perry deconstructs pop culture that visually represents the randomness present in daily life and promotes thinking outside of the box. Perry has sold over six thousand original paintings worldwide and has been nominated by *Pittsburgh City Paper* for best local visual artist four years in a row and in 2020 was a *Pittsburgh Magazine* nominee for Best Artist in the City.

Pittsburgh Public Schools Equity Advisory Panel (Community Member)
Formed in October 2006, the Equity Advisory Panel is charged with monitoring, advising, and reporting on the Pittsburgh Public School District's progress around reducing the racial achievement gap, providing instructional support, and creating an environment of equity for its Black students. EAP Members: Wanda Henderson, Tamanika Howze, Anthony Mitchell, Celeta Hickman, Maria Searcy, James Stewart, and Kirk Holbrook.

Taj Poscé (Visual Artist)
Taj Poscé is an abstract artist from the city of Philadelphia. His work investigates the visceral and cerebral Black experience. He also challenges the status quo, with a vibrant lens of optimism that captures Black imagination.

DaVonna Shannon (Graduate Student)
DaVonna Shannon, PhD, is the director of Research and Impact for the Early Excellence Project. In this role, she designs the strategic research and policy agenda for the organization's efforts to professionalize the early childhood education industry. She also oversees internal programmatic evaluation as well as provides guidance and operations evaluation to Early Excellence Project provider clients. Dr. Shannon is the owner and principal consultant of A. Shannon Consulting LLC. Dr. Shannon's research centers on the activism of Black women educators toward improving the educational experiences and life outcomes of Black children.

Cadence Spruill (Youth Author)
Cadence Spruill is currently a senior at Pittsburgh Milliones 6-12 ("University Prep") and graduated in 2024. She is intensely curious and passionate about learning and enjoys reading, writing, and drawing.

Amber Thompson (Community Member)
Amber is an equity service designer who works with businesses to debias organizational infrastructures and implement systemic changes

bottom-up. She uses multimethod research and deciphers data through an intersectional lens.

Sabina E. Vaught (Coeditor)
Sabina Vaught is professor and director of the Kinloch Commons for Critical Pedagogy and Leadership at the University of Pittsburgh.

Sala Udin (Community Member)
A lifelong Pittsburgher, Mr. Udin was born and raised on the historic Lower Hill District and has decades of leadership and activism in civil and human rights. In 2002, Mr. Udin and Rev. Johnnie Monroe founded the Hill District Education Council.

Nekiya Washington-Butler (Youth Author)
Pittsburgh native Nekiya Washington-Butler graduated in April 2024 with a bachelor's degree in Applied Developmental Psychology from the University of Pittsburgh and is completing a specialized master's degree program in K-12 Special Education and K-4 Early Education.

Chris Wright (Graduate Student and Academic Author)
Christopher M. Wright is a PhD student in the Urban Education program at the University of Pittsburgh. His research centers Black spaces as geographic sites of political struggle and worldmaking.

Appalachian Futures
Black, Native, and Queer Voices
Series editors: Annette Saunooke Clapsaddle,
Davis Shoulders, and Crystal Wilkinson

This book series gives voice to Black, Native, Latinx, Asian, Queer, and other nonwhite or ignored identities within the Appalachian region.

Black Freedom Struggle in Urban Appalachia
Edited by J. Z. Bennett, Christy L. McGuire, Lori Delale-O'Connor, T. Elon Dancy II, and Sabina Vaught

No Son of Mine: A Memoir
Jonathan Corcoran

To Belong Here: A New Generation of Queer, Trans, and Two-Spirit Appalachian Writers
Edited by Rae Garringer

Tar Hollow Trans: Essays
Stacy Jane Grover

Deviant Hollers: Queering Appalachian Ecologies for a Sustainable Future
Edited by Zane McNeill and Rebecca Scott

Reading, Writing, and Queer Survival: Affects, Matterings, and Literacies across Appalachia
Caleb Pendygraft

Appalachian Ghost: A Photographic Reimagining of the Hawk's Nest Tunnel Disaster
Raymond Thompson Jr.